AMERICAN TELEVISION NEWS

AMERICAN TELEVISION NEWS

The Media Marketplace and the Public Interest

STEVE M. BARKIN

M.E.Sharpe
Armonk, New York
London, England

Library of Congress Cataloging-in-Publication Data

Barkin, Steve Michael, 1945–
American television news : the media marketplace and the public interest / Steve M.
Barkin.
    p. cm.
Includes bibliographical references and index.
ISBN 0-7656-0922-3 (hardcover : alk. paper) ISBN 0-7656-0923-1 (pbk. : alk. paper)
1. Television broadcasting of news—United States. I. Title.

PN4888.T4 B29 2003
070.1′95—dc21

2002075887

Printed in the United States of America

The paper used in this publication meets the minimum requirements of
American National Standard for Information Sciences
Permanence of Paper for Printed Library Materials,
ANSI Z 39.48-1984.

MV (c)   10   9   8   7   6   5   4   3   2   1
MV (p)   10   9   8   7   6   5   4   3   2   1

For Wendy

There is no boredom or misery to equal the pursuit of distraction alone. We do not slip into happiness. It is strenuously sought and earned. A nation glued to the television set is not simply at a loss before the iron pioneers of the new collective society. It isn't even having a good time.

—Adlai Stevenson, 1959

So where does that leave us, the readers and the watchers? It leaves us as victims of an intense competition, between and among not only ABC and CBS and NBC, but also PBS and C-SPAN and Fox and Warner and CNN and TNT and Nickelodeon and Comedy Central and QVC and Court TV and A&E and Blockbuster. I grew up believing that competition was good, that it was invigorating, that it promoted research, that it improved the product, that it lowered the price, that it made everybody feel good. Reluctantly and painfully I have concluded that almost the opposite is true in television.

—Roger Mudd, 1995

Human kind Cannot bear very much reality.

—T.S. Eliot, 1935

Contents

Preface

About eight years ago, it became evident to me that American television news had profoundly changed, breaking with decades of tradition. The changes had not happened overnight, and they were not unrelated to developments that were occurring more broadly throughout American journalism. Nevertheless, the practices and purposes of television news, I believed, were different—and the difference was worth understanding. By some point in the 1990s, the center of gravity in TV news had shifted. Neither the stern, unyielding predominance of the profit motive nor the blithe (perhaps even arrogant) rejection of the goals of public service and civic responsibility was new, but, it seemed to me, they had finally carried the day in an unquestioning, and disturbing, spirit. That view was shared, I later learned, by a surprising number of practicing TV journalists. This book is an effort to tell the story of the last twenty-five years of television news in the context of the social and cultural history of American broadcasting. "Trash television" does not emerge from a vacuum; neither do broadcasts of the highest quality.

Chapter 1, "Electronic Journalism in a New Era," presents an overview of television news in the United States today. It focuses on the changes of the last two decades and the concerns those changes have aroused—within the industry as well as among many members of the viewing public.

Chapter 2, "Beginnings: The Ethic of Commercialism," examines the creation of a regulatory and financial framework for American broadcasting. Radio—and subsequently television—were held to a public-interest criterion of service in the law that governed broadcasting, but they were not held to account in practice. Radio and television were defined in the 1920s and 1930s as, above all else, commercial enterprises that would be supported by advertising and provide entertainment. The material in the chapter about the early history of television focuses on the 1950s and 1960s, relating the local and national evolution of television news to the early history of American broadcasting and to considerations of the impact of mass culture on individuals and society.

Chapter 3, "The Era of Network Dominance," traces the arrival of TV news at the center of American public life, with particular attention to the expectations of public service that network news then carried for itself. The era of network dominance ushered in the new prominence of the "anchorman," as American television journalism continued to evolve differently from its counterparts in Western Europe, where the tradition of "news readers" held sway.

Chapter 4, *"60 Minutes* and the News Magazine," examines the economic and cultural impact of the landmark CBS program that premiered in 1968. The success of *60 Minutes* changed assumptions about the role television news could play economically and journalistically, gradually producing changes throughout the industry.

Chapter 5, "Tabloid Television and a World of Talk," examines news and news-related programming that may present ethical and professional questions for journalism practitioners as well as the public. The 1980s and 1990s were characterized by an increased focus on sensational and, in some instances, salacious news coverage that challenged societal assumptions about taste, morality, and objectivity. "Talk" television raised the same issues and underscored an ongoing debate about who, indeed, is a journalist in a society as saturated with information as ours.

Chapter 6, "Hard News—Soft News," looks specifically at changes in the news division of CBS in the 1980s as the tone and timbre of network news began to shift. That analysis sets the stage for a discussion in Chapter 7 of "Prime-Time News Values," as prime-time news-magazine programs multiplied and then multiplied again, bringing about a change in journalistic standards that accompanied the shift of news programming into prime time.

Chapter 8, "The Impact of CNN," traces the history of the Cable News Network and assesses the effect of around-the-clock news. All-news cable programming has in many respects added up to something less than what might have been desired, but the nature of one presidential election and many international crises and domestic issues have been dramatically changed by the omnipresence of CNN, MSNBC, and, more recently, Fox News.

Chapter 9, "Celebrity News," examines a cultural phenomenon: the endless fascination of audiences with celebrities, entertainment, and the lives of the wealthy. The full flowering of celebrity journalism is not unrelated to the growth of tabloid television programs.

Chapters 10 and 11 summarize the outlook for local and national news in the new television environment. Chapter 12 returns to the debate over television's responsibility to society and whether the efforts by electronic journalists to serve the public interest have been meaningful and lasting or halfhearted and self-serving. By 1960, Edward R. Murrow had concluded that, sadly, television journalism was part of an unholy alliance with advertising and show business that made public service all but impossible. In the twenty-first century, some of the historic misgivings about television's role in the United States need to be reconsidered in the light of vast technological and social changes that Murrow could not have imagined.

Acknowledgments

For many years, I have been fortunate to work with supportive and stimulating colleagues at the Philip Merrill College of Journalism at the University of Maryland. This book is an outgrowth of cross-national studies of television news conducted at Maryland with Mark Levy, now of Michigan State University, Michael Gurevitch, and Jay Blumler, superb colleagues all. Along with numerous scholars, I am indebted to Mark Levy for his insights into audience comprehension and into the editorial processes of electronic journalism, and to Michael Gurevitch and Jay Blumler for their pioneering research on public-service journalism.

The dean of the Merrill College of Journalism, Thomas Kunkel, helped in many ways to ensure that this book would be written. I appreciate his friendship, enthusiasm for the topic, moral suasion, and generous financial support. Additional funds to support travel were provided by the L. John Martin Research Fund of the College of Journalism and the General Research Board of the University of Maryland. Professors Lee Thornton, Haynes Johnson, Douglas Gomery, Reese Cleghorn, Carl Sessions Stepp, Judith Paterson, and Gene Roberts read all or part of the manuscript, and each made valuable comments and suggestions.

For more than two decades, I have had the privilege of watching and discussing television news with hundreds of undergraduate and graduate students. Many of them—certainly more than I could or should name— have made direct contributions to this text. I especially appreciate the assistance of Debra A. Schwartz, Kristin Wedemeyer, Laura Hockridge, Lesley Werthamer, Jeff Harvey, Eric Bucy, Kathy Hettleman, Natasha Holmes, Erica Cranston, Jeremy Ritzer, Anna Gawel, and Laura O'Neill.

In the course of writing this book, I conducted more than seventy-five interviews with present and former network news executives, local news directors, local and national anchors, producers, writers, reporters, and critics of television journalism. I cannot thank them all, but for their unusual generosity in carving out the time to see me and their willingness to answer hard questions thoughtfully, I would like to thank, in no special order, Tom Bettag, David Zurawik, Paul Friedman, the late Ed Turner, Gail Evans, Mary Tillotson, Tom Brokaw, Harry Fuller, Bob Reichblum, Barbara Cochran, Randy Covington, Tony Burton, Lori Beecher, Don Dunphy Jr., Jim Van Messel, Jim Hanchett, Carla Wohl, Bob Horner, Sharon Houston, Brian Lamb, Susan Swain, Dick Reingold, Jan Schaffer, Ed Fouhy, Steve Lewis, Roberta Dougherty, Mike Boettcher, and Charles Gibson. I also thank the capable and patient archivists at the Herbert Hoover Presidential Library in West Branch, Iowa, and at the Broadcast Pioneers Library of American Broadcasting at the University of Maryland.

I owe the greatest debt to a group of friends, colleagues, mentors, and family members for their long-standing commitment to me and my work. I cannot begin to do justice to the contributions of my wife, Wendy, and of my children, Joel, Stephanie, and Adam. They provide continuing inspiration for me to do my best.

I

BROADCASTING AND
THE CULTURE OF NEWS

— 1 —

Electronic Journalism in a New Era

On June 1, 1980, a forty-one-year-old champion sailor and former owner of a struggling sign company began a twenty-four-hour-a-day cable television news network in studios set up in a building that had once been a Jewish country club in Atlanta, Georgia. Less than eight months later, on a brisk and biting Washington morning, a sixty-nine-year-old former actor, pitchman, and governor of California became the fortieth president of the United States.

With the passage of time, Robert Edward "Ted" Turner III and Ronald Wilson Reagan would come to be thought of as emblematic of the 1980s. Both men were disciples of individual will and entrepreneurial spirit. Yet their modest educational accomplishments and checkered family histories did not suggest the scope of their ambition or eventual success. Together, it would be argued, they revitalized the "can-do" American ethos in a decade in which a popular movie offered the credo that "greed is good."[1] Both men had been intimately tied to broadcasting for years. Turner, the owner of a barely watched UHF station, was canny, indeed brilliant, in his ability to recognize that the emerging technologies of cable television and satellite transmission could be fused into an entirely new form of television, a "super station" that theoretically could be viewed in every corner of America (and by implication in every corner of the world).

Ronald Reagan had grown up deeply influenced by radio, had worked as an announcer, and through television had achieved his widest recognition. His notion of free enterprise—industry unfettered by government bureaucracy—would lead in the 1990s to the historic deregulation of radio and television, displacing the regulatory apparatus that had been law since 1934.

3

For electronic communication in general, and television news specifically, Turner and Reagan were truly revolutionary figures. Forces set in motion in the 1980s would, in the next two decades, turn television and television news upside down. As a result, the television news viewer of 1980 might scarcely recognize today's TV marketplace:

• The news services of the three principal commercial networks have been joined by a number of other national news-and-information networks on cable television. These include C-SPAN, a cooperative service funded by cable systems around the country; CNBC, a financial-news and talk network owned by General Electric; Fox News, owned by Rupert Murdoch's News Corp.; MSNBC, a coventure of NBC and Microsoft; and Ted Turner's CNN news services, now owned by AOL Time Warner. Headline News and the Cable News Network are a presence in virtually every corner of the globe. The General Electric-owned CNBC provides Wall Street reporting from opening bell to well after the close of trading. Sports news is provided by, among others, Fox Sports Net and the extraordinarily successful ESPN, owned by the Walt Disney Company and valued at well over $2 billion.

• Fewer than ten global conglomerates have consolidated media power on a scale never seen before, virtually turning the communications industry into an oligopoly, similar to the airline and automobile industries, in which power is vested mainly in a few enormous companies. The most powerful media corporations have combined their international reach with a presence in Internet communication, cable television and broadcasting, home video, radio, newspapers, magazines, and book publication. (The Walt Disney Company, for example, is the world's largest publisher of children's books and magazines, with total annual sales of 375 million copies.)[2]

• The combined share of the viewing audience claimed by ABC, CBS, and NBC has dwindled from the 90 percent range to a number well under 50 percent. The network audience has scattered to cable channels, independent stations, to viewing films and other programs on videocassettes, and occasionally to public television. Ratings for each of the three traditional networks' evening newscasts are now typically in the 5 to 7 range (meaning 5 or 7 percent of those homes with television sets). In the 1970s, CBS's top-rated newscast often averaged a rating of 16 or 17. Today it is not at all unusual for the combined network rating for the three newscasts to be less than that of the 1970s CBS by itself. The combined share of the audience for the evening newscasts (the percentage of those people actually viewing at a particular time) is often well below 30.

• The national newscasts themselves face competition from expanded local newscasts that report extensively on national and international news.

Local stations cover major events all over the world with their own personnel. In larger markets, "local" news blocks of two or three hours early in the morning and during each afternoon and evening are not uncommon. The anchors of these newscasts can be expected to interact with each other on the air, conveying warmth and camaraderie; to the degree that network news programs are presented in the same colloquial and collegial spirit, local stations have set a standard for national TV news formats.

• Another source of competition for the networks is the programming of syndicated news magazine shows such as *Inside Edition* and *Extra*, which are widely regarded as practitioners of tabloid journalism for their choice of sensational subjects and their questionable methods of reporting (such as paying sources) and news presentation.

• News has become a staple of prime-time programming. By the 1990s, the four major commercial networks (including the Fox network, owned by media baron Murdoch) offered about a dozen prime-time programs that could be called news magazine shows. *60 Minutes* was the first news magazine to achieve notable ratings success, in the early 1970s; ABC's *20/20* premiered in 1978, struggled at first, and eventually became a solid performer in the ratings. An onslaught of such programs did not occur until the 1993–94 television season. Now ABC, CBS, and NBC all have prime-time news magazine programs from two to occasionally four nights a week.

• At the institutional level, the expectation of regular, substantial profits from news has become shared by every network news division. The ownership of ABC, CBS, NBC, and CNN changed hands, in some cases more than once, in the mid-1980s and 1990s, as a new breed of managers took the reins of network news. One result was a heightened attention to production and payroll costs and, subsequently, a painful process of job eliminations, the closing of foreign bureaus, and a new, stricter financial accountability for reporters, editors, and producers.

***

Taken as a whole, the changes in the news environment are profound, and their implications still are being sorted out. The vast, provocative television coverage of the O.J. Simpson murder case in 1994 and the Monica Lewinsky scandal in the second term of the Clinton administration illustrated some of the new realities in vivid detail. The thorough blending of news and entertainment that characterizes much of television journalism has raised ethical questions at every turn, in virtually every news report, during a mind-numbing series of scandals covered extensively on the networks and on cable news outlets—Robert Blake, Chandra Levy, Tonya Harding and Nancy Kerrigan, Jon-Benet Ramsey, Michael Jackson, Amy Fisher and Joey

Buttafuoco, the Menendez brothers, William Kennedy Smith, John and Lorena Bobbitt, and other figures too numerous to mention. The genre of entertainment news sprouts new programs every year, with *Entertainment Tonight, Access Hollywood,* and *E! News* enjoying growing audiences.

To be sure, the proliferation of news programs has a positive side. Accomplished, long-form documentaries can be seen on CNN, MSNBC, PBS, the Discovery Channel, the Learning Channel, the History Channel, the Arts and Entertainment network, and elsewhere. Every news-magazine program has covered more than a few important stories. National Public Radio and its affiliate stations produce, at the local and national levels, many programs of distinction.

Paradoxically, though, an era of program diversity in news and public affairs has yielded a substantial degree of program convergence: many programs presented under the banner of journalism or at least "nonfiction television" are at best similar and at worst clones of one another. The prime-time news magazines owe much to the network morning programs (not coincidentally, Katie Couric, Barbara Walters, Tom Brokaw, Charles Gibson, Diane Sawyer, and Jane Pauley are all veterans of both prime-time magazine shows and the early-morning wars). The story of O.J. Simpson belonged just as much to *Dateline NBC* as to *Inside Edition. 20/20* covers stories that might just as easily be seen on the confessional daytime talk shows.

When Tonya Harding traveled to the 1994 Winter Olympics in Norway, she was accompanied by a crew from the tabloid news program *Inside Edition,* which had paid a substantial sum for the privilege of interviewing her. A few seats away on the plane sat Connie Chung, coanchor of the *CBS Evening News.* Symbolically, the trip to Lillehammer marked a new destination for CBS News and its flagship broadcast—after decades of representing the best of broadcast journalism, of riding in first class, they had become close to their tabloid competitors in more ways than one.

It is unarguable that a broader range of news and information programs, including all-news programming, daytime talk, prime-time news magazines, and quasi-journalistic tabloid shows and reality-based offerings (usually about crime and police work), is now available to the television audience. *American Television News* is an examination of the broad-based changes in television news now occurring in an unprecedented era of program diversity brought on by fundamental alterations in the corporate and technological climate.

The Cultural Role of TV News

Since its earliest days, television journalism has had a dual personality. When CBS pioneer Edward R. Murrow was at the height of his power and prestige, he was as readily recognized for his celebrity interview program *Person to Person* as for his controversial investigative reporting. Critics occasionally spoke of the "Higher Murrow" and the "Lower Murrow." That early dichotomy has evolved into a range of television news programs, from relatively conventional to clearly sensational, that makes a reconsideration of the character of television news particularly timely.

Journalism, print and otherwise, has its roots in the art of narrative: television news is a form of visual storytelling that adheres to the requisites of plot and character development and the attainment of dramatic unity. Journalism by definition entertains us as it offers compelling portrayals of reality, thus engaging our senses as well as our intellects. Distinctions between "news" and "entertainment" are never easy from the point of view of the audience member, who is likely to be "entertained" at some level by any story that is well-told; distinctions in the *content* of news are perhaps as problematic. Does television news dwell on sensational and extraordinary events at the expense of substantive news? The question is increasingly at the heart of a continuing national debate.

For at least thirty years, television and TV news have been the frequent targets of pointed critiques of mass culture. The intellectual argument of such critics is that television fosters shallowness, simplistic views of society, and a sense of unreality by virtue of its commercial and technical nature. Many intellectuals and social critics find in television news a "lowest common denominator" mentality that reduces information to raw experience and trivializes serious discourse.

Ironically, one of network television's most vocal detractors has been CBS's star anchor Dan Rather. In an address to the national convention of the Radio and Television News Directors Association in Miami, Rather lamented "complacency" and "cowardice" on the part of television journalists, charging that the promise of television had been "squandered and cheapened." The "thoughtful analysis" of the earlier period had been replaced with "live pops" urged by market analysts and others driven by ratings.[3]

Later, in a talk at the Columbia Graduate School of Journalism, Rather expressed the fear that journalism—especially broadcast news—was succumbing to entertainment, to "what I call Hollywoodation," in lieu of "its role in the governmental system, its checks and balances . . . and [it's role in] public service."[4]

Despite Rather's protestations, news and entertainment are as solidly linked on network "news" programs as they have ever been. If that battle for the soul of television in fact was ever waged, it is certainly over by now. A more pressing problem today may be the blurred distinction between mainstream

7

programming and what is widely referred to as "tabloid television."

Reality-based programs that feature crime, sensationalism, sexuality in all its manifestations, and an obsessive interest in celebrity run the gamut from network news magazines in prime time to daytime and late-night talk shows to programs based on newscast formats such as *Inside Edition*. Producers have argued that the overwhelming success and subsequent spread of tabloid news programs can be attributed to the American audience's boredom with fictional television and "hard news."[5]

Such nonfiction television has proved a formula for achieving great success at comparatively low cost. The tabloid programs usually cost between 25 and 50 percent less to produce than Hollywood sit-coms or police shows. Geraldo Rivera, host of his own talk shows, defended the tabloid style he used and that of similar shows at the time. "Non-fiction TV has become more diversified and more democratic," he said.

> Face it, the old-style network news documentaries had become boring. Yes, they were critical darlings, but the television audience got tired of being lectured down to by reporters sitting up on a journalistic Mount Olympus. . . . At some point, even the ivory tower elite will recognize that an audience numbering in the tens of millions is not a lunatic fringe nor a gullible cult. It is America, and it is watching.[6]

Conventional broadcasters appear to have gotten the message. *Nightline* has tackled difficult subjects with skill and insight, but it rode to its highest ratings on the heels of Jim and Tammy Faye Bakker, the colorful (and cartoonish) televangelists done in by their own misdeeds. NBC's failed *Saturday Night With Connie Chung*, then its failed series *Yesterday, Today and Tomorrow*, relied heavily on dramatic reenactment of actual events for the program's content. The E! Entertainment Network routinely uses such reenactments in what purport to be documentaries. For a long while, tabloid subjects occupied the networks as much as any other stories in recent years (according to some reports, ABC devoted more news personnel to the Tonya–Nancy affair than to the 1989 Loma Prieta earthquake in California and the tearing down of the Berlin Wall combined).

For the networks, the prime-time news magazine shows have provided the opportunity to augment traditional journalism with sometimes generous doses of tabloid storytelling. Indeed, when *60 Minutes* first went on the air in 1968, some critics considered the show tabloid television because it was rebelling against the traditional full-hour documentary style used by network news programs.[7] It is indisputable that *60 Minutes* changed the climate for broadcast journalism because it has made a lot of money for a

8

long time—now in excess of $2 billion, more money (excluding income from reruns) than any program in television history.

The Network Dilemma

In 1968, CBS veteran director and producer Don Hewitt created a paradigm for the television news magazine with *60 Minutes*. Not only would its format eventually supplant the documentary as a program form, but the program's success also increased the demand that news deliver a hefty audience. *60 Minutes* has never been surpassed in that regard; the program has long accounted for a large portion of the entire network's profits.[8]

As a programmer, what Hewitt did changed the nature of the TV documentary, which had traditionally been an hour-long program on a single subject narrated by an off-camera reporter. His strategy was ingenious:

1. Structure the program around three approximately fourteen-minute narratives, each with a discernible beginning, middle, and end—and a coherent, engaging story line.

2. Enhance the role of the reporter, so that he or she becomes a part of the story, either its investigative protagonist, guide to the unusual (but not often the bizarre), or companion to an engaging celebrity.[9]

3. Provide most stories with a clear good-versus-evil orientation, so that the viewer is caught up in the cupidity, duplicity, and sheer gall of the wrongdoers.

4. Make profiles of famous people a key ingredient of the mix.

The basic structure of *60 Minutes* is largely the framework on which all magazine programs rest. If anything, the variations on the theme are likely to be stories that are just a bit more lurid, a bit more suited to the tabloid style. ABC's Diane Sawyer began the program *Turning Point* with an unrevealing return to the story of the murderous Manson family of the late 1960s. *Dateline NBC* garnered its highest ratings with an extended interview with mass murderer Jeffrey Dahmer.

Richard Wald, a vice president of ABC News, pointed out one aspect of the network dilemma in a 1994 broadcast of the program *Viewpoint*.[10] Coverage of the O.J. Simpson case presented network programmers with a no-win proposition: leave the coverage of a rather mundane pretrial hearing and lose most of your viewership, or continue with the coverage and become the target of a barrage from media critics. ABC, Wald contends, is simply in the business of mass journalism, and one of its components is attention to celebrity figures; critics of the substance of network news, he says, refuse to accept that fact.[11]

Perspectives on the New Media Environment

Despite widespread criticism, some television insiders and social observers are not terribly concerned about the state of TV news. They find it true that there is more information being provided—on television specifically and in society as a whole—than there has ever been. The United States has perhaps 12,000 specialized magazines, more than 250 devoted to personal computers alone; 10,000 radio and television stations; 5,000 cable TV systems; and 1,500 daily newspapers. The sources of electronic information, in new technologies from digital cable to wireless communication to direct satellite programming, are in a period of explosive growth. That television is faced with a new set of program alternatives is not surprising and should be a welcome development.

Combined with the increased availability of information is a noticeable increase in audience interest in reportage, practical information, and dramatic portrayals of reality. NBC anchor Tom Brokaw says the range of what is covered by television news has expanded considerably:

> When I started in this business, black America didn't exist on television. We didn't cover the black culture. We had begun to cover it in the 1960s as a civil right phenomenon, but we still didn't cover the family, or the school problems, or the economic problems. . . . There are lots of things now that do get covered that didn't get covered then. It was a pretty narrow base, in the old days. It was Washington, London, and New York—and if there was a train wreck in Ohio, that got on, or a farmer's revolt of some kind. But big chunks of the country simply didn't get covered. Now we do pay a lot more attention to a lot more issues that affect people's lives.[12]

Everyone in television news pays a lot more attention also to the audience figures that issue forth not only during ratings sweeps weeks, but during every week—even within an individual newscast, as audience fall-off from one story to another is monitored at the local and national levels. Once a form of "insider information" considered too arcane for the general public, the analysis of television viewing has become regular reading material provided by most local TV columnists. Ratings winners and losers generally are reported weekly in U.S. metropolitan newspapers. A rating is defined as a simple percentage of the total audience, expressed in terms of households with television (i.e., "TV households") tuned to a specific program. If there were 100 million TV households, a program with a rating of 15 would have an audience composed of 15 million TV households. (The number of households has actually grown larger than 100 million, but the simplified figure is used here to make the definition clearer.) The share is a competitive index of how an individual program fared against those in its time period, those on the air at the same time. The population used in computing a share is thus "sets in use," a number always smaller than the total population of TV households. A share of 20 for program X means that 20 percent of however many sets were in use at a particular time were tuned to program X. For the networks, the last twenty-five years have brought both declining ratings and declining shares.

Another explanation of the changing television landscape is concerned mainly with forces inside the television and entertainment industries. Network entertainment has become much more competitive and expensive; competition from cable TV suppliers, independent TV stations, and videocassettes has meant a declining network share of the entertainment audience, while the price of producing or underwriting entertainment remains as high as ever.

Looming Problems

One form of government regulation, referred to within television circles as the financial interest and syndication or "fin-syn" rules, served for many years as a disincentive for the networks to invest in entertainment programming.[13] In the past, the regulations prevented networks from owning more than three hours a week of their own prime-time nonnews programming and from placing into syndication, after a five-year network run, programs they had produced themselves. Networks were thus prevented from reaping substantial profits. With those rules in place, news in prime time was appealing financially because the networks owned it and it was reasonably cheap to produce. With the rules now revised, networks have much more financial clout overall, but the attractiveness of prime-time news, some people believe, may wane. If that is to happen, there are no clear signs of it yet in prime time.

Still, the most prevalent reactions to sweeping structural changes in TV news have been negative. Critical reaction to the increased prime-time popularity of news programming, its frequent brushes with tabloid values, and the related questions of program diversity, taste, and professional standards is abundant and exists on many levels—including critiques of the underlying cultural values of TV news and chagrin over misguided professional practices. At the outset, these perspectives need to be identified. The points of view they represent are often connected and overlap. Some of the many intertwined arguments about the failings of television journalism that have come to the fore are outlined here:

11

News has become dangerously market-driven. In catering to the interests of the largest possible audience, producers and reporters are led astray from their social and civic responsibilities. Walter Cronkite, who was anchor of the *CBS Evening News* for nineteen years, says that, confronted with rising competition from cable, videocassettes, and more aggressive local newscasts and tabloid shows, the network newscasts "frequently go too soft." He notes that "their features aren't interpretive to the day's events, and the time could be better used. We've always known you can gain circulation or viewers by cheapening the product, and now you're finding the bad driving out the good."[14] Cronkite's complaint is allied to a concern with journalism's role in contributing to declining cultural standards.

Television news has chosen to portray the darker side of American society and, in its quest for ratings, has debased notions of what the country really is. Historically, it is fair to assert that news has always been a commodity packaged for an audience and that TV journalism proffers "pictures of reality" for sale to the largest possible public. Some critics of the media fear that what we learn from their refracted images of American society today are lessons that our basest instincts are the ones that really matter, that action supersedes meaning, that distinctions between private and public behavior have become quaint, and that "news value" is enhanced by the value of vulgarity.

The visibility and power of celebrity journalists have distorted television news values. Charles Gibson, the cohost of *Good Morning America* and *PrimeTime Thursday* and a respected former congressional correspondent, was asked what he viewed as the most disturbing trend in the new programming. He spoke of the enormous sum invested in Diane Sawyer by ABC (at the time between $5 and $8 million annually) and the reality that, for the network, "Diane Sawyer cannot be allowed to fail."[15] If that means lowering the standards of her subject matter, so be it, Gibson implied. Whatever had to be done to obtain the necessary audience would be done. Ironically, the two would be paired later both in the morning and at night on two successful programs.

Ed Turner, a longtime news executive at CNN, said before his retirement that the emphasis on building and maintaining "stars" in the network news divisions was a function of how little the regular evening newscasts were allowed to differ. With limited time at 6:30 or 7:00, the three network newscasts must devote most of their news hole—less than twenty-three minutes—to the same stories. Facing an extremely competitive fight for ratings, the single element that distinguishes one program most clearly from another, and consequently one network from another, is the anchor, Turner said.[16]

For every network magazine program, there is a star—or two—at its helm. For more than a decade, anchors have been the reporting stars on their own newscasts, sent literally around the world on a moment's notice to cover breaking news. The anchor's travels play a large role in shaping decisions on story selection and placement.

In the effort to bolster ratings at all costs, journalistic standards have been lowered. Network news magazines were roundly criticized when they began reenacting events for dramatic effect. The technique had already become standard practice for the tabloid and entertainment-news shows. Following reenactments aired on two NBC magazine programs, *Time* magazine charged that television journalists were "trying to locate their ethical bearings in this brave new world":

> At one extreme are the traditionalists, who insist that a staged scene of any kind is inappropriate on a news program, which depends for its credibility on presenting the truth and nothing but. On the other side are a new generation of TV news producers, under pressure from network bosses to come up with programs that will draw prime-time-size audiences.[17]

ABC's Tom Bettag, executive producer of *Nightline* and formerly executive producer of the *CBS Evening News with Dan Rather*, blames the use of questionable production techniques, by the networks and tabloid programs, for confusing viewers, producing doubt in the audience about what they're viewing. "Distrust of the media in this country is well-founded," he says, "and we bring it on ourselves by not making clear what's real and what's not real."[18] He cites the use of sound effects to amplify news footage and the editing in of stock footage from film libraries (without making clear the source of those materials) as production devices that blur the meaning of the story on the air. Bettag reserves his greatest concern, though, for the practices of the tabloid magazine shows.

> There's a real danger there . . . no matter what the subjects are. The paying of people for interviews, the hyping and hoking and distorting . . . I cannot feel more deeply about that. [The tabloid programs lack] the commitment to reportorial honesty.[19]

It is clear that the pressure to succeed can push reporters and producers past the point of honest reporting. In 1993, *Dateline NBC* weathered a storm of controversy after broadcasting a story about allegedly fire-prone gas tanks in General Motors trucks. On the program, tests of the trucks had been rigged to ensure that they would explode; in the story's aftermath, the network issued apologies, producers were fired, and the president of NBC News, Michael Gartner, resigned.

The quality of U.S. television news and of American democracy itself is poorly served by the increasing concentration of media power. Previously unimaginable in their scope and sheer capital worth, global conglomerates such as General Electric, Viacom, News Corporation, Disney, Vivendi Universal, Bertelsmann, and AOL Time Warner are by necessity driven to meet investor expectations, not public-interest obligations. Both vertically and horizontally integrated, these companies have proprietary interests that may stifle competition within each medium, promote editorial timidity, and apparently have already prevented negative news coverage of the flagship corporation by a beholden news division. The most pointed example of network reluctance to cover controversial issues for corporate reasons was the initial failure of CBS to broadcast sensational material on the tobacco industry on *60 Minutes.*

***

Was the infiltration of corporate pressure or "entertainment" values to blame for cases of journalistic weakness, excess, or irresponsibility? I hope to suggest in this book that the reasons for the particular evolution of broadcast journalism in the United States are more complex and are related to economic, cultural, historical, and technological forces.

In 1977, television critic and commentator Ron Powers focused on the "news business as show business" in *The Newscasters*, a book that identified the culprits as managers and news consultants for local stations:

> The biggest heist of the 1970s never made it on the five o'clock news. The biggest heist of the 1970s *was* the five o'clock news. The salesmen took it. They took it away from the journalists, slowly, patiently, gradually, and with such finesse that nobody noticed until it was too late.[20]

Powers wrote that network news was insulated from the market pressures that were common at the level of local stations, but there were clear signs in 1977 that the networks, with ABC at the forefront, were changing their definition of and approach to news.

The careers of three prominent ABC employees—Barbara Walters, Geraldo Rivera, and Roone Arledge—took off in the 1970s, and it is not an overstatement to say that television news has not been the same since.

Roone Arledge utilized his technical and journalistic gifts first to revolutionize sports coverage at ABC and then to revitalize the news division. (*Copyright 2002 ABC Photography Archives*)

Walters' success may be said to represent the ascendancy of celebrity journalism. Rivera championed a style of populist, often confrontational reporting that instilled news coverage with a high degree of emotionalism. Arledge almost singly saw the narrative power that lay in the tools of television. In the 1960s, he began to revolutionize the nature of sports coverage, treating the game itself as raw material that could be shaped into compelling visual drama. "The game was just the starting point," author Marc Gunther noted in a study of Arledge's career at ABC. "It was the show that counted."[21] To cover sports, the tools Arledge employed were the slow-motion camera, the instant replay, stop action, and the creative use of cameras placed wherever the action might be—underwater, at the top of a mountain, in the driver's seat of a race car. Video coverage of news that packaged events as "stories," utilizing the dramatic potential of the medium to enhance, and even re-create, actual events, was not far in coming.

As network news was gradually transformed from a budgetary "loss leader" to a potentially very profitable area of programming, the celebrity status of anchors and reporters grew. That was not an entirely new development: NBC's David Brinkley had stopped most of his reporting years earlier when he found that the clamor his presence created made routine news coverage impossible. Walter Cronkite became in turn a greater celebrity than Huntley or Brinkley. By the 1980s, the three networks' anchors were certifiably "stars" in every sense. Their own work was an exercise in celebrity journalism whatever and whoever their subjects might be. By the 1990s, TV news was solidly moored in the realm of popular culture. Over the course of four decades, broadcast journalism had achieved mass popularity, with all its rewards and limitations.

This book tells a story within a story; both may seem familiar, but neither is well understood by scholars and students of media history in the United States. The first story is the development of electronic news in this country in the last two and a half decades. As I have indicated, the pace of change has been furious, and the landscape of television journalism has emerged barely recognizable. Bellwether federal communications legislation that lasted for more than fifty years is gone. What is the sum of these regulatory and structural changes? Is the American public better off? At the least, this book extends and, I hope, enriches the discussion of that question. The cataclysm in television, moreover, begs the issue of the social and civic responsibility of broadcasting in the United States. Why, almost alone among countries in the West, did the United States opt for a commercial system with almost no practical accountability? What, if anything, has been lost in the bargain? And does the concept of public interest have meaning in a communications environment of 100, 500, or even thousands of channels? Today there is considerable public debate over these matters in Great Britain, Italy, India, Australia, and many other countries. The United States is strangely quiet. Does anyone believe, for instance, that the Internet *should* do certain things? That the marketplace will not provide enough of everything? This book addresses those questions as well, promoting a conversation about the role of television and subsequent technologies in America.

The rapid development of new media technologies in the United States, along with the evolution of new corporate structures for news and entertainment, has made this discussion especially timely. The issues it explores touch on governance, citizenship, commerce, the uses of leisure, and the nature of self-fulfillment. We are at the beginning of a new communications era. It is a good time to pose important questions.

— 2 —

Beginnings: The Ethic of Commercialism

Together with the aeroplane and other of the modern devices,
the radio has taken its rightful place as one of the agencies
necessary to American life.

—Herbert Hoover, 1927

The Introduction of Radio

The scientific history of radio may be said to have begun in the nineteenth
century with the discovery of electrical energy. The commercial history of
radio in America can be traced to a memo written in November 1916 by
David Sarnoff, a young executive with a company called American Marconi,
to his superior, Edward J. Nally:

> I have in mind a plan of development which would make radio a "household
> utility" in the same sense as the piano or the phonograph. . . . The receiver can
> be designed in the form of a simple "Radio Music Box" and arranged for
> several different wave lengths, which would be changeable with the throwing
> of a single switch or pressing of a single button.[1]

Sarnoff, born in Russia in 1891, was a visionary who understood intuitively
that radio had the capability to change the lives of ordinary people. Brilliant and daring as the head of RCA, he became the man most responsible
for shaping American radio in its early years. But radio developed haphaz-
ardly in the United States, without the government control that existed in
Europe and with no overarching plan.

18

From our perspective in the twenty-first century, it is difficult to imagine how the new medium of radio was regarded more than eighty years ago. After all, life was so different then: simpler in many respects, with fewer opportunities for travel or cultural enrichment. Radio was considered wondrous. By some miracle, radio made available to everyone live performances of opera, the music hall, a concerto, a vocal solo, educational talks. Nowadays we may speak disparagingly of "entertainment" in the broadcast media as trivial, mindless, or merely time-consuming, but in 1920, most Americans had no opportunity to be entertained in the way that radio made possible. Indeed, the introduction of radio produced a distinct euphoria, the feeling that more wondrous things were sure to follow.[2]

But managing the innovation called for some degree of oversight. Radio reception required a system of station allocation. Two stations broadcasting in the same geographic area on the same frequency meant no reception for anyone. In Washington, the Department of Commerce granted licenses to broadcast, but without a coherent plan or system of organization. From January through November 1921, it granted five licences; then, according to broadcast historian Eric Barnouw, came "the deluge"—more than 450 licenses in the next eight months.[3]

Chaos was beginning to reign. The secretary of commerce, Herbert Hoover, called a first, then a second, Washington Radio Conference in 1923. He invited "experts and broadcasters," many of whom were amateurs using crystal sets from their homes. Hoover had been a mining engineer and an extremely successful businessman. He believed that radio should not be used for individual communication, but should contain material of interest to large audiences. He expressed concern that private groups might begin to monopolize the wavelengths, but in whatever restrictions he placed on station allocation, he was determined not to exercise censorship.[4]

The key to Hoover's philosophy and to the way the regulation of radio evolved was that he wanted regulation to be "decentralized and largely voluntary."[5] Still, there remained the problem of spectrum allocation. (Radio waves occupy part of the electromagnetic spectrum, which contains phenomena ranging from X rays to visible light to VHF and UHF television.) Stations placed too closely together caused interference on the air and headaches for listeners. By 1926, Hoover was speaking of the need to centralize oversight. According to a Philadelphia newspaper account, he referred to radio as a "spoiled child":

> That radio, carefully nursed from infancy, has grown into a spoiled child and is now "acting up before company" was the assertion of Secretary Hoover, who visited Philadelphia yesterday. "Radio must be put under the control of a central commission, as is proposed, or it will fall into a chaotic state," he said.

"We nursed radio along," continued the Secretary, "and now that it is in a healthy, grown-up condition, it is rapidly getting out of bounds."[6]

In 1926, President Calvin Coolidge urged Congress to remedy the confusion in radio broadcasting. The result was the Dill-White Radio Act of 1927. The radio act established the principle of public ownership of the airwaves. No one party could assert that it owned a particular frequency. Only the public could own such a natural resource. Stations were allowed, in the radio act and in the legislation that followed, to "lease" the frequency for a specified time from its public owners. The radio act also called upon the president to appoint a five-member commission to allocate station licenses, the Federal Radio Commission (FRC). In March 1927, there were 732 stations broadcasting in the United States. Few were network-affiliated; more than 600 stations operated independently. "The majority of these were not selling time. Many were still publicity vehicles, representing newspapers, stores, manufacturers, hotels. About ninety stations were operated by educational institutions, offering concerts and talks, including full college courses. There were also a number of religious stations."[7]

The radio act nullified all existing licenses. But it offered little consideration to the sale of advertising time and barely recognized the existence of networks (then referred to as "chains"). Thus, the legislation took no direct stake in the looming battle between commercial and noncommercial interests. In the granting of a license or in the transfer of a station, the guiding standard was to be the "public interest, convenience and necessity," words that obviously referred to the public's welfare but had little concrete meaning in 1927—or in the years to come. Licenses to broadcast would be subject to renewal every three years. There was to be no censorship with the exception of a ban on obscene language. From its beginning, the FRC was subject to significant forms of pressure from Congress and the broadcast industry. Even with the 1927 radio act, it was unclear how radio would be financed. There remained a clear need for more comprehensive legislation that would be attuned to the realities of American broadcasting.

Corporations and Commercials

Among the interested parties active in the formation of radio were such large companies as General Electric, Westinghouse Electric, and Western Electric, a subsidiary of the American Telephone and Telegraph Company (AT&T). American Marconi, the outright leader in radio, was the source of most of the radio equipment in the country.[8] During World War I (1914–1918), American companies had pooled their patents for military use. After the war, the government urged the formation of a new corporation that would hold all American patents related to radio and act as a service organization for American companies. General Electric set up a fund to buy out shareholders of American Marconi and then joined with AT&T and Westinghouse in ownership of that new company, which was named the Radio Corporation of America (RCA). In the 1930s, the government forced the separation of RCA from its parent companies.

Two companies began to link individual stations together to form networks. AT&T used its own telephone lines to interconnect its flagship station, WEAF in New York, with seventeen other stations. RCA patched together a smaller chain of stations using its New York outlet, WJZ, over lines normally used by Western Union. The AT&T network would eventually become the flagship station of the National Broadcasting Company (NBC), which was created in 1926. By the next year, NBC operated two networks, called NBC Red and NBC Blue. In 1943, following an antitrust action, NBC Blue was sold to Edward J. Noble, the manufacturer of Life Savers candy, and became the American Broadcasting Company. The Columbia Broadcasting System (CBS) premiered in September 1927 as a sixteen-station chain owned by William S. Paley, the heir to a Philadelphia cigar company fortune.

Meanwhile, there were ongoing deliberations about how to fund radio broadcasting. Suggestions included private endowments, local taxation, licensing fees paid by users of the medium (which became the financial base for the British Broadcasting Corporation), taxes on receivers, and commercial sponsorship of programming. AT&T's WEAF was the first station to use commercial funding on a large scale. First, it offered sponsored talks on the air. Then it simply attached the names of products or companies to performing acts, such as the "Lucky Strike Orchestra" named for Lucky Strike cigarettes or the "Interwoven Pair" for Interwoven Socks. Next, it was programs: *The Eveready Hour* for Eveready batteries. WEAF was now rarely available for free broadcasts; it was selling its time to advertisers.[9]

Sponsorship became increasingly common, and advertisers wanted specific data about the size of the audience. National advertisers set up an organization called the "Comparative Analysis of Broadcasting" under the direction of researcher Archibald Crossley. He hired interviewers across the country who called homes to inquire about radio listening. The method of audience analysis was later called telephone recall, and it marked the beginning of the ratings system that would play such an important role in the future.

Early in the 1920s, the large broadcasting companies had assumed that radio might boost profits, but they did not consider the medium a way to make money directly. Amateur operators "had looked to radio as part of their hobby, an active rather than passive enterprise."[10] Educators and others thought that radio held the potential for broad public enlightenment. "Instead, the form national radio took in the United States proved to be directly commercial, passive, and homogenized, promoting consumption as the way to happiness."[11]

The 1927 radio act was replaced with new legislation, the communications act of 1934. The act created the Federal Communications Commission (FCC), made up of seven commissioners appointed by the president and confirmed by the Senate. No more than four of the seven could be members of the same political party. Most of those appointed to the FCC were lawyers with experience in public utilities or government service. The FCC was given the charge to determine if a station's policies and programs were in the public interest, but in practice it dealt very little with broadcast content. (Most cases concerned disputes over station ownership and other financial matters.) Extended to television, the 1934 legislation remained the central framework for the regulation of American broadcasting for almost sixty years.

By the mid-1930s, the nature of radio in the United States—and eventually television would follow the pattern set by radio—was in place. Radio would provide a range of entertainment programs, offered by networks to their affiliated stations. Advertising would be the fundamental base of financial support. News, when it was aired at all, was generally in the form of announcers reading from the newspaper. (That would change as World War II approached, however, when the importance of events and the attendant upsurge in public interest in what was happening abroad meant that actual reporting would be a necessity). Radio would exist to make a profit, and ratings would be used to determine the popularity of programs on the air.

Television News and the Ethic of Commercialism

> Unless we get up off our fat surpluses and recognize that television in the main is being used to distract, delude, amuse and insulate us, then television and those who finance it, those who look at it and those who work at it, may see a totally different picture too late. I do not advocate that we turn television into a 27-inch wailing wall where longhairs constantly bemoan the state of our culture and our defense. But I would just like to see it reflect occasionally the hard, unyielding realities of the world in which we live . . . . This instrument can teach, it can illuminate; yes, and it can even inspire. But it can do so only to the extent that humans are determined to use it toward those ends. Otherwise, it is merely wires and lights in a box.

> —*Edward R. Murrow, 1958*

Edward R. Murrow was the pioneer of American broadcast journalism in both radio and television. At the end of his career, though, he had grown disenchanted with television and with CBS. (*CBS Photo Archive*)

Radio and television journalism have been hesitant and perplexing undertakings from the earliest days of both media. As radio began to develop, most sponsors did not even want news broadcasts. The leading radio network in 1933, called NBC Blue, did not have a single daily news program. Programming at that time was likely to be controlled by the wishes of advertising agencies, and sponsors insisted on veto power over news programming. The news services—Associated Press (AP), United Press (UP), and INS (International News Service)—were prohibited from providing news to the networks, although bulletins were available for a fee to some stations.[12] It has become a cliché that "Edward R. Murrow invented broadcast journalism" in the United States. The truth is somewhat more complicated. American television news sprang from three sources: radio journalism, which was in effect created and shaped during World War II; the history and tradition of the documentary film; and the model of the theatrical newsreel, which combined elements of entertainment with journalism.

Edward R. Murrow

Edward R. Murrow was certainly the most important figure to emerge from radio journalism in the 1930s. The distinctive "Murrow style" was that of the on-air radio journalist as a literate, hard-edged, superbly theatrical reporter. The powerful role of the radio correspondent began with reports from Europe that conveyed for American audiences the reality, and especially the *sound*, of what was happening overseas.

To a degree, Murrow followed the career path of H.V. Kaltenborn, another CBS commentator and news analyst. In the mid-1930s, Kaltenborn did two broadcasts each week and paid for his own travel through Europe. His main income came from lectures given throughout the United States. In 1936, Kaltenborn, who delivered his radio commentaries in an inimitable, high-pitched, nasal voice and staccato tempo, reported on a skirmish in the Spanish Civil War "while hiding in a haystack between the two armies. Listeners in America could hear bullets hitting the hay above him while he spoke."[13] In 1937, twenty-eight-year-old Edward R. Murrow, a native of North Carolina and a graduate of Washington State University who had never worked for a newspaper and had never been a reporter, took a job as CBS European director, arranging educational talks and other broadcasts from his base in London. In March 1938, Murrow, informed that Germany had begun the seizure of Austria, flew to Berlin and chartered a transport plane to Vienna. On March 13, he broadcast his first report to American listeners. This is how it began:

24

> This is Edward Murrow speaking from Vienna. It's now nearly 2:30 in the morning and Herr Hitler has not yet arrived. No one seems to know just when he will get here, but most people expect him after 10 o'clock tomorrow morning. It's, of course, obvious after one glance at Vienna that a tremendous reception is being prepared. I arrived here by air from Warsaw and Berlin only a few hours ago. There was very little excitement apparent in Warsaw. People went quietly about their work. The cafés were full. The drivers of those horse-drawn cabs were muffled up in their fur coats and they seemed pretty remote from the crisis.[14]

Murrow spoke simply and with authority. He had a powerful voice and, as he gained experience as an announcer, became a master at using silences for dramatic effect. His connection with audiences was virtually immediate. Perhaps his most famous wartime broadcasts came during the bombing of London. This report was aired on September 12, 1940:

> This is London at 3:30 in the morning. This has been what might be called a "routine night"—air-raid alarm at about nine o'clock and intermittent bombing ever since. I had the impression that more high explosives and few incendiaries have been used tonight. Only two small fires can be seen on the horizon. Again the Germans have been sending their bombers in singly or in pairs. The antiaircraft barrage has been fierce, but sometimes there have been periods of twenty minutes when London has been silent.[15]

Murrow's impact as a reporter—and, accordingly, the influence of radio journalism—was extraordinary. Broadcast coverage of the war was more timely than newspaper reports, reached a national audience of millions, and identified the institution of CBS with a single individual. Murrow also put together a team of foreign correspondents, regarded thereafter as one of the finest groups of journalists ever assembled. It included William L. Shirer, Eric Sevareid, Charles Collingwood, Alex Kendrick, Howard K. Smith, Larry LeSueur, Richard C. Hottelet, and David Schoenbrun.

After the war, Murrow took an administrative job with CBS News. Returning to broadcasting in 1947, he began a partnership with Fred Friendly, a producer who had worked in radio in Providence, Rhode Island. After working on a series of radio documentaries called *Hear It Now*, they turned to television in 1951; their documentary series for television was *See It Now*.

According to many reports, Murrow was distrustful of the medium of television.[16] Known for a particular brand of personal journalism, he worried about the collaborative nature of television work, the entertainment aspects of the medium, and the importance of technical expertise in putting together programs. According to David Halberstam, he also had misgivings about Friendly, who was certainly a gifted producer: "'Watch out for

Friendly,' Murrow would tell journalistic initiates who might not know of Friendly's instinct for drama, 'he doesn't know a fact.'"[17]

At the outset of his television career, Murrow did have the advantage of a close friendship with the founder and chairman of CBS, William S. Paley. As long-time CBS and ABC correspondent and anchorman Harry Reasoner wrote in his autobiography, largely because Murrow was regarded as important, Paley regarded news as important. Without that relationship, Reasoner observed, American television news might have had a very different tradition:

> We might have very dull and nominal news, as the British do. Or very sexy and trivial and irresponsible network news, as some local American stations do, or the sort of thing the British have in print journalism.[18]

Reasoner made those comments in 1981, before network news would be accused of being both trivial and sensational, but his characterization of the CBS tradition is accurate. At the beginning, executives at CBS accepted the assumption that news would be serious and responsible, free of the direct influence of advertisers. (When Murrow became controversial, though, advertisers stopped sponsoring his programs, and finally the programs themselves became infrequent.) Second, it was assumed early in the history of television that "network news would be free-spending, in spite of the fact that at that time no one foresaw that news could ever turn a profit."[19] Without question, Reasoner notes, Murrow helped establish the dramatic and journalistic importance of the television newsman: "The face the people saw and the voice they heard would be not only the central figure to the audience but a substantial influence in what he was asked to do and how he would do it."[20]

The Documentary Film

The second influence on the birth of television news, the documentary film, can be traced to silent instructional and educational films produced before the beginning of the twentieth century. The first documentary artists were, generally speaking, not Americans; they included the Russian Sergey Eisenstein; Britain's John Grierson, who made films in the late 1920s and brought the word "documentary" into use; and Alberto Cavalcanti, whose principal work was a 1926 silent film of a day in the life of Paris.[21]

Documentary film was rooted in the themes and techniques of social realism. Far from being whimsical or escapist, its tone was exploratory and reformist; throughout his career, Murrow's television documentaries reflected that film heritage. With the beginning of World War II, interest in films about reality, especially interest in their value as propaganda, was heightened.[22] Leni Riefenstahl's 1937 *Triumph of the Will*, a powerful, visually stirring work, is the best known of a large number of Nazi propaganda films. In England, the Ministry of Information assumed control of a film unit and produced feature-length documentaries. Propaganda films developed new techniques for re-creating events after the fact.

The Newsreel

While Edward R. Murrow followed in the tradition of European documentary filmmakers—and was instrumental in establishing a new framework for American television documentaries—the evening network newscasts were more strongly influenced by the theatrical newsreel. In the United States, Thomas Edison, J. Stuart Blackton, Biograph, and Vitagraph began filming actual events around the turn of the century, including the inauguration of President McKinley in 1897, his funeral in 1901, the Galveston cyclone in 1900, and the San Francisco earthquake in 1906. The first regular newsreel series is credited to Charles Pathé and his *Journal* of 1907. By the late 1920s, Metrotone, International Newsreel, Fox Movietone News, and the Pathé Newsreel had news-gathering operations all over the world.

During the 1930s, the conventional newsreel form became established in England and America. Each newsreel contained a number of short, unrelated items, usually between six and eight; the length of a newsreel was about fifteen minutes. They appeared regularly and were changed once or twice a week to maintain topicality.[23] There was some coverage of current events, some "travelogue" footage of different cultures or traditional ceremonies and festivals, and frequently light human interest subjects such as stunts or beauty pageants. Serious filmmakers such as John Grierson dismissed newsreels for their triviality and "postcard" emphasis on the visual. Grierson referred to them as normally containing "just a speedy snip-snap of some utterly unimportant ceremony."[24]

The March of Time, introduced in 1935, was the most successful product of the genre and had a powerful influence on television journalism.[25] The series dealt with a wide range of issues and, at the height of its popularity, between 1936 and 1942, appeared in more than 9,000 American theaters before a combined audience of nearly 20 million people. It certainly had its roots in the newsreel format, but its producer, Louis de Rochemont, sought to make *The March of Time* different. His aim was to achieve more continuity and substance. The series consequently treated fewer stories than the previous newsreels—on occasion, the entire sixteen minutes would be devoted to a single subject—and, although *The March of Time* staged the recreation of events more than a few times, its subject matter and tone were often serious. The series lasted until 1951.

Early Television Newscasts

Regular evening newscasts began inauspiciously. In 1946, NBC presented a filmed report called *The Esso Newsreel*, sponsored by Esso gasoline, which aired for fifteen minutes on Sundays and ten minutes on Mondays and Thursdays. In 1947, CBS introduced a twice-weekly broadcast with Douglas Edwards, by then an experienced radio announcer, as its host. In August 1948, *The CBS-TV News* with Edwards premiered; it was broadcast every weekday evening for fifteen minutes. On NBC, the ten-minute, Monday-through-Friday *Camel Newsreel Theater*, sponsored by Camel cigarettes, began in February 1948 with John Cameron Swayze as host. It evolved into the 15-minute *Camel News Caravan* in February 1949.

When Edwards began the 1948 nightly program, it was seen only in New York, Philadelphia, Boston, and Washington, D.C. The coaxial cable that made nationwide broadcasts possible did not reach the West Coast until 1951.

The earliest television newscasts have been described as "radio with pictures," but that may give them more credit than they deserve. Radio broadcasts probably were more coherent. The newscasts of the early 1950s contained the weaker qualities of the newsreel and remained less important than documentaries for many years. The evening newscasts of CBS and NBC were hardly the flagships of their news divisions. Perhaps they were the tugboats.

Two examples of network newscasts from the early years indicate that nascent TV journalism was a pastiche of some information, some advertising, and some content that today is virtually inexplicable.

On CBS on April 7, 1949, Douglas Edwards began his newscast, sponsored by Oldsmobile, with rapid-fire headlines.[26] The brief items concern price supports for agriculture, the United Nations, guerilla activity in Greece, and an FBI investigation of fraud in the bond market. As the newscast proceeds, there is clearly an emphasis on film for its own sake. The follow-up story on price supports for wheat is accompanied by generic footage of farming. Silent film of Army Day in Washington shows bands parading. We see the arrival of the Brazilian minister of war at West Point, then what are called "very, very dramatic protests" in Reykjavik, Iceland. "Here comes the tear gas," Edwards says at one point in narrating the protest footage.

The application of news judgment is not really in evidence, either in the order of stories presented or in the time allotted to each story. Near the end of the program, Edwards holds up three photographs of nineteen-week-old

Charles, the Prince of Wales. That item is followed by "late news" from Washington concerning the United Mine Workers union.

Another example, a 1950 newscast on NBC, is somewhat more polished but no more coherent. It is September 4. *The Camel News Caravan*, a fifteen-minute program featuring John Cameron Swayze, opens with a story about the Korean War, with a crude map indicating the position of the "North Korean Reds."[27] The second story is a filmed report from WPTZ-TV in Philadelphia in which a casualty of the war, a man from Mt. Carmel, Pennsylvania, whose leg was amputated, tells his story as a microphone is held beneath him; the interviewer remains off-camera. "Films from the battlefield" are presented next. Aerial footage of battleships is accompanied by martial music.

Transitions between stories are abrupt or nonexistent, and commercials are at first difficult to distinguish from news stories; an on-screen title, "The Camel Camera Testifies," marks the beginning of a commercial, which itself seems to be a news story about a smoker who underwent tests conducted "under the supervision of noted throat specialists" who found no signs of irritation brought on by smoking.

Brief stories follow on New York governor Thomas E. Dewey, a primary election in Nevada, an increase in auto industry wages, and a hurricane in Florida. Swayze narrates film of a train wreck in Milwaukee. Other stories are illustrated by line drawings and, in one case, a burning miniature cardboard house is shown as National Safety Council death figures are reported. As far as one can determine, footage of oyster fishing on Maryland's Eastern Shore is unrelated to news.

Baseball scores are followed by another visit from "The Camel Camera," this time focusing on fashion ("plaids are high fashion for fall") with music provided in the background. Swayze then introduces twenty-five seconds of international news with his signature line, "Hopscotching the world for headlines . . . " The program ends with a camera shot of a cigarette burning in an ashtray. No reporter has been identified at any time in the newscast. There have been several references to "Commies" and "Reds."

Murrow's Rise and Fall

While the evening newscasts of the 1950s languished, Murrow and his *See It Now* team flourished. *See It Now*, he first major documentary series on television, soon became the flagship broadcast of CBS News. It had a production budget of $23,000 a week, more than CBS allocated for its evening newscast. According to longtime Murrow colleague and broadcast historian Edward Bliss Jr., "Frequently the cost of a single program exceeded

29

$100,000. Not once during the four years the program was sponsored by the Aluminum Company of America did [*See It Now*] operate out of the red."[28] The shows Murrow and Friendly produced, with the considerable assistance of filmmaker and director of operations Palmer Williams, set a high standard for future television documentaries:

> It was a great team—this band of brothers, as Friendly would often say—and he drove it, and himself, hard. It was not unusual for persons working on the Sunday program to disappear into the film center on Friday and not be seen for 48 hours as they fought the deadline.[29]

After two seasons, Murrow and Friendly had moved beyond the multiple-story format and were concentrating on single topics. "Christmas in Korea," broadcast in 1953, is regarded by film historians as a milestone. The *See It Now* team went to Korea to provide an intimate, personal view of the "faces, voices, sounds, and sights of the stalemate" as soldiers were experiencing it.[30]

It is fair to say that "Christmas in Korea" was an entirely new form of reportage, direct and powerful. The drained faces and tired voices of soldiers gave a vivid, personal dimension to the meaning of war apart from the statistics of the battlefield. *See It Now* was carving out a new role for television. Ed Bliss notes the impressive range of stories covered by *See It Now*—coal mining, Italian land reform, Passover in Berlin, mental health, wiretapping, floods, even the part coffee plays in American life.[31] Yet Murrow and Friendly were not satisfied. Friendly has said that Murrow was marshaling his energies for a story that would fully employ the power of television journalism.

That new battlefield was to be an assault on the career and tactics of the junior senator from Wisconsin, Republican Joseph R. McCarthy. Looking for the right narrative vehicle with which to confront the erratic and often brutal anti-Communist, Murrow found the case of a twenty-six-year-old Air Force reservist and University of Michigan student named Milo Radulovich. Radulovich had been asked to resign his commission because his father and sister allegedly had read "subversive newspapers" and engaged in other "questionable activities."[32] A *See It Now* producer, Joseph Wershba, was sent to Detroit to follow up on the story.

The result was the *See It Now* broadcast called "The Case Against Milo Radulovich, AO589839." After CBS declined to provide funds for newspaper advertising, Murrow and Friendly spent $1,500 of their own money for an ad in the *New York Times*. The program aired live on October 20, 1953. That night the opening of *See It Now* was postponed for an announcement filmed that day by Harold Talbott, the secretary of the Air Force. Talbott said that he had reviewed the Radulovich case and had decided that the lieutenant was not a security risk; he would be retained in the Air Force.

The *See It Now* Radulovich broadcast was an extraordinary success, but it was not without cost. Anti-Murrow attacks on the network continued, and there was intensified pressure on Alcoa, the program's sponsor. Bolstered by their October program, though, Murrow and Friendly turned their sights to McCarthy himself. Their historic report taking direct aim at McCarthy was broadcast on March 9, 1954. It was a straightforward accounting of McCarthy's actions, which for years had gone unchallenged by otherwise responsible politicians of both parties. Murrow closed the broadcast with these words:

> As a nation we have come into our full inheritance at a tender age. We proclaim ourselves—as indeed we are—the defenders of freedom, what's left of it, but we cannot defend freedom abroad by deserting it at home. The actions of the junior senator from Wisconsin have caused alarm and dismay amongst our allies abroad and given considerable comfort to our enemies, and whose fault is that? Not really his. He didn't create this situation of fear; he merely exploited it, and rather successfully. Cassius was right: "The fault, dear Brutus, is not in our stars but in ourselves." . . . Good night, and good luck.[33]

McCarthy was offered time to reply, and did so. On April 6, at the regular *See It Now* time, McCarthy responded with a personal attack on Murrow, whom he called "the leader and the cleverest of the jackal pack which is always found at the throat of anyone who dares to expose individual communists and traitors."[34] A few days later, CBS president Frank Stanton showed Friendly a survey that the network had commissioned. Stanton seemed disturbed that polling done after the McCarthy response indicated that 33 percent of those sampled believed that McCarthy had raised legitimate doubts about Murrow or had proved that the newsman was pro-Communist.

In 1955, *See It Now* presented another program, "A Conversation With Dr. J. Robert Oppenheimer," that related to McCarthyism. Oppenheimer had been the leader of the Manhattan Project, which had created the atom bomb, but he opposed the development of the even more powerful hydrogen bomb. His loyalty was questioned by government officials and eventually he lost his top-security clearance. The CBS program was widely praised despite continuing pressure on Alcoa and CBS and renewed attacks on *See It Now* from columnists for the Hearst newspaper chain.

The McCarthy broadcasts marked a high point for Murrow, for CBS, and in retrospect for television news. The *See It Now* team had been vilified collectively and individually, yet they pursued the matter with personal courage and the corporate commitment of CBS chairman William S. Paley. The programs had a direct influence on public policy. They set the stage for televised hearings on McCarthy's allegations of Communist infiltration of the U.S. Army, which immediately led to his downfall. Following the Army-McCarthy hearings, a broken Joseph McCarthy was censured by the Senate. He died in 1957.

Paradoxically, however, the McCarthy broadcasts set in motion other forces that would in the future place limits on television news broadcasts, especially on the kind of activist reporting that sparked controversy. Sponsors had been drawn in ever larger numbers to television through the *See It Now* programs, but they wanted to be associated with safer material. Murrow himself, attacked by newspaper editorialists all over the country, was infuriated by the network's practice of caving in and granting equal time whenever a politician claimed that a report had been unfair.[35] A program about the issue of statehood for Alaska and Hawaii seemed to pose little controversy, but a New York congressman named John Pillion demanded and received reply time, to the consternation of Murrow, Friendly, and the entire news department. There followed a meeting between Murrow, Friendly, and Paley in the chairman's office. Murrow had written Paley an earlier memo saying that *See It Now* could not continue under present conditions. Paley, in essence, agreed, and Murrow realized he had lost the corporate and moral support that CBS had provided him for twenty years. He asked Paley, "Are you going to destroy all this?" Paley is widely reported to have replied, "I don't want this constant stomach ache every time you do a controversial subject," to which Murrow said, "I'm afraid that's the price you have to be willing to pay. It goes with the job."[36]

The meeting had ended, as had an era in broadcast journalism. CBS canceled *See It Now* in mid-1958.[37] In October 1958, Murrow and Friendly began an interview program called *Small World*. It resembled *Person to Person* in some respects, but was usually more substantive and occasionally controversial; it had the following of neither *See It Now* nor *Person to Person*.

Murrow was invited to address a convention of radio and television news directors in Chicago on October 15, 1958. He took that opportunity to give the major address of his career, stunning his superiors at CBS by issuing a broad-based indictment of television. The commercial imperatives of television, Murrow argued, produced unavoidable conflicts between economics and editorial judgment; "there is no law," he admitted, "which says that dollars will be defeated by duty":

> I can find nothing in the Bill of Rights or in the Communications Act which says that [radio and television stations] must increase their net profits each year, lest the Republic collapse. . . . I am frightened by the imbalance, the

constant striving to reach the largest possible audience for everything, by the absence of a sustained study of the state of the nation.[38]

The tone of Murrow's most remembered words from his Chicago speech is decidedly not optimistic:

> For those who say people wouldn't look [if television were seriously committed to news and information useful to the public]; they wouldn't be interested; they're too complacent, indifferent and insulated, I can only reply: There is, in one reporter's opinion, considerable evidence against that contention. But even if they are right, and this instrument is good for nothing but to entertain, amuse and insulate, then the tube is flickering now and we will soon see that the whole struggle is lost. This instrument can teach, it can illuminate; yes, and it can even inspire. But it can do so only to the extent that humans are determined to use it to those ends. Otherwise it is merely wires and lights in a box.[39]

Executives at CBS were furious that Murrow, the country's most respected broadcaster, had chosen to foul his own nest. Following his speech and the angry reaction in New York, Murrow was physically depleted and at a low point emotionally. His contract with the network allowed him to take a one-year sabbatical leave of absence, and on August 26, 1959, he left with his wife and son for Europe. Rumors swirled about that Murrow had resigned or been fired, but the truth was different, though harder to pin down. Murrow had been defeated by Paley, ultimately disillusioned in his work, and he needed rest and distance from CBS. He got little rest on his sabbatical, however, for he was a man who never really learned how to relax. He returned to New York the following May, almost two months before his sabbatical was to have ended.

His career at CBS was nearing an end. He was paired with Walter Cronkite as a coanchor at the 1960 Democratic convention, but that turned into an unhappy experience for everyone involved. He and Cronkite did not work well together, and covering American politics was clearly not one of Murrow's strengths. When President John F. Kennedy offered Murrow the position of director of the U.S. Information Agency, he resigned from CBS. His last years were marked by failing health. Suffering from cancer, he died in 1965, two days past his fifty-seventh birthday.

Murrow and the Culture of Television News

Murrow's life and career were unique. He was, it can be argued without much difficulty, the first person to do meaningful television journalism. Yet a strong case can be made that no one did it so well again. Broadcast journalism reached its full flower in that early springtime of Murrow's career, then, to overstate the case only slightly, never blossomed so beautifully again. Biographer Joseph E. Persico captures the perplexing notion that Murrow's career failed in some measure because he was too good—for his time (or for any time?), especially too good for the medium of television:

> After he was gone, there followed at CBS what Harry Reasoner called "The Great Correspondent Sweepstakes." Who was to be the next Murrow? But there was, however, never to be another Murrow. . . . The man who had built the temple had, for all practical purposes, been driven from it. There was no place left for him in broadcasting to match his stature. And so the founder and then reigning master left. It was an irony wrapped in an absurdity.[40]

But what was the meaning of Murrow's personal travail? There have been many interpretations of the "lessons" of his career, some of which are contradictory. In the broader context of what has happened since in the development of broadcast journalism, that is understandable: to assess the implications of Murrow's work and his frustrations is inevitably to stake out a position about the merits or evils of American broadcasting.

Murrow himself summarized much of his predicament in the Chicago speech. Television was, he said, an incompatible mixture of news, advertising, and show business. The nature of the corporate structure would indeed demand that financial managers make the final decisions about issues related to news and public affairs. Profits, and ratings, would be paramount. Murrow also demonstrated in his career that there were tangible limits to the freedom that would be granted to individual journalists who worked within a network structure. No single journalist would operate so independently again. Perhaps despite his own wishes, Murrow's career showed as well the inextricable tie between television news and celebrity. "Show business" values were rooted in the American culture of television news.

— 3 —

The Era of
Network Dominance

Television news first occupied a central place in American life in the 1960s, when developments in technology allowed for much more immediate transmission of news events. With the advent of lightweight cameras, communication satellites, and videotape, the power of television news to convey important news and issues and to set the national agenda increased dramatically. There followed a remarkable period of domestic and international turbulence that began with the assassination of President John F. Kennedy. Although television coverage of the civil rights movement in the Deep South technically came earlier and introduced television news as a profound social and political force, the networks' brilliance in covering the Kennedy story cemented the relationship between television journalism and American public life.

The Kennedy Assassination

November 22, 1963, was a Friday. In Washington, D.C., CBS News bureau chief William J. Small was in his office making up the invitation list for a Christmas party. In New York, Walter Cronkite ate lunch at his desk. Several blocks away at NBC, Julian Goodman, the president of NBC News, and anchor Chet Huntley were giving a business lunch in the executive dining room. At 12:25 P.M. Eastern Standard Time, Air Force One, carrying President Kennedy, touched down at Love Field in Dallas. The ABC affiliate in Dallas, WFAA-TV, was at the airport with cameras and a mobile unit. The CBS affiliate, KRLD-TV, was prepared to cover Kennedy's luncheon speech at the Dallas Trade Mart with three cameras set up in the balcony. Three experienced network correspondents were traveling with the president.[1]

As the president's motorcade passed the Texas School Book Depository Building, shots were fired, and the motorcade changed direction and sped toward Parkland Hospital. At 1:34 P.M. Eastern Standard Time, United Press International interrupted a story being filed with this message: THREE SHOTS WERE FIRED AT PRESIDENT KENNEDY'S MOTORCADE TODAY IN DOWNTOWN DALLAS.

Six minutes later, Cronkite was on CBS television, audio only, reporting that the president had been "seriously wounded." In Dallas, CBS bureau chief Dan Rather, holding several telephones at the same time, told the radio editor in New York that he had information that Kennedy was dead. The CBS radio network reported the story seventeen minutes ahead of anyone else. At 2:37, Cronkite was handed a piece of Associated Press wire copy. Sitting at the anchor desk, his voice breaking, he said, "From Dallas, Texas, a flash, apparently official. President Kennedy died at 1 P.M., Central Standard Time, two o'clock, Eastern Standard Time." He hesitated. "Some 38 minutes ago."[2]

Thus began an extraordinary period of four days in American life. The momentous events in Dallas were followed by the swearing in and return to Washington of a new president, the arrest and subsequent murder of a suspect named Lee Harvey Oswald, a national rite of suffering and pageantry commingled in the state funeral in Washington—a series of unforgettable images that stayed frozen in the minds and hearts of an entire generation. At the center of the ordeal was television. The networks carried no commercials from Friday through Monday, and at times nine out of ten Americans were watching.[3] Over the years since, the coverage has been called the finest hour in the history of television news and, some have said, the most important. Many people believe that television held the country together during the tragedy. Two researchers, William A. Mindak and Gerald D. Hursh, reported that television coverage had in fact relieved viewers of their immediate anxiety about rumors of a conspiracy against the government:

> [Television] served as a catalyst to speed up adjustment to the finality of the President's death and to renew faith in the future. . . . People who on Friday exhibited emotional reactions that usually precede collective disorder appear to have acquired after the funeral a more realistic appraisal of the assassination's implications for the future of the country. . . . The reversal in mood and in perspective was aided considerably by the presence of television.[4]

The funeral was to be held on Monday. The networks pooled resources to cover the event, planning to use about fifty cameras. On Sunday, as the president's casket was about to be transferred from the White House to the Capitol, Lee Harvey Oswald was about to be moved from Dallas police headquarters to the county jail. NBC broadcast Oswald's movements live. The startling images showed a man, Jack Ruby, fire his pistol at point-blank range at Oswald. Viewers for the first time saw a murder as it happened, then a scene of panic and disorder.

The coverage returned to Washington, where President Kennedy lay in state, and continued through the night. Monday's somber ceremonies were watched by unprecedented millions. For those in the television industry, thoughts about the medium's power were changed forever. Historian Eric Barnouw writes of those dawning perceptions:

> Some television people have slept as little as six hours in three nights. They go on, almost welcoming the absorption in the task at hand. Their dignity, intelligence, and judgment are extraordinary. Did the networks have any conception of the talent submerged in their news divisions, squeezed into daily one-minute and two-minute capsules?[5]

Coverage of the Kennedy assassination showed for the first time the full capabilities of television journalism. And the audiences were huge. A.C. Nielsen reported that the average home in its viewing sample had television tuned to the events of the weekend of November 22 for 31 hours and 38 minutes. Approximately 166 million Americans in more than 51 million homes tuned in. In some homes, people watched for more than eleven hours a day. NBC was on the air with coverage for 71 hours and 36 minutes, ABC for 60 hours, and CBS for 55 hours. Portions of the broadcasts were seen in twenty-three other countries.[6]

By 1963, television news actually had arrived at a position from which it would be able to fill a new and compelling role in public life. In that year both NBC and CBS expanded their evening newscasts from fifteen minutes to a half hour. The year before, CBS had launched four new domestic bureaus, joining those in Washington and Chicago. ABC lagged well behind its two competitors: it would not expand its evening newscast to a half hour until 1968.

Vietnam

Our cultural memory of the 1960s is that of a trail of national cataclysms that in retrospect seem to have flowed naturally from one to another. ("The Sixties" itself has become a metaphor for what began in Dallas in 1963 and ended with the conclusion of Watergate, the Nixon resignation in August

Table 3.1

Television Comes Into Its Own: Top Special Events in the 1960s

1960   Kennedy-Nixon election results
        Viewers: 91.8 percent of TV homes
        Average viewing time: 4 hours, 30 minutes

1961   Kennedy inaugural address
        Viewers: 59.5 percent of TV homes

1962   John Glenn's orbital flight
        Viewers: 81.4 percent of TV homes
        Average viewing time: 5 hours, 15 minutes

1963   Kennedy assassination/funeral coverage
        Viewers: 96.1 percent of TV homes
        Average viewing time: 31 hours, 38 minutes

1964   Johnson-Goldwater election results
        Viewers: 90.6 percent of TV homes
        Average viewing time: 2 hours, 51 minutes

1965   Gemini-Titan IV Launch
        Viewers: 92.1 percent of TV homes
        Average viewing time: 4 hours, 47 minutes

1966   Congressional election results
        Viewers: 84.4 percent of TV homes
        Average viewing time: 6 hours, 10 minutes

1967   Johnson's State of the Union address
        Viewers: 59.6 percent of TV homes

1968   Democratic National Convention in Chicago
        Viewers: 90.1 percent of TV homes
        Average viewing time: 9 hours, 28 minutes

1969   Apollo XI moon landing
        Viewers: 93.9 percent of TV homes
        Average viewing time: 15 hours, 35 minutes

Source: *Variety*, August 27, 1969, p. 39.

1974.) At the time of Kennedy's assassination, the president was actively engaged in the problem of what to do about the war in Vietnam. Soon enough, the problem was Lyndon B. Johnson's, and television news was once again at the center of an American agony.

The nature of television's role in Vietnam was controversial. For at least a decade there were persistent arguments that TV coverage of Vietnam not only influenced events, but substantially distorted them. By contrast, in the late 1950s and throughout the 1960s, television news coverage of the civil rights movement was not often the subject of intense debate as either right or wrong. TV news was increasingly important in making clear the extent of America's racial problems and in pressuring presidents from Eisenhower on to take remedial action, but Vietnam was a different matter. At some point the Vietnam War and television news became inseparable, joined in a relationship of suspicion and hostility between the government, the American public, and broadcast journalists.

War coverage demonstrated the power of pictures, often close-up, searing images of death and destruction. Writer Michael Arlen called it the "living-room war," and for more than seven years families watching the evening news saw a conflict that frequently lacked an internal or even an on-the-field logic. American soldiers wanted to go home; military commanders became the objects of scepticism or worse.[7] All of this was entirely new for American journalism. No previous war had been so accessible to reporters. In the early years in Vietnam, reporters in the field received great cooperation from the military and there was little direct censorship, although cameramen were not permitted on bombing strikes against North Vietnam.

As the war continued, official displeasure with the coverage began to mount. The American command in Saigon reviewed network footage regularly and, if unhappy, would complain directly to correspondents. Occasionally a single story would resonate powerfully—and provoke doubt about the entire American mission in Southeast Asia. In 1965, CBS correspondent Morley Safer aired a report in which Marines burned down a South Vietnamese village said to have been a launching area for enemy guerrillas. The story was deeply upsetting, and the Defense Department reacted angrily against Safer and CBS. In a CBS documentary, "The World of Charlie Company," correspondent John Laurence presented a unit of soldiers on the verge of mutiny, unsure of their military objectives and unimpressed by their own officers.

In 1966, a Senate hearing on Vietnam produced a startling result—at CBS News. Edward R. Murrow's former partner at CBS, Fred Friendly, had in 1966 been president of CBS News for two years when network executives refused to show live coverage of congressional hearings on the Vietnam War and instead aired a rerun of an ancient *I Love Lucy* episode. Friendly was infuriated, accused the network of breaking its long-standing public-service obligations, and resigned. According to one journalist writing years later, "Fred Friendly quit his job in 1966 rather than betray his principles, and for that he became a hero to an entire generation of television journalists."[8]

Coverage of the Tet offensive in 1969 marked a turning point. At least from the perspective of television news, it was no longer certain that the United States was winning the war and that it would eventually prevail. Tet was the lunar New Year, and on that night, North Vietnamese forces, aided by Vietcong guerrillas, staged a coordinated series of attacks on all of South Vietnam's population centers. Militarily, it was convincingly argued afterward, the American enemy sustained a huge setback, losing every battle of consequence. But the United States suffered a much more serious psychological blow at home. If America was winning, it didn't look like it. If we were to be committed to victory in the long run, the run would be long, indeed. Popular loss of faith in the military mission in Southeast Asia paved the way for congressional resistance to funding the war.

And what were the powerful forces that eroded national resolve? Pictures. The unrelenting, nightly scenes of suffering both caused and sustained by Americans: an almost naked child running from the fighting, her eyes a mirror of unspeakable terror; the brutal and seemingly instantaneous on-street assassination of a suspected Vietcong by an officer of the South Vietnamese army; correspondents in Saigon under fire themselves in a war that was said to be not only winnable, but "under control." Vietnam revealed the power of television news in a new light, its ability to portray an event so powerfully that the images could not be shaken, no matter what had really transpired. During the Vietnam War, television changed the practice of American statecraft. In the future, no protracted military action was possible—the American people wouldn't stand for it—unless there were tight control of what reporters could see and photograph.

Watergate

Television journalists did less to uncover the misdeeds during the Nixon presidency that are collectively known as the Watergate scandal than did their newspaper counterparts. But as the story moved to its conclusion, the Senate hearings on Watergate and the resignation of President Nixon, television was again at the center of a shaken society. Countries that have a young president killed on their streets are often subject to revolution and chaos, Fred Friendly later commented about the Kennedy assassination. Television news, he believed, saved the republic in November 1963. Much the same logic applies to Watergate in the late summer of 1974. Television news explained the unthinkable, and Walter Cronkite's CBS evening newscast outlined what was known, by whom, and when. Americans seemed reassured that the country could withstand the resignation of a president. On the evening when Richard Nixon announced his resignation, during the farewells of the following day, and during the swearing in of a new president, Gerald Ford, television news went beyond its journalistic role of reporting breaking news. Television kept the country together once again.

The Anchorman Ascendant

In his 2001 memoir, *Tell Me a Story*, CBS producer Don Hewitt recalls that the term "anchorman" was coined during the coverage of the 1952 Republican convention in Chicago. "It had nothing to do with boats," he remembers, but everything to do with the concept of a relay team. CBS planned to use four broadcasters, including a new and promising reporter, Walter Cronkite.

> The idea was that they would hand off the coverage to each other, more or less the way a relay team hands off a baton. And just as the fastest man on a relay team runs the "anchor leg," Cronkite would run the anchor leg for us and became from that day on, not just "an anchorman," but "*the* anchorman." And now, "anchorman" is what everybody calls anyone, man or woman, who sits at what has become known as an "anchor desk" and presides over a newscast.[9]

The *idea* of the anchorman, though, would over time transform American television news. Among the first men who presided over network newscasts were Douglas Edwards at CBS and John Cameron Swayze at NBC. Edwards was taciturn and business-like; Swayze theatrical and flamboyant. They were, to some extent, personalities—Swayze especially. But what they were not was working journalists, men who had had distinguished reporting careers and were identified as the alpha males for their networks' news divisions. They were news readers. There was, of course, precedent for this role: European newscasts to this day are presented by news readers. With the notion of the anchorman, American TV journalism began to veer toward something much different than, for example, the British structure of news broadcasting. In the United States, news would feature a star system that relied on the popularity of its anchorman—on occasion, its team of anchors.

Cronkite's performance at the 1952 convention garnered many positive reviews, but Murrow still stood apart within CBS News. Murrow and his staff were "larger and better paid than the entire CBS television network news operation, of which [they were] not really a part."[10] The first true anchormen "stars," matinee idols really, were NBC's Chet Huntley and David Brinkley.

Huntley was little known to the public, and his experience in national political reporting was thin. Brinkley was a twelve-year veteran of NBC News, a former newspaper reporter who understood the ways of Washington. His intelligent, wry remarks played off well against the more somber, direct delivery of Huntley. Together, they made television magic. NBC executives paired them for the 1956 political conventions, and, under the direction of senior producer Reuven Frank, they conquered the audience. Huntley was a thorough professional, serious and well-prepared. Brinkley

Chet Huntley (left) and David Brinkley led NBC to news leadership through much of the 1960s. *(NBC/Broadcast Pioneers Library of American Broadcasting, University of Maryland—College Park)*

was a brilliant television writer. Moreover, he had a keen eye for the absurd, and a political convention offered uncounted opportunities to use it. Following their success at the conventions, it was only natural that Huntley–Brinkley take over the struggling *NBC Nightly News*.

When they premiered on October 29, 1956, they initially made no impact on the ratings, but after some months they took the lead. More importantly, they enlarged the importance of the evening newscast on every network. Unlikely as it may seem, at the outset of the Huntley–Brinkley broadcast, the program had only two reporters regularly assigned to it. Producer Frank decided to make the evening newscast more serious and more substantive.

> Frank broke once and for all with the old newsreel clichés—the ship christenings, fashion shows, and baby parades. He hated verbal clichés, too, insisting on a care and accuracy in writing news that was previously unknown on television. . . . The *Huntley–Brinkley Report looked* like a news program for grownups.[11]

The NBC program also was noted for its signature sign-off: "Good night, Chet." "Good night, David." "And good night for NBC News." The close was Reuven Frank's idea. Although controversial at first, it became part of the cultural landscape.

With Huntley–Brinkley on top, NBC president Robert Kintner decided to make news the instrument of his network's fight to overtake CBS (there was little alternative; the CBS entertainment lineup was unassailable). He sought to make reporters, including Edwin Newman, Frank Reynolds, and John Chancellor, stars as well as his anchors. "He pushed the news department simply outrageously," David Brinkley said. "He insisted, demanded, that we be the first on the air, sometimes behaving quite brutally. He would call people at 4:00 A.M.—he was one of those people who never slept—but we didn't object to his tactics. We liked it because it was paying off beautifully."[12]

Executives at CBS—which principally meant Chairman William S. Paley and network president Frank Stanton—knew it was time to regroup. By 1962, Edward R. Murrow was gone and Douglas Edwards was faring poorly in the ratings. It was decided that Cronkite would replace Edwards in April 1962. In 1966, for the first time, Cronkite edged ahead of NBC in the ratings, but only briefly. Then CBS went ahead to stay—from 1967 until Cronkite ceded the position to Dan Rather in 1981. In those fourteen years, Cronkite came to personify the role of anchorman, earning a place for many as "the most trusted man in America." As his own stature grew, television news seemed to become more and more pivotal in American life. Television, and Walter Cronkite, were there: for the assassinations of Martin Luther

King Jr. and Robert F. Kennedy, for moon landings and urban riots, for the turmoil in Chicago at the 1968 Democratic convention, with out-of-control police action in the streets and "a bunch of thugs," as Cronkite called them on the air, in the convention hall.

As Vice President Spiro Agnew resigned in disgrace, as the Nixon presidency unraveled, as Vietnam changed from a limited action to a war widely regarded as unwinnable, CBS and Cronkite became the sounding board for most American viewers of television news. Neil Armstrong's first steps on the moon were accompanied by Cronkite's infectious "Wow!" In a much more serious vein, Cronkite, in an unusual on-air commentary, urged that America leave Vietnam and seek a negotiated settlement. When President Lyndon B. Johnson, having lost his base of political support because of opposition to the war, announced that he would not seek reelection, he explained to associates that "If I've lost Cronkite, I've lost Middle America."[13]

Icon as well as anchor, Walter Cronkite was forty-five years old in 1962. By training and talent, appearance and demeanor, he was the right man at the right time—an experienced reporter with a passion for accuracy and an instinct for breaking news. As he aged, he looked increasingly distinguished, so it was not difficult to see why he was called a father figure for America or, more fondly, "Uncle Walter."

Walter Leland Cronkite II was born in St. Joseph, Missouri, the son and grandson of dentists. He grew up in Kansas City and worked as a part-time reporter while attending the University of Texas.[14] He quit school in his junior year to take a full-time job on the *Houston Press*. In 1937, he joined the United Press wire service, and after a stint in Kansas City, he was assigned to London, where he caught the attention of Edward R. Murrow. When the Korean War broke out in 1950, he joined CBS.

Twenty years later, Cronkite sat at the helm of the finest broadcast news organization in America. In 1959, when CBS News was formed as a separate division within the corporation, it had 437 full-time employees. A decade later, the number had grown to 816.[15] CBS News president Richard M. Salant liked to say that, in addition to Cronkite, he had "an infield, an outfield, and a strong bench."[16] The players included Eric Sevareid, Harry Reasoner, Roger Mudd, Dan Rather, Mike Wallace, and Charles Kuralt. Cronkite, who played an active role in the operation of the *CBS Evening News*, selecting which stories to use and carefully editing his copy, held the title of managing editor.

By 1980, the star system would be, if anything, more firmly entrenched. Rather would replace Cronkite after an unprecedented bidding war with ABC, winding up with a contract worth more than $1 million a year. Within CBS, his competition had come from Roger Mudd, an experienced political reporter and the man who had filled in for Cronkite for years. Mudd may or may not have been the better journalist; that question was and is open to debate. But Dan Rather, who had drawn attention as a local reporter in Texas, who was in Dallas as CBS bureau chief during the Kennedy assassination, who was physically assaulted at the 1968 Democratic Convention, and who had been a lightning rod for praise and criticism repeatedly while covering the Nixon White House, was unquestionably the bigger "star." Mudd was bitter when CBS passed him over. For many of the twenty years he had worked at CBS News, he was considered to be the logical heir to Cronkite. On the afternoon when CBS announced the choice of Rather, Mudd released a brief statement: "The management of CBS and CBS News has made its decision on Walter Cronkite's successor according to its current values and standards. From the beginning, I've regarded myself as a news reporter and not as a newsmaker or celebrity."[17] Mudd remained under contract with CBS for another eight months—never appearing again on the network, though—then worked for NBC, PBS, and the History Channel on cable television. He was never comfortable with anchor stardom.

NBC's Tom Brokaw and ABC's Peter Jennings completed a long-standing triumvirate with Dan Rather. Each man was a seasoned professional with extensive reporting credentials. And each man was a "star." Barbara Matusow summarizes the development of the anchor as "a process abetted by the networks in the hope that the anchors' prestige would rub off on the organization as a whole, i.e., boost ratings and advertising revenues. At the same time, anchors began to take charge of their own programs, gaining the upper hand over producers."[18] To authors Robert Goldberg and Gerald Jay Goldberg, "they could be members of the family, their faces are so familiar to us":

> The aggressive Dan, who fronts the CBS cameras like a heavyweight, with hard, determined eyes and punches out the news. Likeable Tom with his easy smile and colloquial style, the gray-haired choirboy eager to win our approval for NBC. And urbane Peter of the receding hairline and flashy breast-pocket foulard, ABC's spit-and-polish wing commander, clipping his words as they quick-march past us with military precision. Who doesn't know Rather, Brokaw and Jennings?[19]

II

SEISMIC SHIFTS IN TELEVISION NEWS

— 4 —

60 Minutes and the News Magazine

The symphony of the real world is not a monotone, and while this does not mean you have to mix it all up in one broadcast, it seems to us that the idea of a flexible attitude has its attractions. All art is the rearrangement of previous perceptions, and we don't claim that this is anything more than that or even that journalism is an art, but we do think this is a sort of new approach.

—Harry Reasoner on the first broadcast of 60 Minutes

The revolutionary CBS news program *60 Minutes* was largely the product of one man's energy, imagination, and, undeniably, his unrelenting ego. Throughout a news career that has lasted more than fifty years, Don Hewitt has demonstrated a unique sense of what works on the air—and has stepped on more than a few toes in doing so.

Hewitt began his journalistic career by working briefly for the Associated Press. He worked next for the *Pelham* (NY) *Sun* and Acme Newspictures (a wire photo service for newspapers) before joining CBS News in 1948. Eventually he became the producer-director of *Douglas Edwards with the News*, the network's nightly fifteen-minute broadcast. He was also the studio director of the Murrow–Friendly program *See It Now*, but was never considered a member of the Murrow inner circle. His colleagues on the Edwards program included Sidney Lumet and John

Frankenheimer, later distinguished film directors, and a director-turned-actor named Yul Brynner. Hewitt went on to direct the award-winning arts-and-public affairs program *Omnibus*, covered the launch of Sputnik in the 1950s, and produced and directed CBS coverage of the coronation of Queen Elizabeth II.

Hewitt earned a place in the history of political communication when he produced and directed the first Kennedy–Nixon debate in 1960. According to Hewitt's personal account, he suggested to Richard Nixon's campaign managers that their candidate needed to apply makeup for the debate because of a noticeable "five o'clock shadow." Nixon's handlers declined, and viewers saw a particularly haggard-looking Nixon. Studies conducted after the debate indicated that audience members who listened on radio thought that Nixon had won, while those who saw the debate on television believed Kennedy was the winner.[1]

One of the original *60 Minutes* correspondents, Harry Reasoner, called Hewitt "an authentic genius of television news."[2] He had a voluble personality and could be rash, but no one has denied that Hewitt had an uncanny sense of how television connected with its audience. Before he developed the idea for *60 Minutes*, Reasoner wrote, within CBS News Hewitt was considered "smart, maybe brilliant," but not serious enough.[3]

What became Hewitt's big professional break occurred when Fred Friendly, always a professional rival at CBS and then the president of the network news division, removed him in 1965 from the staff of the *CBS Evening News with Walter Cronkite*. Hewitt noted in 2001 that he and Friendly were never on good terms:

> A barrel of laughs he [Friendly] wasn't. Fred was now my boss and acted like nothing good had ever happened in television until he got there. . . . Nothing about either of us rubbed off on the other. The problem was that he didn't really approve of me.[4]

Friendly told Hewitt he was being reassigned to a special unit to produce news programs, but Hewitt realized that he was indeed being "relegated to [a] backwater to produce . . . what can best be described as hour-long snoozers."[5]

> I ended up doing public-affairs shows and making holier-than-thou documentaries that no one watched, or not many people anyway. The truth was that all the documentaries got about the same share of audience—maybe 8 percent, which wasn't much—regardless of whether they were on CBS, NBC, or ABC. People don't like reading documents. Why would they want to watch something called a documentary?[6]

Hewitt had another idea. In 1967, he proposed an alternative to the traditional documentary. His idea was to split an hour into three briefer reports, thus catering to the viewers' limited attention span and allowing for a new form of personal journalism. He wanted to present news, but to "package" it differently. He sent a memorandum to the new president of CBS News, Richard S. Salant. "Why don't we try to package sixty minutes of reality as attractively as Hollywood packages sixty minutes of make-believe?" he asked.[7] Hewitt explained later that he was trying to retain the audience of news buffs who were interested in documentaries while reaching out to a far larger audience of average viewers. Hewitt imagined a television program similar to *Life* magazine at the height of its popularity, "serious and light-hearted" in the same issue.[8] Of the three major stories broadcast on each program, one was usually a hard-edged investigative piece that uncovered wrongdoing of some sort, often something outrageous and/or malicious. Another story was lighter fare—either a profile of a celebrity or something humorous in tone.

The result was a program that, at the very least, changed television journalism. A persuasive argument could be made that, over time, the model and lessons of *60 Minutes* changed and probably are still changing journalism of all kinds everywhere. The impact of the program was based on several factors, the most important of which were these:

- *60 Minutes* demonstrated that television journalism could be massively profitable.
- It cast reporters as the protagonists in fourteen-minute minidramas, capitalizing on and redefining the narrative power of television news.
- It accelerated the demise of the hour-long, single-subject television documentary.
- It made newsworthy topics entertaining, and entertaining issues newsworthy, eventually contributing to a blurring of the line that traditionally had separated the two.
- It introduced effective and dramatic techniques in editing and investigative reporting, raising ethical questions in both areas while expanding the power of broadcast journalism.

Despite the recollections of many people, *60 Minutes* was far from an overnight success. The first program, with Mike Wallace and Harry Reasoner, aired on September 24, 1968, a Tuesday night, opposite the extremely popular drama *Marcus Welby, M.D.* In closing the broadcast, Mike Wallace spoke to the range of stories *60 Minutes* would attempt to cover in future editions:

"Our perception of reality roams, in a given day, from the light to the heavy, from warmth to menace, and if this broadcast does what we hope it will do, it will report reality."[9] The first program's ratings were marginal, and initial reviews were unremarkable. *60 Minutes* was scheduled to air once every two weeks.

In 1970, Morley Safer, a Canadian who had distinguished himself reporting for CBS from Vietnam, replaced Harry Reasoner.[10] Wallace recalls that by the time the third season drew to a close in the spring of 1971, "CBS programming executives had run out of patience. Three years of prestige and low ratings in a precious hour of prime time were enough."[11] That fall, the program opened in a new time slot, 6:00 P.M. on Sunday. It was broadcast once a week, except during football season when it was often preempted.

With each season, the program attracted greater critical acclaim and a larger audience. In 1975, it returned to prime time, given the 7:00 slot on Sundays. (*60 Minutes* benefitted from a slight loophole in the definition of prime time, it must be admitted. On Sundays, as far as the ratings were concerned, prime time began at 7:00 P.M.) Wallace and his coauthor Gates recall what happened next as a "phenomenon" that no one could have predicted. Over the next two years, *60 Minutes* became one of the ten top-rated programs on the air. By the fall of 1978, it had advanced to the head of the pack, and when the season ended, it had established itself as the highest-rated show on television.

> Don Hewitt's once-fragile magazine broadcast had evolved into a colossal contradiction in terms: a news program that consistently attracted a larger audience than the most popular entertainment shows, including such long-running blockbusters as *M*A*S*H* and *Dallas*. Nothing like it, or even close to it, had ever happened before in the thirty-year history of network television.[12]

In his autobiography, Harry Reasoner noted that one of Hewitt's most important decisions in structuring the program was that there would be reporters, but not hosts. "Only Mike [Wallace] and Morley [Safer] and Dan [Rather] and Harry go everywhere—from Hoboken to Libya, from Palm Springs to Rapid City."[13] Hewitt's notion of "personal journalism" meant not only that reporters would become associated less and less with dispassionate third-person objectivity. It meant that they would be identifiable personalities whose stories had a particular flavor. Moreover, the packaging of reality in order to capture the interest of ordinary viewers involved making the reporter part of the story, a key actor in each fourteen-minute playlet. Using the magazine rather than a newspaper as a model, *60 Minutes* blurred the distinction between fact and fiction, between the journalistic report and the short story.[14]

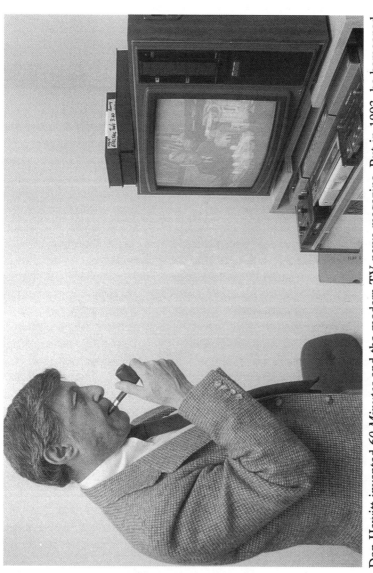

Don Hewitt invented *60 Minutes* and the modern TV news magazine. But in 1993, he bemoaned what the magazine shows had become. "*60 Minutes* has single-handedly ruined television," he told an interviewer. "No one can report news today without making money." (*CBS Photo Archive*)

Hewitt was not the first producer to understand the narrative power of television journalism. Reuven Frank, a president of NBC News, once wrote a famous memo in 1963 to the staff of the *NBC Evening News* in which he outlined the dramatic structure to which each television news story should adhere:

> Every news story should, without any sacrifice of probity or responsibility, display the actions of fiction, of drama. It should have structure and conflict, problem and denouement, rising action and falling action, a beginning, a middle and an end. These are not only the essentials of drama; they are the essentials of narrative.[15]

Edward Jay Epstein's 1973 study of NBC News, called *News from Nowhere*, is one of the earliest examinations of television news narrative. He notes that events are routinely reorganized by producers and editors in the process of what he calls "the resurrection of reality."[16] At the time Epstein studied the production of news at NBC, film was still used instead of videotape. But the fundamental tenets of story construction were already in place: more footage is shot that can be used; events can be re-created through interviews with individuals who either participated in the event or have some connection with it; passages that are dull or difficult to understand will be edited out; establishing shots convey the atmosphere and setting; silent footage and reaction shots are used to maintain the illusion that an actual event is being witnessed.

That is the grammar of visual storytelling. But grammar is not enough. The raw materials of a story must cohere—there must be syntax as well, a structure that will be meaningful and readily understandable to viewers, that fits news developments into predetermined molds and maintains stable audience expectations. Referring to these formulaic aspects of a story as "the story line," Epstein cites a former NBC reporter, Sander Vanocur, speaking about the narrative structure of television reports. "Network news is a continuous loop," Vanocur said. "There are only a limited number of plots— 'Black versus White,' 'War is Hell,' 'America is falling apart,' 'Man against the elements,' 'The Generation Gap,' etc.—which we seem to be constantly redoing with different casts of characters."[17]

60 Minutes brilliantly presented information as narrative, with each program containing three self-contained minidramas each with a beginning, middle, and end. And one of Don Hewitt's most significant innovations as a news producer was to cast the correspondent in a key role in each of these scenarios. Elsa Walsh writes that one-time *60 Minutes* correspondent Meredith Vieira was uncomfortable with her own prominent position within each story: "[Vieira] hated being at the center of a story and purposefully kept herself out of the piece. But that was atypical of the *60 Minutes* formula, which had correspondents showing up as many as 30 times—in about a quarter of the shots. Meredith appeared in [one story called] 'Thy Brother's Keeper' only eight times."[18]

It is not much of an exaggeration to say that the star of each story was its correspondent. That might not have been strictly true in a personality profile, but even then, the stars might have been both Lena Horne and Ed Bradley, for example. Mike Wallace has defended *60 Minutes* against the charge that the program is more an exercise in show business than in journalism. He regards such comments as "elitist" and asserts that "we are, after all, a magazine broadcast that is committed to a multi-subject format, and we have never pretended to be anything else."[19] Wallace then retreats a bit, concluding that the program is certainly meant to be entertaining:

> There's no denying that we go after the most articulate, the most persuasive, the most villainous and the most heroic figures we can find to people our stories. For we have learned, through trial-and-error over the years, that the most effective way to deal with complex subjects—like chemical warfare, the insanity plea, new economic theories, or the question of safety in nuclear power plants—is to place them in the context of graphic and compelling stories, stories told engrossingly by the participants, the people who have first-hand knowledge of the tale we're telling. If that's show biz, then so be it.[20]

60 Minutes eventually set a standard for investigative reporting on television. Aggressive correspondents, interviews edited for maximum dramatic effect, on-the-street confrontations between reporters and wrongdoers (Hewitt would over the years rely less on such "ambush" tactics), tightly framed camera close-ups of investigative targets, and the use of hidden cameras in time would be parodied on *Saturday Night Live*, but more often would be techniques borrowed over and over by other news magazine programs and then borrowed again by entirely new genres of tabloid television and entertainment-based reality programming.

The elaborate, journalistic "sting" operation was an early feature of *60 Minutes*. In 1976, in a story called "The Clinic on Morse Avenue," producer Barry Lando worked with the Better Government Association of Chicago to demonstrate how medical labs in Illinois that billed Medicaid for tests illegally took kickbacks from the clinics that sent blood work to their lab. Lando rented a store on Chicago's South Side and set up a phony clinic equipped with a camera installed behind a one-way mirror. Lab owners who came to the bogus clinic were met by someone posing as a doctor. The lab owner would offer to kick back money to the clinic, following which Mike Wallace would step out from behind the one-way mirror and confront the lab owner. Wallace would sternly reprimand the wrongdoers: "You're talking kickback. I heard you talk kickback." On a special *60 Minutes* broadcast devoted to examining its own investigative techniques, Don Hewitt was himself lectured by a panel of other journalists who argued that encouraging breaking the law was counterproductive and not a good model for investigative reporting. The editor of the *St. Petersburg Times*, Eugene Patterson, was especially outspoken, noting that *60 Minutes* was exposing its subjects as criminals, in effect denying them a fair trial. In his autobiography, Hewitt defended the tactic:

> What is the morality, the ethics, of that kind of journalism? I, for one, have no trouble with it. I am a great believer in everyone's right not to be snooped on. I don't think the Constitution guarantees anyone the right of privacy while he or she is committing a crime.[21]

An even more famous hidden-camera investigation, titled "This Year at Murietta," was aired in 1978. Produced by Marion Goldin, the story concerns a health resort in California that was bilking its patients for huge amounts of money. The spa was run by a huckster named R.J. Rudd. The scale of the deception was impressive. Three *60 Minutes* staffers—Goldin, cameraman Greg Cook, and sound man James Camery—enrolled at the clinic, posing as a wealthy investor and his two aides: a traveling photographer portrayed by Cook and a long-time secretary played by Goldin. Camery, who played the patient, was dubbed "the Colonel" and was presented as having just learned that he was suffering from leukemia. The three imposters arrived in a rented Rolls-Royce. The Colonel was subsequently enrolled for nine days in a program "that consisted, in its entirety, of living on distilled water and lemon juice and having his urine analyzed at regular moments—which they used as opportunities to report remarkable progress in curing his leukemia."[22] On two occasions, the *60 Minutes* team substituted Cook's urine for "Colonel" Camery's and on one occasion provided producer Goldin's. Mike Wallace then arrived with another film crew, only to spring the trap on a flustered R.J. Rudd, who was exposed as a charlatan with phony college degrees from institutions he had difficulty remembering on camera. After the report was broadcast, the state of California put the Murietta spa out of business.

Over the years, *60 Minutes* would use hidden cameras less and less frequently. But the other network news magazine programs made hidden-camera reports a staple.

In 2001, ABC's *PrimeTime Thursday* was using the hidden-camera template almost identically. Two stories presented by Chris Wallace (Mike Wallace's son) were typical. In a report on the inflated cost of antiques, *Primetime* staffers sold a number of valuable objects to antique dealers in the New York City area. Two experts were consulted beforehand to vouch for the actual worth of the items. One antique dealer bought a Tiffany tray for $25 and was caught on camera saying there was very little buyer demand for such trays. About three hours later, different *PrimeTime* staffers purchased the same tray after negotiating the price down from $800 to $650: the dealer had sold the tray for twenty-six times the price he had paid. Several other objects were then sold at considerable multiples of their worth by the dealer. The two experts called these markups more than excessive. The purchases and sales were photographed with a hidden camera. Then Chris Wallace returned with the videotape to confront the dealers. One dealer denied that he had been a party to the sale at all, which the videotape proved was clearly untrue. Two of the dealers told Wallace to get out of their stores; one of them struck the camera repeatedly. A fourth dealer was unapologetic, claiming that he had simply engaged in "good business."[23]

In a separate story, *PrimeTime* joined forces with the district attorney's office in Nassau County on New York's Long Island. In this sting operation, a typical-looking house with typical-looking middle-aged owners (actually, employees of Nassau County) was rigged with seven hidden cameras. A variety of repairmen were called to fix extremely minor problems with appliances. Their failure to properly check the appliances or their charging for unmade repairs was documented. In a number of cases, the county took legal action against the offenders.

The hidden-camera scenario may have been used by investigative reporters prior to *60 Minutes*, but Don Hewitt's program unarguably had introduced the technique to millions of viewers and to more than a generation of television news producers. The dramatic elements of the story have remained unchanged: plot, character, tone, and theme. The hidden-camera story is best understood as a particular kind of narrative that carries a powerful punch no matter how many times we see it. The plot is one of rising action (the sale of the antique, for example, at an absurdly low price), a climax (the purchase made at a comparatively obscene markup), and a resolution (the villain is confronted and forced to account for his or her cheating ways). Legal action against a scam artist may be the payoff for the viewer, but more often, and more viscerally, the payoff is the humiliation the offender is compelled to undergo, and his or her pathetic and transparent attempt to rationalize or simply squirm out of the situation.

What makes *60 Minutes* work so successfully—and what has made it an iconic form of television storytelling—is a combination of ingredients, certainly not the least of which is the skill with which such narratives are carefully crafted. Don Hewitt chose to title his 2001 autobiography *Tell Me a Story*, and he undoubtedly knows a good story when he hears one. During his tenure at *60 Minutes*, he has been able, as executive producer, to identify the dramatic high points of a story and to work with producers to create narratives with staying power. The "sting" narrative, which can be labeled "Cheater Gets Caught," has a clear villain and hero, particularly when the correspondent—who doesn't arrive until it is time to indict the wrongdoer—is a famous television figure such as Mike Wallace or Ed Bradley or Leslie Stahl.

Those individuals who are caught in the act meet their comeuppance when *60 Minutes* walks through the door in the person of a famous television reporter. We are watching news as theater, a meticulously constructed drama with a forceful resolution. The news magazine story thus contains many of the same attributes as the so-called "nonfiction novel" and other "docudramas." It uses the techniques of fictional narrative, of entertainment, to tell a story that is true. Like the novelist, the producer and the reporter manipulate point of view (using both script and camera) and manipulate dialogue, to a degree, in the editing process.

Don Hewitt's original brainstorm—to package reality as Hollywood packaged entertainment—was to have far-reaching consequences. Famed journalist David Halberstam expressed considerable worry, though, that *60 Minutes* was venturing into dangerous territory:

> At *60 Minutes* there is an almost pathological fear of being boring, which reflects Hewitt's obsession with ratings, and therefore a comparable lack of proportion or balance. But the real challenge for talented journalists has always been to take subjects which are seemingly boring and make them interesting and thereby show ordinary people their stake in something complex. Almost anyone can take a crime or a petty corruption piece and make it sexy, or at least semi-sexy.[24]

The Furor Over Tobacco

Over the years, *60 Minutes* has been sued repeatedly by some disgruntled subjects of its stories. It has won the vast majority of those lawsuits. Occasionally it has reached out-of-court settlements with plaintiffs. The darkest hours for *60 Minutes*, though, came because of one of its own producers—perhaps its premier producer, Lowell Bergman—and a scientist named Jeffrey Wigand. The incident embarrassed CBS many times over, first as it unfolded in stages and then, for a much larger public, as it was retold in the film *The Insider*, starring Al Pacino as Bergman, Christopher Plummer as Mike Wallace, and Russell Crowe as Wigand.

Dr. Jeffrey Wigand was a biochemist with a Ph.D. who had been vice president for research and development at Brown & Williamson Tobacco Company, one of the nation's largest cigarette makers. In March 1993, Wigand was fired. As part of his separation with the company, he signed a confidentiality agreement, which, among other things, allowed him to keep his family's health insurance policy. Under the terms of the agreement, he could say very little or nothing at all about his years of employment, specifically the nature of his work, and nothing about the terms of the severance contract.

At the time CBS first became involved with Wigand, employing him as a consultant to *60 Minutes* on tobacco-related stories, the company was controlled by Lawrence Tisch, himself an owner of another major cigarette manufacturer. In addition, Tisch was then in the process of arranging the sale of CBS to Westinghouse. In 1995, events began to move very quickly. *60 Minutes* intended to interview Wigand and use the material on the air as part of a story about the practice of "nicotine-spiking"—a tobacco company tactic to manipulate the levels of nicotine in cigarettes to ensure that smokers would stay addicted and keep smoking. Wigand had clear-cut, empirical evidence that spiking was common throughout the industry.

After ABC broadcast a story about nicotine-spiking, the Philip Morris Company sued ABC for $10 million and settled the case out of court. Wigand had been interviewed for a *60 Minutes* story that expanded on the topic, but there was the problem of his confidentiality agreement. Don Hewitt was told by the chief legal counsel for CBS that if Wigand appeared, there might well be a trial, and the damages for CBS could be $1.5 billion. He was told that no story, whatever the circumstances, should put the network at risk, as this one would. On November 11, 1995, CBS broadcast a story about tobacco-spiking, in which admittedly "critical information" was left out and Wigand was not identified despite the vague mention of a "tobacco insider." At the end of the story, Mike Wallace added an extraordinary "personal note":

> We at *60 Minutes*—and that's about a hundred of us who turn out this broadcast each week—are proud of working here and at CBS News, and so we were dismayed that the management at CBS has seen fit to give in to perceived threats of legal action against us by a tobacco-industry giant. We've broadcast many such investigative pieces down through the years, and we want to be able to continue. We lost out, only to some degree on this one, but we haven't the slightest doubt that we'll be able to continue the *60 Minutes* tradition of reporting such pieces in the future without fear or favor.[25]

What was the truth behind the story? Did the upcoming merger with Westinghouse make CBS jittery? Did board chairman Lawrence Tisch wish to protect the tobacco industry from damaging revelations? No one knows, but Hewitt chose to emphasize that *60 Minutes* had taken a poke at its own network on the air. But in January 1996, when the *Wall Street Journal* made everything public in a long story that quoted and named Wigand, CBS and *60 Minutes* both looked weak when confronted with the resources of Big Tobacco. In 1999, when *The Insider* began playing in theaters across America, CBS and Wallace looked cowardly. Hewitt and Bergman, who was no longer with CBS, disagree on most of the facts concerning the whole incident, especially on the details of the movie depiction. Whatever the truth was, it was not a proud moment for anyone at *60 Minutes* or at the network. The famous CBS eye was left more than a bit discolored.

— 5 —

Tabloid Television and a World of Talk

The questions of what is and what isn't newsworthy have their own considerable history. News judgments reflect both professional standards and cultural values, so journalistic practice can offer telling insights into society at large. Gossip, for example, has always been a component of news. Troubadours and minstrels (along with Shakespeare, Dickens, and many other celebrated authors) treated gossip as the essence of what people wanted to know and what made a good story. As journalism became professionalized, with more established codes of conduct and training that was more formalized than the earlier apprenticeship system, gossip became increasingly suspect in the mainstream press. It eventually garnered the label of "tabloid" journalism ("tabloid" referred originally to the size of a page in a newspaper; papers were either "broadsheets" or tabloids; tabloid papers had smaller pages, opened as a magazine did, and often contained sensational content). At the same time, a strengthened concern for privacy has brought certain kinds of personal information into question. Is gossip newsworthy? The answer is constantly shifting. It depends on when the question is asked.

The answer also depends upon the nature of the story. Journalistic standards always have been based on relativistic criteria. If the people involved in a story are prominent enough, or if the acts are extreme enough, or if the local angle is compelling enough, then the gossip can be judged newsworthy.

The O.J. Simpson case and President Clinton's affair with Monica Lewinsky have been cited as prime examples of the "tabloidization" of television news. But a plausible argument can be made that while both stories contained sensational, even tawdry, elements that are usually associated with tabloid journalism, they were both important, undeniably newsworthy stories.

The O.J. Simpson story was about a famous celebrity, a Hall of Fame professional football player who appeared in movies and was a fixture on television programs and commercials. The Simpson story concerned two brutal murders, sex, jealousy, alleged drug use, eventually celebrity lawyers, and much more. The Monica Lewinsky story dealt with the most important individual on the American news landscape, the president of the United States, and was about infidelity, lying, and stunningly detailed accounts of sexual liaisons. But the lurid qualities of both stories do not obviate their news value. Simpson probably was the most famous American ever charged with first-degree murder. The Lewinsky matter resulted in the impeachment of an American president.

What was historically noteworthy was, at least in part, the unprecedented time allotted to the stories on television broadcasts. For the first time, all-news cable channels existed that could devote days and months to wall-to-wall coverage, "all Monica all the time." The Simpson case featured complete coverage of a nine-month-long trial, and the Lewinsky story was discussed for hours night after night on cable.

The 2001 Chandra Levy–Gary Condit story received a similar coverage—without the involvement of a president or the known commission of a crime. Levy, a college-age intern, was the mistress of Condit, a married California congressman. Her murder was not discovered for months after her disappearance. In fact, hours of commentary on cable television programs plowed the same ground over and over again, because nothing had happened during the previous day or week. By 2002, the murder charge against actor Robert Blake would arouse much less interest.

The Simpson and Lewinsky stories were especially relevant to a debate over journalistic propriety because they dealt with sensitive subject matter more explicitly than network television had dared to do before. Now, types of stories that the networks would have covered much more sparingly in the past—for example, the case of the "Long Island Lolita," sixteen-year-old Amy Fisher, and her lover, Joey Buttafuoco—are reported more extensively. (Fisher was jailed after she shot Buttafuoco's wife in a failed murder attempt.)

Changes in the content of newscasts were apparent first in local programming. NBC engaged in nearly two years of extensive audience research before unveiling *News Center 4* on WNBC in New York City in 1974. The research concluded that "television news had become too important to be left to the news people."[1] With *News Center 4*, the lines between news and entertainment were deliberately blurred. The program premiered with an elaborate set, the largest staff in local television news, and an anchorman, Tom Snyder, who was as much a television personality as a newsman.

While previous newscasts had centered largely on events, audience analysis suggested that viewers responded better to personality-driven news.[2] Programmers attempted to make viewers connect on a personal level with both the newsmakers and the broadcasters. Instead of focusing on a complicated issue raised in a political campaign, for example, programmers decided that it would be more effective to cover the candidates themselves. In the studio, anchors were featured as regular people to whom the audience could relate. Their likable "regularity" was displayed through "happy talk" between the members of the studio team, such as the exchange of hearty banter between stories, segments of the program, or while going into commercial breaks.

In a 1973 statement, Frank Magid, a news consultant, reminded programmers that "the vast majority of our viewers have never seen a copy of the *New York Times*. The vast majority do not read the same books that you and I read . . . in fact, many of them never read anything."[3] Thus, in a way similar to the approach taken by popular newspapers in the nineteenth century, television news in the late twentieth century was being reconfigured for the "common man."[4]

The patronizing undertones of Magid's statement are underscored by New York City station WABC's creation of a more "accessible" image for long-time anchorman Joel Daly. In the mid-seventies, Daly, a Yale graduate with a six-figure salary, was reconstructed as a "hillbilly."[5] Ads featured Daly wearing blue jeans and smoking a cigarette while humming "I Turned 21 in Prison Doin' Life Without Parole." At a 1976 country music concert, Daly actually took the stage in full cowboy attire and read a poem paying homage to hillbilly life. Although the strategy was a success with viewers, it reflected the lengths to which stations would go to become more viewer-friendly.

As local news began to change, so did nationally syndicated news programs in the 1990s. They pushed the networks to become much more explicit in their treatment of once-taboo subject matter. In the longer view, critics had for years predicted that television standards would not only change, but disappear altogether.

In the 1976 movie *Network*, screenwriter Paddy Chayefsky and director Sidney Lumet fashioned a vision of a morally bankrupt and maniacally reckless society drawn from their trenchant satire of network news run amok. In the film, anchorman Howard Beale attracts huge audiences after abandoning the news to become a ranting, latter-day "prophet of the airwaves." When his ratings slump, executives have him murdered. A television news magazine on the same network meanwhile enters into an agreement with a terrorist group and broadcasts its crimes—kidnapping, robberies, hijackings— on the program each week.[6] In the 1970s, some called *Network* Hollywood's revenge against television. But thirty years later, the apocalyptic vision of the movie would seem strangely prophetic.

In the 1990s, "Trash TV" was the title of the cover story run by one news magazine, "tabloid TV" the generic label for real television *really* run amok. Historically, it may be surprising that television, in some ways the most accessible and populist of media, aimed at the largest possible audiences, took so long before offering up sensational and populist versions of the news. News has always been a matter of commerce, and it has always entertained as well as informed. Historian Mitchell Stephens traces an audience appreciation for tabloid content to the sixteenth and seventeenth centuries, when pamphlets and broadsides for the less educated masses began to be widely distributed. One contemporary critic described such material as "trifles, pieces of nonsense, fables, frivolities, drolleries, charlantries and pranks."[7] In the 1990s, tabloid TV contained all of those items, but the mix is more easily described as news about crime, sex, scandal, and celebrity— with an emphasis on any combination of the four.

In recent media history, a direct line leads from English-language tabloid newspapers (mainly in Britain and Australia) to tabloid TV in the United States. The connection was forged by Australian media magnate Rupert Murdoch and the program *A Current Affair*. Murdoch, whose News Corporation is one of the largest communications conglomerates in the world, first got a foothold in U.S. television with the purchase of Fox Broadcasting. In 1986, *A Current Affair*, a nightly thirty-minute program, began to take shape. Murdoch met with the man he wanted as anchor, Washington-based talk-show host Maury Povich, in New York. Povich recalled the conversation in his autobiography:

> What kind of a show will this be? I asked.
> A news show that will make news and break news, [Rupert Murdoch] said. Unique.
> I was stupid, I said, this is what you brought me here for? It sounds like every other television news show I've ever heard about. What's different?
> He looked at me with those cool, deadly eyes and replied simply, "You'll work it out."
> And when will you want this program to go on the air?
> A man introduced as Ian Rae jumped in. He said in about a month, which was crazy. Starting up a television show took time—a year, six months, at least. Nobody did that kind of thing in a month. You had to get staff, you had to get stories, you had to have trial runs.
> Or two weeks, said Murdoch. If you can.[8]

64

Over the next few weeks, Murdoch's team of Australian executives put together a staff of twenty producers, reporters, and researchers. Povich wrote later about the "undiminished and happy zest for vulgar truth" that bound the program's creators together.

> No comforting euphemisms, no sappy evasions—life, in all of its messy incarnations was, for us, endlessly fascinating. Somewhere along the line each of us had been thwarted by those careful guardians of taste and style known in the industry as "the suits." Each of us had run up against the brittle rules of engagement in the timid news divisions of local stations ("Don't take sides"; "Don't show emotion"; "Be sure to get both sides").[9]

Were those antiquated industry rules really about taste and style? Or did they have just as much, or even more, to do with accuracy, balance, and fairness? The terms of the inevitable debate—indeed, the fundamental question of *what was being debated* as news programs were reconstituted— were being established.

A Current Affair premiered in New York on July 28 at 11:30 P.M. Soon afterward, John Corry of the *New York Times* reviewed the program, saying, in part: "'A Current Affair' is tabloid journalism. Forget now the pejorative notions that cling to the phrase. 'A Current Affair' is tabloid journalism at its best. It is zippy and knowledgeable, and when it falls on its face, at least it's in there trying."[10] Elated by the blessing of the *Times*, Murdoch moved the show to 7:30 P.M., replacing his most popular show, *M*A*S*H*.

A Current Affair, along with the syndicated programs that followed it, adopted the look and feel of a newscast—and then changed, not at all subtly, the content of a newscast and many of its accepted techniques of information-gathering. There was, to be sure, an anchorperson behind a desk and there were clearly people functioning as reporters. Much of what was broadcast, though, the *New York Times* notwithstanding, used the appearance of journalistic methods to make something that was not quite journalism seem valid. The on-air sources used on tabloid programs were often vaguely identified as "experts" or unaffiliated reporters or "entertainment journalists." What they reported was often unattributed gossip. Still, the TV tabloids set the pace for the rest of the news media, especially on stories based in Hollywood, where their sources might be extensive and, yes, could be correct.

A Current Affair took the blurring lines between news and entertainment and erased them altogether. Excerpts from popular films and songs were routinely inserted into news programs. Photographs of Jerry Lee Lewis and his teenage bride were included in a 1989 story, for example, about a girl, with no connection whatsoever to the singer, who was expelled from school for getting married.[11] Chuck Berry's "You Can Tell" played in the background. In a 1990 story in which actor William Shatner of *Star Trek* fame was being sued by a former lover, *A Current Affair* deftly blurred the line between fact and fiction, showing images of Shatner's Captain Kirk character while a voice-over intoned:

> California Supreme Court: The Final Frontier. Captain Kirk had been brought down to earth. And now, with all those fierce intergalactic forces behind him, he faces one of his most daunting duels: a showdown with a human Klingon—a woman determined to cling onto what she thinks is rightfully hers.[12]

A Current Affair often added a layer of subversive irony to its presentation through the physicality of anchor Maury Povich, who rejected the stoic, serious-minded demeanor of the traditional news anchor in favor of a collection of facial expressions that included scowls, head shakes, and raised eyebrows to, in his words, give his "unconcealed opinion about my own show." He described his style as "Lenny Bruce as anchorman"—indicating that he was no different than a politically charged comedian who used humor to vent his own feelings.[13]

According to one report, *A Current Affair* had gross revenues of $850,000 a week with production costs of about $260,000.[14] Murdoch's program would not have the field to itself for long—that was certain. The King World production *Inside Edition* began broadcasting in 1988. (Roger King was considered the king of syndicated television. His programs eventually included *Oprah*, *Wheel of Fortune*, *Jeopardy*, and *Geraldo*.) Paramount readied a program called *Hard Copy*, which debuted in 1989. Soon afterward, *American Journal* was on the air.

By 1994, with the arrival of a new group of network news magazine programs, apparent new standards in daytime talk, and breaking news of the O.J. Simpson murder case appearing everywhere, tabloid television had become a topic of national concern. *Time*, *Newsweek*, and *U.S. News & World Report* led an assault on the methods of tabloid TV (while, of course, using the superheated tabloid story about tabloids to enhance their own circulations). *U.S. News* featured tabloid TV in a gaudy story headlined "Tabloid TV's Blood Lust."[15] (Did it occur to the magazine editors that their entire approach was the very thing they were decrying?)

The new programs were changing the news, it was argued, in a number of ways. Paying sources (a long-accepted practice of the tabloid press) had reached a new level of competitive fury with television now in the fray. A potential witness in the Simpson case received $5,000 from *Hard Copy*. Rupert Murdoch defended the practice of making payments to news sources, while so-called mainstream journalists said that the result of news-for-cash was the airing of more and more unsubstantiated and suspect rumors.

Tabloid news programs were prone to use subjective forms of editing and cinematography, background music, and occasionally reenactments. Extreme close-ups or slow motion were employed to heighten dramatic tension, for example. Or grainy footage was used to impart a documentary or hidden-camera feel to video that was neither. The line separating fact from fiction was invisible, and it was obvious that less "serious" news was displacing stories of substance. One critic referred to the resulting content as "reality lite."[16] The new approach, it was said, meant that sources could be coached and complicated stories reduced to simple morality tales (an argument that can be made about virtually all journalism of almost any time).

An analysis of one program, *Inside Edition*, during six weeks in the summer of 1995 is instructive.[17] Stories were coded for content as indicated in Table 5.1. Clearly, *Inside Edition* was a program devoted to stories about crime and about celebrities.

In addition to this particular (and, I believe, broadly representative) mix of topics, tabloid television news is characterized by a set of thematic structures and narrative conventions. In a 1996 study called "The Journalism of Outrageousness," Matthew C. Ehrlich identifies four recurring frameworks in tabloid TV:

Sensationalism. The example Ehrlich cites is a story on *A Current Affair* about the actions of a criminal gang. The topic and its treatment are both sensationalized. Close-ups and slow-motion video are used to retrace the movements of the gang's victims, accompanied by evocative music. A murder scene is shown in red-tinted video.

Innocent Victims/Guilty Villains. Crime and sex stories portray the victims as devoted children or loving parents, people with all-American values. Perpetrators are sick, evil, or both.

Irony and Sarcasm. Ehrlich refers to a story about Prince Charles and Princess Diana's marital troubles. The story contains a dramatization of a sexually tinged conversation between Charles and his lover, Camilla Parker-Bowles. Reporter Steve Dunleavy narrates the story with a sneer:

> Frankly, the tape sounds like a disgustingly smutty conversation between two dopey adolescents. And yet these are the people who think they're better than you and I.... All this from the man born to be king. Some king he'll make!

Irony is also used as a distancing device, such as the anchor's use of wry disclaimers to accompany more outrageous stories, such as accounts of UFO sightings.

Table 5.1

Tabloid Topics

Topic	Number of stories	Percentage of all stories
Crime	29	30
Celebrities	28	28
O.J. Simpson	9	9
Fashion/beauty	6	6
Health/safety	6	6
Sports	6	6
Animals	3	3
Sexual aberration	3	3
Other	8	8
		99
		(Total less than 100%)

Sentimentality. In stories about terminally ill patients or tearful reunions, emotions are often reinforced by music and slow-motion video.[18]

In the 1990s, as a growing number of talk-show hosts seemed to specialize in tabloid subjects, mainstream news itself became more sensational. In April 1991, a woman alleged that she had been raped by Senator Edward M. Kennedy's nephew, William Kennedy Smith, at the Kennedy estate in Palm Beach, Florida. NBC News took the unusual step of breaking ranks with other major news organizations by reporting the name of the alleged victim, Patricia Bowman, without her consent. The story received a great deal of coverage, including broadcast excerpts of the courtroom testimony. At that time, such coverage of an alleged rape—even one involving a prominent defendant—was unprecedented.

NBC News president Michael Gartner defended his decision to name the victim. He argued that although a rape was rarely a national story, in this instance suppressing the victim's name would be akin to participating in a conspiracy of silence. The suspect's name had been known at the outset—as was customary—and had been widely disseminated. Indeed, his name and family had made the story newsworthy in the first place. Gartner contended that naming the victim was journalistically fair, despite the dissenting views of many of his colleagues, both within and outside NBC News.

Later in the decade, a news story that was nothing if not lurid was widely covered, breaking new, and literally and ethically uncomfortable, ground for many. A Virginia woman, Lorena Bobbitt, told police that her husband John had raped her. In an act of reprisal, she sliced off his penis with a kitchen knife. Although the major networks did not cover the story extensively on the evening newscasts, many syndicated and network news magazines did. So did the *New York Times*. Writer Howard Fast noted that no part of the Bobbitt story was off-limits to the public:

> News stories have dwelt on every aspect of this curious tale—the sharp edge of the knife; the casting aside of the dismembered organ out of a car window onto a vacant lot; Mrs. Bobbitt's pleas that she had no memory of committing the attack; her testimony of the pain and beating and rapes and further indignities she said were bestowed upon her by her husband; the physicians' scientific explanations to the court concerning the restoration of the organ in question and the possibilities of its further use.[19]

Changing news standards were everywhere. A once unthinkable national story could now be expected to receive an enormous amount of coverage—from *Time* magazine, the *New York Times*, the television networks.

Another remarkable trial received frenzied interest in California. Two brothers, Erik and Lyle Menendez, were accused of murdering their parents, José and Kitty, in Beverly Hills. The 1989 murders were especially brutal and unexpected: the Menendez parents were well-to-do and apparently had been close to their twenty-one- and eighteen-year-old sons. They lived in a twenty-three-room mansion protected by an elaborate security system. The brothers' first trial ended in a hung jury; in the second trial, they were convicted of first-degree murder and sentenced to life prison terms without the possibility of parole.

The coverage of the Menendez brothers, the Bobbitts, and William Kennedy Smith demonstrated the appeal of sensational material, and also the appeal of a trial in which cameras were allowed in the courtroom. The trials were prepackaged melodramas that lasted weeks or months, were inexpensive to produce, and built toward a dramatic outcome.

In 1990, communication researcher Elizabeth Bird conducted a study of tabloid readers. She found that readers of supermarket tabloids shared a "class-based feeling of powerlessness and alienation from the mainstream" that breeds a distrust of the traditional media.[20] Perhaps contrary to popular belief, Bird found tabloid readers to be "fairly well-educated and interested in the world around them."[21]

If we assume that viewers of tabloid television fit a similar profile, then the embracing of tabloid news in the electronic media, whether it be a reported sighting of Bigfoot on *A Current Affair* or the exploration of alternate sexual lifestyles on a daytime talk show, may be seen as the insistence of at least some viewers that there is more going on in the world—or more interesting things going on in the world—than what the mainstream media allow. Some viewers may be well aware of the journalistic shortcomings of some of this information, but believe that it can be accessed only outside the mainstream.

In retrospect, it seems that by the summer of 1994, a large part of the news media, particularly the tabloid press, the daily entertainment-news programs on television, CNN, Court TV and other cable outlets, and the network news magazines, were ripe for a sensational and scandalous story. It also can be said that a large part of the American public was probably ready for such a story, its appetite whetted by the increasing attention given—mainly on television—to scandal.

The floodgates burst during the second week of June, when Nicole Simpson, the ex-wife of former football great O.J. Simpson, and a friend, Ron Goldman, were brutally murdered in Brentwood, California, a fashionable section of Los Angeles. Detectives investigating the crime scene found what seemed to be an abundance of evidence linking O.J. Simpson to the two murders, including blood spatters and drops, a bloody glove, and bloody shoe prints and socks that apparently tied him directly to the crime. Through his attorney, he was told to present himself to the police as a suspect in the murders. When he failed to do so, Gil Garcetti, the Los Angeles district attorney, declared that O.J. Simpson, once a hero to millions of Americans, was "a fugitive from justice."[22]

The stunning developments that followed were unprecedented in the history of American culture and journalism. Facing arrest, Simpson apparently fled in a white Ford Bronco van with a friend, A.C. Cowlings. Police soon took up pursuit on the freeway. News helicopters provided pictures of the thirty-mile-an-hour processional, referred to as a slow-speed "chase," to an estimated 95 million viewers.[23] In an instant, the Simpson case became a story of unheard-of proportions. At the networks, brief updates gave way to full-scale live coverage.

The story itself was barely believable. Simpson had told a police dispatcher by cellular phone that he was holding a gun to his head, and a letter from Simpson was released to the press that for all purposes was a suicide note. NBC News decided to cut into a live telecast of a professional basketball playoff game. David Bohrman was in charge of special events for NBC News. According to Bohrman, network news president Andrew Lack decided to switch live to the scene in California:

> "We knew it was going to be a difficult night and it was," Bohrman said. "No one had thought through this scenario before. This was not a geopolitical crisis, this was just an incredible story which was happening while we were there. The most famous person ever charged with murder in this country, a beloved athlete, someone everyone knew. It had taken this turn and for all

these reasons we were all drawn to it as people who wanted to put a news story on the air."[24]

As author Paul Thaler points out, coverage of the story was strongly influenced by legal commentators and other analysts. No story in memory had been turned over so thoroughly to so-called experts, pundits who were free to personally interpret virtually every aspect of the story. O.J. Simpson became a campfire around which countless hours of opinionated talk were presented.[25] As weeks turned into months, television became inseparable from the events before and during the trial. On-air analysts applied the methods of "horse race" journalism, commenting on who "won" a particular day during the trial, who was leading, and who was behind. In the midst of the story, a backlash against the tabloid nature of the coverage, or against the sheer journalistic overkill, began to grow. Analysis became a cottage industry for lawyers who liked the camera and could ably comment on the legal maneuvering. When the *National Enquirer* paid witnesses for their story about the purchase of a knife by Simpson, the paper was singled out for criticism by the "mainstream" media. But the mainstream media went after the same story.

> The tabloids also exploited the violent aspects of the case, with re-enactments of the murders featuring actors disguised as victims and as the assailant. But a Los Angeles KCBS report went further to re-create the murders using a computer-animated figure, depicted as an African-American, slashing the throat of another computer-animated figure, white and blonde.[26]

Indeed, there was little to separate the allegedly mainstream media, especially prime-time network news magazines, from the tabloid press. On ABC, *20/20* reveled in the most lurid aspects of the story, in fact expanding upon them when Barbara Walters asked about a purported lesbian relationship between Nicole Simpson and a friend, again when she asked O.J. Simpson's first wife if the couple's son were gay, and again when she asked if O.J. had lost his sexual desire for Nicole. In his book *The Spectacle: Media and the Making of the O.J. Simpson Story*, Paul Thaler notes that Walters was at her tabloid best (or worst) in an interview with the family of Ron Goldman, in which, by innuendo and suggestion, she trashed the reputation of Goldman, the victim who had been in all likelihood a hapless bystander:

> WALTERS: You know, we have read about Ron being in the fast lane, you know, driving Nicole's white Ferrari. What does that mean, the "fast lane"? What was his life like, as much as you know?
> FRED GOLDMAN [Ron's father]: Well, I don't know. I guess that some people could hear the term "fast lane" and I guess it could bring about some negative images. But knowing Ron, I mean, he liked to dance, he liked to be

around people. I don't . . . I never got the impression that . . . you know, that Ron saw himself as quote-unquote in some sort of fast lane.

WALTERS: Or a ladies' man?

FRED GOLDMAN: But I don't . . .

KIM GOLDMAN [sister]: But my brother . . . my brother wanted to be married and he wanted to have a family.

WALTERS: Did he have a girlfriend?

KIM GOLDMAN: He was dating a young lady.

WALTERS: Did Ron ever mention Nicole Simpson?

PATTI GOLDMAN [stepmother]: Never.

MICHAEL GOLDMAN [brother]: Never.

KIM GOLDMAN: Never.

WALTERS: Did you ever know. . .

FRED GOLDMAN: Never.

WALTERS:. . . that she existed?

PATTI GOLDMAN: No.

FRED GOLDMAN: I had never heard of her.

WALTERS: You know, so many rumors. First there were rumors that Ron and Nicole were lovers. Then there were rumors that he was gay. Did you hear these, too?

KIM GOLDMAN: Far from it.[27]

The Simpson trial became a national obsession. Viewership on CNN and Court TV rose to unprecedented levels. CNN's ratings increased fivefold during the trial. The all-news network offered 631 hours of trial coverage to an average audience of 2.2 million. Court TV, which began in 1991, was carried in 22 million households by 1995. That may not have been a good thing in the Simpson case, though. Legal commentator Lincoln Caplan finds fault with the Simpson coverage provided by CNN and Court TV. He has harsh words especially for Court TV, which, he says, made little effort to be coherent to the general public, instead "highlighting the machinations of the legal process and the lawyers who move[d] it along, rather than [covering] the substance and the drama of ideas."[28]

Talk, Talk, Talk

> We have lowered the thresholds of civility and tolerance, and
> we have replaced them with the raised voices of gratuitous
> denigration and intolerance. Daytime television has become
> an electronic forum for the kinds of people the society was
> once free to dismiss as trash, with no greater interest in their
> cheap and mindless disputes. The petty dysfunctional now has
> become the electronic icon.
>
> —*Tom Brokaw, 1995*

72

The Development of the Genre

Television talk shows have been in existence at least since the 1950s. Originally the format consisted of celebrity guests sitting at a coffee table and sharing recipes and other personal information.[29] The modern talk-show format originated in the late 1960s in an unlikely place for a broadcast revolution: Dayton, Ohio. Phil Donahue, then thirty-one, with experience as an announcer and radio and television journalist in Adrian, Michigan, and Dayton, began a local interview program on WHIO-TV on November 6, 1967. On his program that day he had only one guest, Madalyn Murray O'Hair, the country's best-known atheist.[30] The second program featured single men talking about what they looked for in women, the third a Dayton obstetrician and a film showing the birth of a baby. Lacking easy access in Dayton to entertainers, Donahue and his producer turned to local news and current events to supply guests. By necessity, they improvised, and in so doing they expanded the range of topics that could be addressed on daytime television.

After two years as a local program, the show was syndicated to other stations in Ohio, then to several other cities in the Midwest. The Donahue show was different—that was clear. Unlike other local programs, it had no light entertainment, no band. Usually there was only one guest, and the audience members actively participated, challenging the guest or arguing with the host or among themselves. Donahue says in his autobiography that it took perhaps three years to realize that what he was doing was special.[31] In the mid-1970s, *The Phil Donahue Show* moved to Chicago, where it grew from being seen in 38 cities to more than 200, and then in the 1980s it moved to New York.

In 1986, Oprah Winfrey began a syndicated talk show that would surpass Donahue in the ratings and produce for her an income in excess of $50 million a year. Along the way, Donahue and Oprah were joined by Sally Jessy Raphael and Geraldo Rivera. By the mid-1990s, the number of daytime talk programs had soared to at least two dozen.

Talk shows have come under criticism for their obsession with bizarre and deviant behavior; with sexuality and personal relationships that range from unconventional to outrageous; with frivolous "female" topics on one hand and bitter family disputes that have led to fisticuffs on the other; with the featured testimony of "experts" on the mundane as well as on the antisocial antics of maladjusted people; with hate groups, the occult, and whatever else can be found at the underside of American life.

As a gay man, Joshua Gamson has written of daytime talk shows:

I think they are a wretched little place, emptied of so much wisdom, and filled, thank God, with inadvertent camp, but they are the place most enthusiastically afforded us—a measure of cultural value. We are taking, and being given much more public media space now, but only because we forged a path in there, and we had best understand the wretched little space where we were once honored guests.[32]

At one time, the shows indeed seemed to be expanding the boundaries of daytime television so that a new kind of journalism might be emerging. Broadcast pioneer Fred Friendly once called Phil Donahue "the people's journalist" before deciding that Donahue had joined the competitive rush to fill the airwaves with whatever would draw a crowd. Oprah Winfrey presented pragmatic issues in day-to-day life as well as traditional journalistic stories, celebrity interviews, and shows devoted to forms of self-enrichment. Sally Jessy Raphael specialized in self-improvement and personal healing; her show was most often a kind of television therapy session. Geraldo Rivera, on the other hand, was from the outset consciously testing the limits of what had been considered acceptable broadcast fare. His syndicated program dealt with bizarre and even occult topics, outrageous personal relationships, crime, gang culture, and sex. In a show on racial prejudice, Rivera's nose was broken in an on-air melee. A news magazine covered the episode with the cover story titled "Trash TV." It proved to be only a beginning.

A World of Talk

In the wake of the first hosts came a far larger group, including Maury Povich, Jenny Jones, Ricki Lake, Jerry Springer, Richard Bey, Montel Williams, Carnie Wilson, Gordon Elliott, Leeza Gibbons, and Tempestt Bledsoe. By 1995, Geraldo Rivera, in an interview, repositioned himself as a talk-show moderate criticizing his successors:

> The sex topics have really been relegated to the back row by the established, brand-name programs. [The newer shows] are doing topics that I wouldn't go near now. We've gone into the middle of the road.[33]

Rivera then took the opportunity to critique the new ratings leader, Ricki Lake.

> Ricki Lake is a program that is insulting to its audience. People are yelling at each other, and every topic is a sexually themed topic. I think that there is a tendency to underestimate the intelligence of the daytime audience, and I think that is unfortunate. I do think that there is a tendency among the audi-

ence to go for the visceral topics rather than the intellectual topics, and I think that's also unfortunate.[34]

Talk-show success, Rivera added, was a matter of walking a fine line between "being competitive" and "pandering" to the audience. Those shows that were able to "walk that tightrope successfully," he said, would endure.

By 1995, however, too many hosts had crossed too many lines far too often for the tastes of many critics and social observers. Jerry Springer had taken the form to new and, to some viewers, deeply upsetting levels of on-screen violence, vulgarity, and deviance. Any number of outrages had been specifically documented: the same people appeared as interview subjects on several programs and presented completely different life histories, none of which were true upon later examination. Audiences were routinely stirred to a fever pitch and guests apparently had to be protected from the studio audience (although in many cases this behavior was staged for effect). A man named Jonathan Schmitz was charged with the shooting death of thirty-two-year-old Scott Amedure after both had appeared for a taping of *The Jenny Jones Show*. The topic was "secret admirers," and Schmitz had expected that his admirer was a woman. Instead, he was confronted with Amedure, who reportedly had a crush on him.

The television critic of the *Washington Post*, Tom Shales, called the Jones taping an exercise in "humiliation television," observing that "the talk shows are part of America's cultural pollution, and now it appears that the pollution can be deadly."[35] Later that year, William Bennett, a former secretary of education under President Reagan and the author of best-selling books on moral values, joined with Democratic senator Joseph Lieberman of Connecticut in a bipartisan attack on "lurid" daytime talk shows. The two men emphasized that they were calling neither for censorship nor for boycotts. But they explained that they were "petitioning producers to acknowledge their responsibilities toward their viewers, both children and the general public, rather than just the profits they may stand to gain from them." Implicitly they were calling for Americans to pressure advertisers, distributors of programs, producers, and the programs themselves to change.[36]

By the year 2000, the audience had fallen off substantially for Springer-style mayhem, although it remained a subgenre that clearly had an audience among the young and, to some extent, the "down-market" demographic. But the profusion of rude and crude talk shows had passed, to be replaced by Oprah and her ideological look-alikes, all providing heartwarming stories, a large dose of self-reflection and self-therapy, and, of course, the occasional celebrity interview. There were also Martha Stewart, Rosie O'Donnell—the "Queen of Nice"—and other, more conventional hosts and programs.

Pundits Galore: Talking About the News

"News talk" on television began with figures in the news, usually politicians, responding to questions from a panel of Washington, D.C., reporters. In 1947, *Meet the Press* moved over to NBC Television from radio. Its format, at least until the 1980s, remained for the most part unchanged. The CBS program *Face the Nation* and ABC's *Issues and Answers* were both venerable programs that, along with *Meet the Press*, appeared on the slowest news day—Sunday—and could be counted on to provide a story, and occasionally a major story, for that evening's network newscast. But they were interview shows, not really *talk* shows. When David Brinkley left NBC for ABC, the network built an hour-long program with a somewhat less structured format, *This Week with David Brinkley*, around its host. There were, at the time, two reporters' roundtables that had been on the air for more than a decade: on PBS, *Washington Week in Review*, with host Paul Duke, and the syndicated *Agronsky & Company*, with veteran newsman Martin Agronsky. Thus there were interview programs and others in which reporters summarized and interpreted the week's news. All that was about to change.

The tabloid screamfest met the news of the day in the person of John McLaughlin, a one-time Jesuit priest, failed Senate candidate, and radio talk-show host. In 1982, he began *The McLaughlin Group*, a half-hour program based neither on interviews nor on reporters discussing the stories they had covered. *The McLaughlin Group* was about heated opinion, expressed loudly and in short bursts of air time. Liberals Eleanor Clift, Jack Germond, and Morton Kondracke were pitted against conservatives Pat Buchanan and Bob Novak, and later Fred Barnes, Tony Blankley, and the hard-to-categorize publisher Mort Zuckerman, among others. The program began locally on the NBC station in Washington, D.C., but caught on and was syndicated around the nation.

Meanwhile, the Brinkley show featured a roundtable discussion that, although markedly less ferocious than McLaughlin's, was grounded in the counterpoint of opposing opinions. Most often, ABC's Sam Donaldson squared off against conservative columnist George Will. Brinkley moderated his program, but McLaughlin domineered over his. He was blunt, rude, verbose, sarcastic, loud—and always had the last word.[37]

Two disturbing trends were put in place in the news-talk programs of the late 1970s and early 1980s. First, opinion was presented so often and with such certainty that it easily could be confused with fact. Opinions were directly presented as facts—or the two were so intertwined in their delivery as to be inseparable. Second, not all of the participants were actually journalists. Pat Buchanan, George Will, and Tony Blankley, to name a few, did or had done some journalism, but they could be defined at least equally as political operatives. On ABC's Brinkley show, the overlap of journalists with politicians caused one especially embarrassing moment when reporter George Will offered his opinion on the air that Ronald Reagan had soundly defeated President Jimmy Carter in a televised debate. It became known only afterward that Will—the political operative—had been part of the Republican team that had prepared Reagan for the debate, using the Democratic briefing book that other political operatives had managed to steal. ABC News never apologized.

What *Washington Post* media reporter Howard Kurtz calls "the reach of the televised shout"[38] found a home on CNN, first with *Crossfire*, which originally pitted liberal Tom Braden against Buchanan.[39] *Crossfire* placed a guest in the studio between the two ideological combatants. Novak, John Sununu, Tucker Carlson, and Mary Matalin were among the conservatives who faced off against Christopher Matthews, Michael Kinsley, James Carville, and other liberals. The fight was over issues, but it was often clear that the *Crossfire* opponents did not care for each other personally. Mary Matalin expressed her disgust with Michael Kinsley, the former editor of *The New Republic* and of the online magazine *Slate*:

> Kinsley is symbolic of everything we loathe and despise. He's a hypocrite and a fraud. He criticizes other people for "spin" and then he becomes Mr. Showbiz. Mr. Sound Bite. When you speak to a conservative audience, you can get the same applause trashing Kinsley as trashing Saddam Hussein.[39]

As a matter of fact, virtually all the television talk warriors became "personalities" in demand for lectures to civic and trade groups around the country. Sam Donaldson took some heat for accepting $30,000 for a lecture given to one industry group that he had reported on, at least indirectly. A group of print journalists now were certifiably stars. But the characterization of talk journalists as either conservative or liberal itself was a vast oversimplification, as was much of the discussion of national and international issues. *The McLaughlin Group* sped by with one-word answers, ratings from zero to "absolute metaphysical certitude," and predictions; it was as if public life were a multiple-choice quiz in which there were right and wrong answers to every question.

Television had created a new class of journalists, or semijournalists, called the punditocracy.[40] The programs made more traditional journalists uncomfortable. The Washington editor of the *New York Times*, Andrew Rosenthal, called them

> silly. . . . They are just entertainment. The problem is that a lot of people watch them. . . . They think they're going to get reporting. And they get opinion. I don't think that's particularly fair to viewers. These shows are so navel gazing and egotistical. All those people sitting around there just blowing gas out of the television tube. I find it very distasteful.[41]

After the success of *Crossfire*, CNN introduced *The Capital Gang*, a program featuring many of the same faces from *Crossfire* and *McLaughlin*. More news-talk shows would be needed on Fox News and MSNBC. They had become a permanent part of the landscape.

— 6 —

Hard News–Soft News

With the passing and the retirement of the old time television anchormen with whom the nation had formed a comfortable bond—Edward R. Murrow, Walter Cronkite, Chet Huntley, John Daly—came a new generation of anchors chosen by the networks more for their marketability and acceptability than for their thinking and pondering and writing skills, chosen also with an eye to what networks knew would be a very protracted decade or two of intense competition, which had been brought on by the deregulation of the television industry under the Carter and Reagan administrations. The new corporate owners of and investors in television, with scant regard for the independent vitality of their own news departments, demanded that the news pay its own way. That meant merchandisable anchors, ubiquitous anchors, omniscient anchors willing to engage in endless self-promotion. . . . It meant sending the evening broadcast out of New York to originate around the country so that anchors could connect with the people as if they were goodwill ambassadors or network hustlers and not journalists whose very profession is singled out for protection by the Constitution.

—*Roger Mudd, 1995*

From Cronkite to Rather

Douglas Edwards had been the anchor of the *CBS Evening News* from 1948 to 1962, when he was replaced by Walter Cronkite. By 1967, when Cronkite's ratings passed those of NBC's *Huntley–Brinkley Report*, Cronkite held a unique, indeed unprecedented, place in American journalism. He was perceived widely as the most trusted man in America, and his popularity in a sense liberated CBS News from daily concern over ratings and news expenditures.[1] In 1978, Cronkite told CBS News president Bill Leonard that he wanted off the *Evening News*. A salary increase to about $1 million a year, and a plea from Leonard to remain, kept Cronkite on the air.[2]

In the meantime, Roone Arledge, the great innovator of sports television, had become president of ABC News in 1977 and was intent on equaling and then surpassing the news divisions of CBS and NBC. That meant, among other things, acquiring on-air talent and paying handsomely for it. He set his sights on Dan Rather, who by then had served as White House correspondent in the Johnson and Nixon administrations, anchorman for *CBS Reports*, coeditor of *60 Minutes*, chief of the London bureau, and correspondent in Vietnam. Rather had been a lightning rod for controversy, especially during the Nixon administration, and now he became the object of an extraordinary bidding war between the three networks. Rather was represented in the negotiations by New York agent Richard Leibner, who skillfully played Arledge against the news heads of the other networks, Bill Leonard at CBS and Bill Small at NBC.

The loser in the anchor sweepstakes was Roger Mudd, who had been with CBS somewhat longer than Rather and who for years had sat in for Cronkite as the substitute anchor. Mudd thought he was the logical successor to Cronkite. After losing the job to Rather, Mudd eventually left CBS for NBC and then public broadcasting, disillusioned with the commercial networks and what he believed was their surrender to tabloid values.

Rather had decided to remain at CBS for the then-unheard-of sum of $22 million over ten years. In 1981, Cronkite retired as anchorman and signed a long-term contract as a special correspondent. His last newscast came on March 6, 1981.

There had been very little planning for the transition from Cronkite to Rather. It had been assumed that changes were probably not necessary. But Rather was uncomfortable in the Cronkite chair and on the Cronkite set, and it showed. His on-air performance was erratic, and the ratings slumped. Television critics reacted harshly to the new anchor, and he slowly began to lose the ratings lead of 2.5 points he had inherited from Cronkite. Just six months after he assumed the anchor post, there was talk of replacing Rather. Eventually CBS would find itself in last place in the ratings.

Van Gordon Sauter: A Different Kind of News Executive

For Dan Rather, relief came in the person of a new president of CBS News. He was Van Gordon Sauter, a former newspaperman and local radio manager in Chicago, a long-time CBS executive who had been bureau chief in Paris and vice president of standards and practices at the corporate level, a man who had revitalized two CBS-owned and-operated affiliates, WBBM in Chicago and KNXT in Los Angeles. Sauter was by every account a colorful figure, a man with an outsized personality and a distinctive, somewhat eccentric personal style. He served two tours of duty as the head of CBS News, the first term lasting from 1981 to 1983, the second from December 1985 to 1988.

During Sauter's tenure as network news director, interrupted by a period of service at CBS corporate headquarters, personnel were classified as being either "yesterday" people (which generally meant past the age of fifty or at least well-connected to the previous CBS News administrations) or, conversely, what Howard Stringer, then the executive vice president for news, called "the television generation."

> The standard-bearer of the new breed is Van Gordon Sauter. Schooled largely in local television, Sauter came to New York convinced that the networks were out of touch with the rest of the country.[3]

Ed Fouhy, then a CBS senior vice president for news, believed that the combined effect of Sauter and Ed Joyce, another CBS News executive thoroughly disliked by a number of his colleagues, was the "triumph of the ethic of the local newsroom over the values of the network newsroom." Both Sauter and Joyce had previously been news executives for company-owned stations and were experienced in taking news programming "down-market," which Fouhy defines as "dropping serious coverage of things like public affairs and foreign news in favor of more personality-oriented, celebrity-oriented, crime-oriented coverage."[4]

Sauter saw his first task as reviving the Dan Rather evening broadcast, and he made clear that his first allegiance was to Rather.

> The elevation to absolute precedence of Dan Rather and his broadcast ("It was my intention to put him at the center of the universe," Sauter said) was at the heart of Sauter's plan for CBS News. It was a carefully calculated strategy that was designed to bring fast results. And it would. But in the long term it

proved to be a disastrous course for CBS News, exacerbating old frictions and creating new ones.[5]

A Different Kind of Newscast

The Sauter plan meant, first, the aggressive marketing of the Rather newscast. A promotional campaign sought to portray Rather as the lineal descendant of the CBS tradition of excellence. "The best remains unchanged" was the tag line of the campaign fashioned by Sauter and a former ABC advertising and marketing executive named Joe Pasarella.

But the content of the newscast itself also had to change, Sauter believed. The Cronkite *Evening News* had contained a heavy dose of bureaucratic, Washington-based news. That newscast reflected the hard-news, wire-service background of Cronkite himself. Sauter wanted the program to be less a reflection of newspapers in general and the *New York Times* in particular. While Sauter was drawn to the coverage of popular culture, Cronkite essentially saw no place for it on his program. In 1977, CBS had chosen not to lead with the story of Elvis Presley's death nor to run a special program later that night on Presley. By contrast, ABC and NBC had treated the story as a landmark cultural and historical event.

Sauter would promote dramatic changes in the evening newscast. He wanted stories that were visual, rooted in human interest, and evocative of the American experience. There was a shorthand designation for such stories; somehow they would capture a "moment" that would have resonance for the audience. Rather told a reporter at the time: "Van keeps saying we need stories that reach out and touch people. Moments. Every broadcast needs moments."

"What is a moment," the reporter asked.

"When somebody watches something and *feels* it, *smells* it and *knows* it," Rather said. "If a broadcast does not have two or three of those moments, it does not have it."[6] Peter Boyer, in his sharply negative history of Sauter's career at CBS, *Who Killed CBS?*, says the doctrine of moments was a

> deftly designed cover for the infiltration of entertainment values into the news. It completely changed the way CBS reported the day's news because it completely changed what news was. There were no moments to be found in a fifteen-minute report on unemployment told by a CBS reporter correspondent standing outside the Department of Labor in Washington, D.C.[7]

Does the focus on human interest constitute an "infiltration of entertainment values"? Perhaps it is fairer to say that Sauter advocated a "soft news" approach that, in hindsight, ultimately characterized changes in the industry as a whole. It is more likely that Sauter anticipated his colleagues at the other networks than that he single-handedly "killed CBS" and the tradition of responsible broadcast news. Sauter is nonetheless an easy target. In making known his opposition to virtually all stories that might be considered boring, he broke with the prevailing set of news values at CBS, which stipulated that news judgments would be made by professional journalists assessing what was important, never primarily by audience considerations of what was interesting.

Another guideline for selecting stories on the Rather broadcast became known as "the back-fence principle," the notion that the most important stories were those that typical neighbors were likely to discuss in a casual setting. Additionally, it became increasingly important under Sauter that CBS cover people and events outside Washington. Stories from the American heartland became known as "South Succotash" stories, a name that an aide to President Reagan gave sarcastically to stories that conveyed the feelings of "real people." Often those people were faced with economic hardships, which Reagan administration officials believed reflected poorly on the incumbent president.

Michael Massing of the *Columbia Journalism Review* assessed the content of the *CBS Evening News* in a 1986 article.[8] The first phase of the Sauter-inspired make-over, he said, focused on replacing official Washington news with local stories containing strong elements of human interest. The second phase "involved changing the texture of the broadcast"—developing a bank of longer stories intended to give viewers context, crisper graphics, a softer-looking Rather.[9] Massing examined a month's broadcasts and found some examples of effective "populist" television, stories that showed the impact of institutional structures and decisions (such as the tendency of private hospitals to turn away indigent patients) on the lives of real individuals in society. More often, he found a national version of local television news. The CBS broadcast was now increasingly trivial, repeatedly covering stories about the weather, about the likelihood of a white Christmas, about snowstorms in Denver and fog in Dallas. The average length of a CBS sound bite was between seven and eight seconds. On one newscast that had more than thirty sound bites, the longest was thirteen seconds.

But if interviews had been pared down, the writing of Rather's news copy had become anything but spare. Ordinary stories had been weighted down with rhymes, alliteration, and cluttered adjectival clauses:

— "the top-to-bottom, border-to-border tax overhaul affecting every pay-
check in America"
— "a House vote tonight on one of the most heavily lobbied, heavy-

money, heavy-pressure issues up in Congress"
—the "special-interest, high-powered, big-bucks lobbying over every-thing from tax overhaul to the budget deficit to toxic waste cleanup"[10]

Coverage of foreign news was severely limited, Massing found. Although CBS gave serious attention to major breaking news overseas, there was little coverage of Asia, Central America, or many other parts of the world. In one three-day period, there were seven stories about medicine and only two foreign stories. Stories about the Soviet Union usually pointed out that the country could not be trusted or was up to its bad old ways again. One report concluded with this sentence: "It calls to mind the old Russian proverb, 'What's good for the goose is good for the propagander.'"

The Demise of the Documentary

As controversial as any of Sauter's actions was the decision to end the active life of *CBS Reports*, the documentary unit that was the direct heir to the Murrow tradition. Sauter wanted to move away from the serious, hour-long, single-subject documentary, nor did he wish to produce the sober, probing investigations that Bill Moyers, one of his chief rivals at CBS, had produced in the past and was advocating now. Instead, Sauter envisioned a different sort of weekly program, an hour of public affairs that would reflect a younger sensibility. The result was *West 57th*, a sort of *60 Minutes* for the video-immersed younger generation.

West 57th Street was the New York location where the carefully chosen cast of reporters worked. For *West 57th* had been put together like a fictional prime-time show about journalism. It had style and attitude; moreover, it was *all about* style and attitude. The program featured upbeat music; young, dashing, and sexy correspondents; a distinctive style of quick edits and transitions. Andy Lack (later the president of NBC News) was the producer of *West 57th*. Internally at CBS, *West 57th* was derided as "light summer fare" by veterans of the news division, including Moyers, Don Hewitt, and Andy Rooney.

Sauter's regime at CBS News coincided with a series of financial upheavals at the network. At one point, Hewitt attempted a purchase of the network with a group of CBS colleagues. A serious takeover attempt was mounted by Ted Turner and turned back. In withstanding the Turner takeover effort, the network had incurred massive debts. In the late fall of 1986, Lawrence Tisch of the Loews Corp., a holding company with most of its interests in real estate, took control of the network. In January 1987, the CBS Board of Directors considered drastic cutbacks in the budget of CBS News.

[Tisch had] seen the figures, the estimates that the CBS News budget would approach $300 million in 1987, up from $89 million in 1978. Even allowing for inflation, Tisch figured, the CBS News budget shouldn't be much more than $200 million and certainly not more than $250 million.[11]

On February 6, the *New York Times* reported that substantial new budget cuts were in the offing at CBS. One month later, the most significant cutbacks in the history of CBS News were announced. The news division budget was cut by $33 million, and 215 people, including 14 on-air reporters, lost their jobs. It was the third major cutback in sixteen months. Bureaus were closed in Seattle, Warsaw, and Bangkok. Chicago was reduced to two correspondents; Paris, to one.[12]

Dan Rather denied strongly that the mission of CBS News had been changed. "We were hard news yesterday," he told an interviewer. "We're hard news today, and we'll be hard news tomorrow."[13] By 1988, *West 57th* had been canceled because of poor ratings, but there remained a commitment to do more prime-time news programming aimed at a wider audience—in other words, more soft news. Van Gordon Sauter had resigned as president of CBS News and became a producer of syndicated programs in Hollywood.

Former CBS executive Ed Fouhy says the move to soft news was an attempt to engage people with only a marginal interest in public affairs and the events of the day. Thus, Fouhy argues, Sauter and his aides "alienated the most regular and most faithful viewers of television news." Since then, he adds, the networks have gone even further down-market in "what proves to be a fruitless pursuit of a disappearing audience."[14]

The changes at CBS News were a watershed for television journalism. What had worked for more than twenty-five years seemed not to be working now, at least in terms of audience loyalty. The size of the audience for network news had begun to steadily diminish. The reasons for the decline were not confined to programming decisions; in fact, the structure of television itself was changing inexorably: the introduction of cable television in large cities gave audiences new options and siphoned off viewers from the networks. Ted Turner's Cable News Network had established a strong commitment to foreign coverage along with a twenty-four-hour-a-day presence. What Fouhy calls the "choke-hold" the three networks had held on television news was ending.[15]

— 7 —

Prime-Time News Values

A Turn to News Magazines

The critical and commercial success of *60 Minutes* was the source of much more than envy at ABC and NBC. News magazine programs were markedly less expensive to produce than entertainment shows. It was a generally accepted fact that it cost less than $500,000 to produce an hour-long news magazine, while an hour of comedy or drama might run more than $2 million. News magazines also earned nearly as much in revenue, an average of $85,000 per thirty-second commercial, in contrast to the prime-time entertainment average of $110,000.[1] And if *60 Minutes* could attract a huge audience, why couldn't a comparable program on another network? Doing news magazine programs was not like producing the evening news, though. It meant adopting a new mind-set. All of CBS's competitors realized that success in prime time meant adjusting the content of "reality-based programming" (the phrase itself was almost twenty years away) to a broader audience than that of the evening news. Former CBS vice president and director of news Ed Fouhy says that in seeking a different audience for prime time, the networks disappointed those viewers interested in serious, substantive news coverage.

> [The networks] are pursuing a group of people who watch a lot of television and who may have only a slight connection with the civil society in which they live, people with only a marginal interest in the events of the day that engage the vast middle of the television audience, which is a mass audience. They're trying to engage people who are not normally engaged by television news, and in trying to do that, I think they alienated the most regular and most faithful viewers of TV news.[2]

Seeking larger audiences and taking on entertainment programs in a battle for ratings meant, depending upon one's point of view, either expanding the definition of news or diluting the product with a large number of soft or tabloid-oriented stories. Paul Friedman, the senior vice president of news for ABC, defends the aggressive pursuit of ratings as only one aspect of what a network news division does:

> I think it's fair to say that there are programs on the air on all the networks now that go more towards tabloid journalism that we ever would have conceived years ago. That primarily has to do with the advent of the magazine programs and the fact that they are in prime-time spots, which means that they have to aggressively pursue ratings. But to some extent all the network news divisions have become like the great publishers. We publish lots of different kinds of programs. I don't think that at ABC News the fact that we do magazine programs in prime time has affected the quality of the work that we do on *World News Tonight* or coverage of special events or elections or whatever. I think it's just something else that we do on news magazines.[3]

Ed Turner, the late executive vice president for news at CNN in the 1990s, was a critic of the genre, arguing that "news magazines have taken the place of serious news-gathering":

> Sure, news magazines make money. They make money because they are so efficient; they only cover the stories that they are going to put on the air. But that's not hard news-gathering. In hard news, you go and stake out Somalia, you go and live in Bosnia, plop down in Haiti with a crew, producers, and reporters, and follow the stories as long as it takes. Let's not forget here what serious news-gathering is all about. It's going to unscripted events where you don't have control and seeing them play through to some kind of end. It's not easy. It's not cheap. It's not a lot of giggles. It's understandable to see why magazines are so attractive to the networks.[4]

The counterargument comes from Alan Wurzel, the senior vice president for news magazines at ABC News:

> Our news magazines are additive. These are programs that add more news out there. It's not as though the programs are taking away the resources or air time of what people consider to be traditional news. . . . As to the criticism about whether this is real news with a capital N, it's as much real news as the Style section of the *Washington Post* or, you know, the real second or third feature section of a newspaper is. It serves a somewhat different purpose day to day, although, obviously, on a hot breaking story, it will in some ways try to break news as well. But, for the most part, it is more feature-driven than it is hard news."[5]

Diane Sawyer and Charles Gibson of ABC News were extremely popular with viewers, both on *Good Morning America* and on their prime-time news magazine. *(Copyright 2002 ABC Photography Archives)*

The Competition Becomes Heated

In the high-stakes news magazine wars, ABC struck back first at *60 Minutes* with a popular program.[6] The premiere edition of *20/20* aired on June 6, 1978. With veteran producer Av Westin at the helm and with Hugh Downs as the anchor, *20/20* was soon a solid ratings success. The show succeeded by "applying the techniques of investigative reporting to a red-hot, sensational topic to produce huge ratings," according to journalist Marc Gunther.[7] Barbara Walters contributed reports to *20/20* for four years before becoming cohost with Hugh Downs in 1984. In 1989, the show was moved to Friday nights at 10 P.M. Its audience numbers grew, then grew more after Victor Neufeld was named executive producer. Its success, according to Paul Friedman, was rooted in a format that focused on "issues that people find matter in their lives or are just plain interesting."[8] Thus, Friedman articulates one of the principles of prime-time news value: most of the time, audience interest trumps any "objective" measure of importance. According to Gunther, the *20/20* process of selecting stories was a key element in making the show work:

> Av Westin's push for control and efficiency meant that more stories had to be plotted in advance, pre-sold, and market-tested before producers and correspondents could commit time and money to them. This dramatically reduced the likelihood of embarking on an open-ended quest for a story and being surprised along the way. . . . Westin's approach worked.[9]

The Trials of NBC

Meanwhile, NBC was simply incapable of putting a news magazine on the air that did work. It tried one magazine show after another, using different hosts or different combinations of hosts or the same hosts time after time in different formats. In house, NBC staffers named one news magazine "Seven Is a Charm" (it was the seventh try) and another "Thirteen Better Be the One" (it wasn't). By most counts, NBC's streak of failure extended to seventeen canceled news-magazine programs—or twenty-two. (The difference is probably caused by confusion over the definition of what actually was a new program. Some were renamed continuations of existing shows.) A summary of just some of the programs is a lesson in prime-time values.

First Tuesday was NBC's first attempt at a prime-time news magazine. First anchored by Sander Vanocour and then by Garrick Utley, *First Tuesday* was a monthly, two-hour show that aired between January 7, 1969, and September 7, 1971.

Chronolog brought Garrick Utley back to the anchor desk for nine months

Table 7.1

Prime-Time News Magazines: Rankings and Ratings

Here's how the news magazines ranked in 1993. The first number is the show's rank among 118 prime-time shows. The second number is the show's audience, expressed in the number of households tuned into the program.

Program	Rank	TV households tuned to show (in millions)
60 Minutes	2	19.9
20/20	13	14.1
PrimeTime Live	16	13.5
Turning Point	23	13.2
48 Hours	38	11.1
Dateline NBC	48	10.3
Eye to Eye With Connie Chung	53	9.9
Day One	61	9.5

Source: A.C. Nielsen for 1993–1994 network season.

between October 1971 and June 1972. In addition to using the same anchor, the show followed *First Tuesday*'s two-hour format, although *Chronolog* was broadcast on Friday nights.

First Tuesday was put back on NBC's prime-time schedule in September 1972. There were, however, some differences between this program and the original *First Tuesday*. Though it still ran monthly, the 1972 program was shortened to one hour, and it did not have a dedicated anchor. This version of the show lasted just under a year.

NBC News Presents a Special Edition kept the no-anchor trend alive during its November 1973–August 1974 run.

Now lasted only one hour in 1977. Hosted by Linda Ellerbee and Jack Perkins, it was canceled after its pilot episode. From its opening segment on reggae music (which had been popular for a while although the show treated it as a brand-new phenomenon) to the anchors' chairs, described by Ellerbee as "pillows that looked like giant marshmallows," *Now* should have been called "Never," according to Ellerbee.[10]

Weekend began in 1974 as a late-night news program. It moved to prime time in December 1975 and was hosted by Linda Ellerbee and Lloyd Dobyns. Then president of NBC News, Fred Silverman originally promised the show a two-year run, but *Weekend* lasted for less than six months.

Prime Time Sunday was anchored by Tom Snyder and aired during the last half of 1979. By the early 1990s, CBS was enjoying success with *48 Hours*, as was ABC with *PrimeTime Live*. *Prime Time Saturday* was the continuation of *Prime Time Sunday*. There was no difference between the two shows with the exception of their nights of broadcast. Despite the switch to Saturday nights, or perhaps because of it, the show lasted only six months longer and was pulled from the air in the beginning of July 1980.

NBC Magazine with David Brinkley premiered in late September 1980, and its cancellation was not the direct function of ratings but of the loss of its anchor. Without David Brinkley, there could be no show called *NBC Magazine with David Brinkley*. As such, this show's last air date was September 18, 1981.

NBC Magazine was the no-anchor show that resulted from David Brinkley's defection to ABC News. Although the name changed, the format and content of the program remained relatively stable, but the loss of Brinkley was something from which the show could not recover. Interestingly enough, *NBC Magazine* continued to draw an average rating of 17 (a rating, remember, is the percentage of all households with television, approximately 100 million, tuned to a particular program).

Monitor, an hour-long program, anchored by Lloyd Dobyns, was another version of the program initially conceived of as *Prime Time Sunday*. This format lasted just five months during the spring and summer of 1983.

First Camera aired between September 1983 and April 1984. Anchored by Lloyd Dobyns, the show was the final reincarnation of the *Prime Time Sunday–Prime Time Saturday–NBC Magazine–Monitor* family line of news magazines. It offered a calmer, more varied mix of stories than *60 Minutes*, against which it was pitted (as *Monitor* had been) in the Sunday night lineup. That it was aired opposite *60 Minutes* was made even more disastrous by the fact that 7 percent of NBC's affiliates, including the local stations in large markets such as Boston, San Francisco, and Detroit, did not run the show. *First Camera* often finished last in the prime-time ratings.

Summer Sunday USA, a live, hour-long program aired during the summer of 1984, featured anchors Linda Ellerbee and Andrea Mitchell broadcasting from a different part of the country each week. In addition to impromptu "man on the street" interviews, the show included segments such as "Trading Places," in which newsmakers interviewed the people who usually interviewed them, and viewer quizzes. The format was unique or experimental or just desperate, depending upon how one looked at it. Linda Ellerbee titled the chapter about the show in her autobiography "And Now for Something Completely New and Different."[11] One of the program's major problems was its time slot—it, too, aired opposite *60 Minutes*. *Summer Sunday USA* had the lowest rating of any news magazine aired after 1980: a rating of 3.6.

American Almanac ran once a month between August 1985 and late January 1986. The show, anchored by the respected Roger Mudd, was the first NBC news magazine to be broadcast from Washington, D.C. The decision to air the program did not enjoy the unanimous support of NBC executives, some of whom were reluctant to tamper with what had become a fairly successful evening entertainment lineup. This basic conflict added to an already serious problem regarding story development. The show had vowed to stay away from "flash and trash," but its staff had a very difficult time coming up with good story ideas and an even harder time deciding how the stories would be presented.

1986 was a midyear reincarnation of *American Almanac*. In addition to the name change and a new set, Roger Mudd was joined by coanchor Connie Chung. Touted by its creators as more "hard-edged" than *American Almanac*, the show still was plagued by its predecessor's story-development problems. When asked by a *Washington Post* reporter if he had any message for the show's audience, Ed Fouhy, executive producer of *1986*, said, "Yes, if they have really good story ideas, our phone number is 885-5002."[12] *1986* was canceled after twenty broadcasts. The show's failure (although it averaged a respectable rating) was largely attributed to decreasing support from affiliate stations, which had started to preempt the program with some degree of regularity. Roger Mudd chastised the network for axing the program. He was quoted in the *New York Times* on December 10, 1986, as follows: "Canceling an hour of public affairs in prime time is akin to killing a newspaper. It silences one more voice in a society which depends on voices and opinions and ideas to survive. Once again, the pressure for profits has proved irresistible."[13] NBC executives denied that money had anything to do with their decision to cancel the show.

Yesterday, Today and Tomorrow, anchored at various times by Maria Shriver, Chuck Scarborough, Mary Alice Williams, and Connie Chung, often is not cited as one of NBC's failed news magazines. Perhaps the reason is that its run was very, very brief, even by NBC standards. *Yesterday, Today and Tomorrow* was aborted after just four pilot episodes during the last half of 1989, primarily as the result of the controversy over dramatic reenactments of real events.

Real Life With Jane Pauley, like the failed shows before it, was expected to break NBC's "news magazine jinx," yet expectations were perhaps even higher for *Real Life* because of Jane Pauley's tremendous popular appeal at the time. NBC's decision to take Pauley off the *Today* show proved harmful both to the morning show and to the network's reputation. "Jane Mania" was expected to carry the new program, which, like Pauley herself, was touted as down-to-earth, not glitzy, real. The set was plain yet homey—no anchor desk or high-tech gimmicks. The show and its stories about real-life problems, such as juggling family and career, survived its five-week trial in the summer of 1990, winning its time slot on four of five broadcasts. The ratings began to slip as the summer ended, however, and when *Real Life* was brought back the following January, its ratings fell precipitously. The program was canceled by November.

Exposé made its debut in early January 1991 with host Tom Brokaw. The half-hour program followed *Real Life With Jane Pauley*, and, like that show, was canceled at the end of the season. *Exposé* was an interesting concept, but it was essentially flawed from the beginning in that "it was not only intense, but overpowering. It proved to be excessive," says John Grassie, who was with the program from its inception and later became a producer for *Dateline*.[14] Grassie says its cancellation was related to the untenable demand its relentless series of exposures, undercover investigations, and sniffed-out "conspiracies" put on the audience. "We never gave the audience a chance to breathe. From the opening moment to the closing credits, it was as if you were sprinting. . . . We have no right to expect the audience to deal with that during prime time. It was a fatal flaw."[15]

NBC's *Prime Story* premiered on June 23, 1993, as NBC's "second" news magazine, following *Dateline*, and boasted seasoned reporters Faith Daniels and Mike Schneider as hosts, joined at the anchor desk by former NBC Pentagon reporter Fred Francis. It faded soon thereafter.

Despite its run of failures, NBC had a solid hit with *Dateline*. Moreover, it still appeared as though news magazines could be every bit as competitive as entertainment programs in attracting an audience. Andrew Heyward, former executive producer of *48 Hours* and later president of CBS News, remarked that there had been an "astonishing boom in new TV magazines" in the 1990s.[16]

Street Signs joined the CBS stable; *Day One* premiered on ABC; NBC offered another version of *Now*, this time with hosts Katie Couric and Tom Brokaw, probably the two highest-profile anchors at the network, and *Dateline*, with hosts Stone Phillips and Jane Pauley. *Now* was incorporated into *Dateline* not long afterward, and *Dateline* became a twice-weekly program. Surprisingly successful, it aired three and then occasionally four times a week. Contributors included Maria Shriver. An NBC on-line description of the "flagship" program notes that "the flexibility of 'Dateline NBC' allows for multipart features, full-hour documentaries on single subjects, or series of continuing reports."[17] Multipart features in turn allowed the network to promote Wednesday's program on Monday, which was done frequently, if not excessively. Appearances by Couric and Brokaw became less frequent. But there were more problems, first with the use of inaccurate video footage or generic images not directly related to the content of the story. Ultimately, NBC's missteps with *Dateline* were the gravest that beset any news magazine.

Dateline Under Fire

"Staged Blow-Up Rocks NBC News"
—*New Orleans Times-Picayune*, February 11, 1993

"NBC Faces Struggle to Climb Back from Mistakes, Embarrassment"
—*Reuters Business Report*, February 11, 1993

"Apologetic NBC Tries to Regroup Amidst Criticism"
—*Cleveland Plain Dealer*, February 12, 1993

"*Dateline NBC* Burns Media Credibility"
—*The Washington Post*, February 23, 1993

"*Dateline* Executive Producer, 2 More Axed"
—*Daily Variety*, February 22, 1993

"NBC Calls GM Show 'Failure,' Network Releases Harsh Internal Memo"
—*St. Louis Post-Dispatch*, March 23, 1993

"*Dateline* Staffers Leave Network over Rigged Explosion"
—*Chicago Tribune*, March 23, 1993

"NBC Report Rips *Dateline*"
—*Daily Variety*, March 23, 1993

"Three More Depart in *Dateline* NBC Fiasco; Producers of Controversial Documentary on General Motors Trucks"
—*Broadcasting & Cable*, March 29, 1993

"NBC News Takes Action to Put *Dateline* Debacle Away"
—*St. Louis Post-Dispatch*, March 28, 1993

On November 17, 1992, *Dateline* broadcast an investigative report on the danger of fuel-tank explosions in accidents involving some General Motors trucks with a particular gas-tank configuration. The story was supported by video showing just such an explosion. Flames engulfed the truck and shot up into the air. And that was the crux of the problem. To achieve a clearly visible and dramatic explosion, producers had inserted igniting devices near the gas tanks. Viewers were not told about the devices. It was an outright case of news tampering, and it could not be explained away. In the firestorm that followed the story, despite a public apology to General Motors and to the American public, three NBC producers were fired, including the producer of the exploding truck story. But the damage went deeper. The ruse had tarnished the reputation of NBC. The next domino to fall was the president of the news division,

Michael Gartner, a highly respected journalist and former newspaper editor, now out of a job.

Some observers saw in the *Dateline* fiasco the inevitable outcome of blending news with entertainment. Producers had data that showed the fuel tanks might explode on impact. Did they need to produce five or fifty accidents to get one explosion that would work on television? No, they figured, these explosions did happen—and some of them looked just like the one they had enacted. It may have made sense to them, but it wasn't journalism. *American Journalism Review* concluded that the underlying culprit was the profit motive: news magazines had become popular as part of an overall strategy of cost-cutting; when it became too expensive to get reality on camera, the need for compelling visuals overwhelmed ethical concerns, shattering credibility in the process.[18] The general manager of an NBC affiliate, calling for Gartner's resignation, said the demand for exciting video was no excuse for misrepresentation. Ellen Hume, a senior fellow at a press and policy center at Harvard, said, "The difference to me [between news and entertainment] has been news is supposed to be based on facts that have been verified. That is the first critical difference."[19] *Dateline* had become a case study in the challenged ethics of television journalism. Perhaps it was the pressure to achieve ratings. Perhaps it was the pressure to do so many stories for so many programs. Commentary in the print media was adamant in its condemnation of the networks.

By the fall of 1994, news magazines presenting minute details of the crime or scandal du jour had become the "centerpiece of the networks' news division," according to some critics.

Soon enough, news in prime time was provoking more concerns, especially about taste and appropriateness.[20] Remarkably, *Dateline* itself recovered from the exploding-truck scandal and celebrated its third anniversary in 1995 with a new, $1 million set.

Questions of Taste and Ethics

In the period from the late 1980s to the mid-1990s, news magazines frequently came under fire from critics of what some called "mass news," that is to say, news for the mass audience. *Time* magazine was offended by the use of dramatic reenactments on the programs *Yesterday, Today and Tomorrow* and *Saturday Night with Connie Chung* (both later canceled). In a *Time* magazine story headlined "TV News Goes Hollywood," Richard Zoglin complained that "as the real and only-looks-like-real are mixed with abandon, a viewer can get confused."[21] The confusion, Zoglin wrote, was shared by the television journalists themselves:

95

At one extreme are the traditionalists, who insist that a staged scene of any kind is inappropriate on a news program, which depends for its credibility on presenting the truth and nothing but. On the other side are a new generation of TV news producers, under pressure from network bosses to come up with programs that will draw prime-time-size audiences.[22]

Zoglin worried that dramatic re-creations both stray from the nature of journalistic work and undermine it. "Journalists are in the business of conveying reality; re-enactments convert reality into something else—something neater, more palatable, more conventionally 'dramatic.'"[23] The executive producer of ABC's *Nightline* and former executive producer of the *CBS Evening News with Dan Rather*, Tom Bettag, worries that the era of news magazines is marked by journalistic confusion: "The definition of news is changing so fast that nobody is clear what a news division should be doing. Distrust of the media in the country is well-founded, and we bring it on ourselves by not making clear what's real and what's not real"[24]

One news-magazine story that met with strong objections was a report on *20/20* by ABC correspondent Lynn Scherr on women's preoccupation with having large breasts. In a *Washington Post* story headlined "Big Breasts and a Bogus Broadcast," reporter Richard Morin said the story was presented as being based on the results of polling. Yet he concluded that the purported data were weak in the first place and were ignored if they ran counter to the theme of the story:

> "Today you don't have to dream about looking like a D-cup, you can lie down on the operating table," Sherr said in the broadcast. "Sex sells, and the number one way to get sexy, in many women's minds, is with larger breasts." . . . Sherr chose to rely on pseudo-statistics collected from readers of a women's magazine to buttress anecdotes from women whose stories fit more comfortably in the tale that '20/20' wanted to tell.[25]

A Repertory of Narratives

In an interview with the author, NBC anchor Tom Brokaw said the news magazines offer correspondents the opportunity "to exercise their story-telling ability, which you can't do on the *Nightly News*." He believes the popularity of the genre arose because "the quality of entertainment on the three networks has diminished. I think that's indisputable. And I also think that people are interested in reality. They want to know what's going on around them in a variety of ways."[26]

To understand the patterns of story selection and narrative strategies of the news magazines, I reviewed a number of them over a period of years. Here are some examples from the fall of 2000:

Dateline, November 13, 2000. The first story reports the quest of two men, Larry Williams and Bob Cornuke, who, taking the Bible literally, set off for parts unknown in an effort to find holy sites. The story is a follow-up to one that had appeared two and a half years earlier. The second story, "Cliffhanger," is an update on the contested 2000 presidential election. The third story, "Cape Fear," is about two fishermen caught in a "monster storm." What appeared to be an unavoidable tragedy was found to be, on later inspection by authorities, a suspicious death and a survivor story that left too many questions unanswered.

Dateline, November 13, 2000. The program begins with a "Consumer Alert" about the safety of sport utility vehicles (SUVs). The investigative report, by Lea Thompson, centers on information developed by the Insurance Institute for Highway Safety. The introduction sets the tone of the piece:

> SUVs. They're popular because they're tough. But are they tough enough? How do SUVs hold up in a high-impact crash? The safety of you and your family may be riding on that very question. Tonight we take a look at how well some popular models perform when it matters most. So strap yourself in for an SUV crash course. . .

The story shows the test crashes of four different vehicles into a wall at forty miles an hour and then reviews the likely effects on a driver. The results shows a serious problem with the Isuzu Trooper: a fuel line had ruptured in the collision. Each company is given the opportunity to respond to the findings. The featured story is an "exclusive" profile of the McCaughey septuplets, reported by Ann Curry. The story gives an inside look into what it means to raise seven children, all just under three years old, some physically and mentally challenged. Each day is portrayed as another drama to face for the parents, who cried several times during the piece. The third story of the night is an update on the contested 2000 presidential race, focusing on what could happen if everything were not resolved by the date of the inauguration. Stone Phillips also reports the latest NBC poll results on public attitudes about the likely outcome of the election.

PrimeTime Thursday, November 23, 2000. The first story is called "Children at Risk?" and is a treatment of the policy of the Walt Disney Co. toward licensing its characters to appear on cell phones. Involved in the issue is the controversial question of whether cell phones pose a health hazard, especially to young children, from the effects of high-frequency radio waves. The story reports that the Disney company's concerns have led it to stop licensing the use of its cartoon characters on the phones. Scientific conclusions about the risk remain unclear, however. The second story is a sentimental interview by correspondent Diane Sawyer of famed musician Paul

McCartney. It is a follow-up to an earlier interview about his wife Linda McCartney's fight against cancer. Now that his wife has died, the former Beatle reminisces about Linda, his trouble in getting past the fact of her loss, and his "return to joy" through music and a new relationship. The third story, reported by Chris Cuomo and titled "A Diabolical Mystery," describes a young mother and her baby, who vanished fifteen years earlier. The report shows that fears that the two were victims of a serial killer were misguided. It is a story "full of twists, turns, and tantalizing clues."

20/20, November 24, 2000. The first story is "Loretta Young's Confession," in effect a televised excerpt from a new biography of the 1930s–1940s movie star and 1960s television icon. Her biography reveals the checkered personal life of an actress who had an image of perfection but a weakness for her leading men that led to numerous relationships—and pregnancies that were subsequently covered up. The second story, "A Lethal Weapon," is introduced as follows:

> Would you put a powerful weapon into your child's hands? Many unsuspecting parents do, when they buy some kinds of BB guns. Before you shop for the holidays, see what Brian Ross discovered about BB guns. . .

Ross tells the story of Tucker, a child injured in an accident with a BB gun, which was a birthday present. The BB hit Tucker in the head with enough force to blow through his skull and penetrate his brain, an injury that left him unable to walk, talk, or even swallow on his own. A third story is "From Castoff to Star," reported by Bob Brown. This is the story of Phuong Thao, one of Vietnam's most popular singers. As the daughter of an American serviceman in the aftermath of the Vietnam War, she was hurtfully teased and even reviled. Amerasian children were frequently referred to as "bui doi"—the dust of life. The story shows her rise to stardom and an emotional encounter with her father, James Yoder. A final story is "The Mummy's Secrets," reported by Tom Jarriel. It is the profile of a scientist's efforts to re-create the process of Egyptian mummification, which preserved "the faces and the secrets of the past."

This may be a thin sample of programs from which to draw, but it presents at least an introduction to the narrative concerns and methods of prime-time news. It should be noted that *Dateline* adds factual tidbits, including features before and after commercials, such as a quiz that asks the viewer to choose the year in which three incidents occurred. An NBC producer confirmed to the author that such devices had proved through audience research to be effective at retaining viewers, so, after the year 2000, they began to be incorporated into the *NBC Nightly News*.[27] News magazines often include updates on breaking news, but they tend to be brief and do not constitute the bulk of the programs. In general, there are a few basic narratives that can be counted on to appear in almost every program. The "consumer alert" metanarrative provides practical information presented as the result of an investigation and shaded with threat. Sometimes the threat is intended to scare viewers silly. The BB gun story is an example of that. Cell phones may cause cancer (there is no definitive finding to support such an assertion) but the point here is that a large corporation took the threat seriously enough to stop licensing its cartoon characters. The information is thus somewhat tentative and the risk unsure, but, for the viewer, the threat is nonetheless real. The SUV story also was introduced with the strong suggestion that millions might be at risk.

The Paul McCartney interview combines two basic narratives, the celebrity interview and the story of "coping with loss." This may be said to create another metanarrative, the "troubled celebrity profile." Syndicated tabloid programs make the troubled celebrity profile a staple, and one can be sure they made much of the loss of Linda McCartney. Diane Sawyer offers empathy and understanding, and the story offers triumph over adversity. That is also the story of the Vietnamese performer Phuong Thao. Loretta Young's story is one of "Celebrity Unmasked," a tale of the foibles of the rich and famous.

"A Diabolical Mystery" is just that—and prime-time magazines are full of such mystery narratives. Often told at length and separated by commercials, this type of story has a cliffhanger aspect that keeps viewers "turning the pages." The mummification story blends mystery with a saga of personal adventure. The mystery and adventure stories as a rule break no new ground, but recapitulate events well-known to authorities and local or specialized journalists. "Cape Fear" melds the adventure, the mystery, and the investigation.

The story of the septuplets is a profile of people who are remarkable, a form of human-interest storytelling as old as journalism. The parents are remarkable because they are ordinary people faced with extraordinary circumstances—another often-used prime-time news-magazine narrative. The tale of the BB gun victim has significant elements of this form of human interest.

The News Magazine Editorial Process

In the 1980s, as prime-time news shows proliferated, there was a noticeable change in the procedures of news-gathering. Whereas a network's evening news staff consisted of reporters, many of whom were assigned to regular "beats," a news magazine staff had a sizable number of "bookers," people whose job it was to line up subjects for interviews. The "hottest" guests— celebrities who were in great demand, people caught up in a wildly publicized scandal, or, even better, any combination of the two—were referred to as a "get" when landed by a particular program or host. Diane Sawyer, then of CBS News, "got" murderer Charles Manson, pop-music star Michael Jackson (accused at the time of child molestation), Olympic ice skater Tonya Harding, and years later, on ABC, TV celebrity Rosie O'Donnell to consent to interviews about explosive or delicate subjects. Barbara Walters, who "got" the leaders of Egypt and Israel, was said to have facilitated the Camp David peace agreement reached by Anwar el Sadat and Menachem Begin during the Carter administration. Thirty years later, she was at it again: she "got" the Crown Prince of Saudi Arabia to consent to an interview about *his* Middle East peace proposal.

"Bookers" had worked for the networks since the early days of television. Barbara Walters had been one herself in the 1950s, when she arranged guests for the *Today* show. Every host of a late-night talk show, from Steve Allen to Johnny Carson to David Letterman, employed staffers to line up guest appearances. The point, however, is that those were, at least originally, entertainment programs. Guests were referred to as "talent." The prime-time magazines not only blended news and entertainment in the material they chose to broadcast, but structurally reconfigured themselves so that they acted not like the evening news, but more like *The Carol Burnett Show* in the way they put a program together. Actually, the morning news shows were the real template for prime-time news magazines. Since their beginning, they had blended news with entertainment. Their staffs consisted in part of people working the telephones to line up guests. They had personable hosts who were also credible news personnel. It is no coincidence that so many news-magazine hosts— Jane Pauley, Tom Brokaw, Charles Gibson, Diane Sawyer, Barbara Walters, Hugh Downs—were first hosts of morning programs.

But experienced journalists for the news magazines were not always comfortable in going after a "get." Katie Couric, in a 1994 interview, lamented the hoops she had to go through to secure an interview with Tonya Harding:

> It is so ridiculous. I remember I would have to call Tonya Harding's attorneys two or three times a day. At certain points I would be calling them from rental-car phones when I was away with my family for the weekend because I'd have to call at certain times. Some of the times you wanted to hang up the phones and take a shower, just because you felt like, God, this isn't why I got into journalism—to try to convince Tonya Harding's attorneys that she should talk with me. Basically, I try to be as charming and ingratiating as I can without making myself vomit.[28]

Dan Rather agrees that the pressure for getting the big interview has never been greater. "Not too long ago, in rare instances, maybe some-

100

body would make a telephone call to put us over the top," but now, Rather says, a telephone call frequently isn't enough to secure an interview. It requires a personal visit and a response to the subject's question, "Tell me why I should do it with you." There, Rather says, "the slope starts to get slippery. The temptation comes with the thought, If I don't agree to their conditions, maybe they won't do it with me; maybe they'll do it with Sue or John."[29]

Producers of the news magazines—as a rule, each program has twenty-five or thirty—eventually become specialists in certain kinds of stories. Some producers work general assignment, while others do only celebrity interviews. "Crashers" do breaking stories on deadline and others specialize in "larger-than-life international human dramas."[30] When he was reporting for *Dateline*, correspondent Mike Boettcher, a veteran overseas reporter now with CNN, says he was given "crash" stories in which he "parachuted" in for two or three days to do a breaking story, often in a foreign country, such as the caning punishment planned for an American, Michael Fay, who had damaged a number of automobiles in Singapore. Boettcher said he was often assigned "stories of people facing some sort of crisis—especially women who've gone through a crisis."[31]

Each magazine program contains a carefully chosen mix of usually three and sometimes four stories. As a rule, one of the stories is particularly hard-edged: either a story about an especially heinous crime, perhaps, or an investigative piece on some serious wrongdoing. That story is normally balanced with a softer story with a "feel good" quality—a touching or heart-warming story or one that features time spent in the company of a delightful person. The third and fourth stories generally lack the strong emotional resonance of the other two. If news is breaking, one or more stories may relate to the ongoing issue and produce a program that has a hard-news feel. (That certainly was the case for at least two months after the destruction of the World Trade Center on September 11, 2001.) If not, the program may be lighter in tone overall.

The Impact of News-Magazine Journalism

The formulaic aspects of news-magazine programs suggest one of their most significant weaknesses. Some narratives, it seems, have lost their power out of sheer repetition. Stories about auto- and home-repair scams are noticeably wearing thin, but they appear just about as often as they ever did. The faked death of an individual followed by the revelation of a second secret life (with or without a flight from justice or a prolonged child-custody case) has been aired over and over again. There are many similar cases of repetition breeding overfamiliarity.

In a *New York Times* column, writer Jeff MacGregor presented a wide-ranging, trenchant critique of news-magazine journalism on television. He observes that the programs are unabashed exercises in making a profit, with no connection to the common good, just recycled and lowbrow assemblages of a "pillow's worth of featherweight stories":

> Our Government is bad and stupid. Politicians are, too. Welfare is bad except when it's not. Likewise, defense spending and the National Endowment for the Arts. Celebrities photograph well, but auto mechanics don't. Modern medicine is a miracle until it kills someone, then it's a menace and something must be done. We are all victims, so here's a label to help you live. Blame the A.D.D. or the P.C.B.s or the NAFTA or the N.T.S.B. Next week you can blame someone else. Brave sick children are a humbling lesson to us all; especially if they're sick because of our Government or modern medicine or the N.E.A. If you paid more than $18,000 for a cordless phone in Times Square, you should try to find the receipt and return it. *Everyone* is ripping you off. Everyone. But it's *not your fault* because, like we said, you're a victim. In what year did Art Carney win an Academy Award for 'Harry and Tonto'?[32] [emphasis his]

News magazines are at least part of a trend toward softer news that is evident in both magazine shows and in the evening newscast. There is not much doubt that many news-magazine stories are relatively simpleminded melodramas. Also, one suspects that news magazines on more than a few occasions have done something to harm, or at least alter, the credibility of their hosts (*60 Minutes* would have to be an exception). NBC's decade of musical anchors leaves an unmistakable impression that reporters are just like the other "talent" on television—canceled at a moment's notice, placed into another set with different furniture or teamed with another cohost, and recycled all over again.

Prime-time news has resulted in the frequent, and intentional, commingling of reality and fictional or quasi-documentary entertainment programming. In 2002, when Tom Brokaw hosted an hour-long documentary about a day in the Bush White House, it was titled "Inside the Real West Wing" and ran adjacent to and was promoted along with an episode of *The West Wing* that aired after the presumably sober view of a White House at war. In promoting that evening's programming on the *NBC Nightly News*, Brokaw suggested that the documentary would be appreciated more by viewers since they could match George Bush and his team against the cast of the popular NBC program. Or perhaps more serious viewers would enjoy the fictional drama by weighing it against the reality. In other cases, networks have gone to unusual lengths to make available reality-show contestants, especially from *Survivor*, as interview subjects on local newscasts, and local stations for years have tried to follow up the Oprah Winfrey show with a "news" story that is related to that day's topic. The magazine shows are subject to the same promotion that entertainment programming gets. Once, when *Dateline* featured a long story on a murder, it was scheduled to run between *Unsolved Mysteries* and *Law and Order*. NBC promoted the evening as "a night of arresting television." Sometimes the amalgamation of fact and fiction is beyond description.

— 8 —

The Impact of CNN

All-news, twenty-four-hour television channels may be taken for granted today, but in 1980, when the Cable News Network (CNN) pioneered the first all-news service, it profoundly changed the character of American TV news. Executives at the traditional networks tended not to say that at the time, perhaps because CNN's effects were not so obvious at first. All-news television's influence, moreover, went far beyond its ratings, which were—and remain today—only a small fraction of the ratings of ABC, NBC, CBS, and Fox.

Twenty-four-hour news changed the playing field very soon for the traditional networks' news divisions. CNN could jump immediately to breaking news at any time of the day. It also had the benefit of reciprocal arrangements with hundreds of local stations, many of which were also affiliates of other networks. It might switch to a catastrophic fire in a Kansas City, Missouri, hotel and stay with the local coverage for ten or twenty minutes—or for two hours. The competitors, who did not have that degree of freedom when it came to time, gradually realized that they were being beaten on major stories. And if the story were important enough, the difference would show in the news division's reputation, if not in the ratings.

CNN became more and more polished in its ability to handle developing news, so that when a Trans World Airlines flight crashed soon after taking off from New York or when John F. Kennedy Jr. and his wife were reported missing on a flight to Hyannis Port, Massachusetts, there would be an almost instantaneous viewer reaction to see what CNN had on the story. Other network newsrooms were constantly monitoring CNN. According to ABC's Paul Friedman, that alone made CNN significant as an "early warning system":

> During the Gulf War, when [CNN's] ratings were up, people were using it as a cue, as an early-warning, easy-update system to tune into us [ABC News] when there was a major development. When we broke into the evening prime-time schedule with no advance notice, no promotion, we had the largest audiences of the night.[1]

But CNN was more than that. Its highly flexible news hole made it possible to turn most of a day's attention to a single story. Sometimes, the coverage was certainly warranted; sometimes, perhaps, it was not. The networks could cover protracted (and provocative) court cases, but not to the saturation point. The Jon-Benet Ramsey and Chandra Levy cases would never have become so important had it not been for the amount of time devoted to them, seemingly hour after hour, on CNN and other cable television outlets. Saturation coverage might also take the form of expanded coverage that created greater understanding. In their coverage of the Persian Gulf War and subsequently in their attention to Pakistan and Afghanistan after the World Trade Center terrorist attack, CNN and, to a lesser degree, MSNBC made news coverage of breaking developments more comprehensible and complete.

CNN came to occupy a unique place in international crises and in the practice of diplomacy. Available virtually everywhere via satellite, CNN was often the first source of international news for the leaders of countries and for diplomats who viewed it in their embassies. Its global reach and significance soon outdistanced its national impact in the United States. It was thus a source of information for global elites and provided an important avenue of communication between them. By 1994, Tom Brokaw of NBC believed that CNN was influential despite its small audience numbers: "In the television universe, CNN has a fairly small audience. But it raises news consciousness, and I think that it has made us [NBC] more competitive internationally."[2] Tom Bettag, the executive producer of *Nightline*, says CNN "keeps everybody sharper, better, smarter."[3]

The Start-Up of CNN

The founder of CNN, Ted Turner, was an unlikely television pioneer. Robert Edward Turner III was born on November 19, 1938, the son of an alcoholic, abusive, and demanding father. Sent to a military academy in the fourth grade, young Ted Turner was already a handful. By the seventh grade, he was the youngest student who boarded at the prestigious McCallie School in Chattanooga, Tennessee. He continued to be a disciplinary problem; he was also deeply affected by the terrible illness of his sister, Mary Jane, who was three years younger and died at fifteen from lupus. His parents' marriage ended in divorce in 1959.

Turner also caused problems at Brown University, where he learned how to sail and excelled in intercollegiate racing but apparently little else. He was suspended for various pranks and for drinking, then was expelled for breaking the rule against having women in dormitory rooms.[4]

His erratic and often distant father, Ed Turner, owned a successful billboard advertising company in Atlanta. After acquisitions in 1962, his company was one of the largest in the country. But Ed Turner was an alcoholic and was subject to deep depression. The next year, while his second wife and a company employee remained in the kitchen after breakfast, Ed Turner went upstairs to his bedroom and committed suicide, shooting himself with a revolver.

Years later, Ted Turner said that, although his father had made millions of dollars, he had set his sights too low: "My father always said to never set goals you can reach in your lifetime. After you accomplish them, there's nothing left."[5] It was a mistake the son would not make. Not content to own just a billboard advertising company, he decided to invest in television. His first steps were far from monumental. Turner bought an independent UHF station in Atlanta, Channel 17, then named WTCG. He wanted to rename it WTBS to represent "Turner Broadcasting System," but a radio station in Boston had those call letters. Turner bought the call letters eight years later. A few years after that, Channel 17 acquired the television rights to broadcast the games of the Atlanta Braves baseball team. WTCG was the first UHF station to carry major-league baseball.

In 1974, Turner purchased the team, which had been losing money, for $11 million to be paid over eleven years. Cable television stations needed programming, and Turner could offer them 162 Braves games a year. With satellite transmission, it became financially feasible to offer Channel 17 to cable systems throughout the United States. Not long afterward, it became known as the first "Superstation," a national network unlike any other, made possible by satellite interconnection.

Meanwhile, Turner earned substantial fame—and the nickname "Captain Outrageous"—by winning the America's Cup yacht race in Newport, Rhode Island. In Newport, he was seen everywhere, drank often, and cavorted until the wee hours of the night. For his accomplishments as well as his antics, he appeared on the cover of *Sports Illustrated*.[6]

In 1977, a man named Reese Schonfeld approached Turner at a cable television convention. Schonfeld had years of experience in television. His

Ted Turner created the first twenty-four-hour all-news channel, the Cable News Network, in 1980. CNN is now a part of AOL Time Warner. *(Courtesy of Photofest, New York)*

specialty was providing news to cable and independent stations. He had got his start with United Press Movietone News (and, like Turner, had been expelled from college, in his case for gambling at Harvard Law School). Turner reportedly said: "Reese, you know what my motto is? No news is good news."[7] By the next year, Turner had changed his thinking entirely; now he was actively considering an around-the-clock all-news channel. A number of his employees tried to dissuade him. The cost of such a venture seemed insurmountable. Turner himself thought an all-news channel would require an initial investment of $100 million.

He called Schonfeld and asked if it could be done.

> It could be done, Schonfeld thought, if they built an all-electronic newsroom, its systems tied together by computer, with row upon row of videotape editing machines. It could be done with a staff of three hundred, the bulk of the people at headquarters in Atlanta and the others mainly in domestic bureaus. They needed offices in New York, Washington, Chicago, and Los Angeles, at the very least.[8]

Schonfeld told Turner he would need to make an investment of between $15 and $20 million before start-up and then several million dollars each month to keep operating. They would need to use satellites for both incoming material and outgoing transmission. Turner was convinced. He would locate the channel in Atlanta, away from the stifling labor costs of New York, where broadcasting was unionized.

In April 1979, he put his Charlotte, North Carolina station, WRET, up for sale in order to use the proceeds to pay for what he now called the Cable News Network. He hired Schonfeld to be his chief lieutenant for news. The start-up date was set at June 1, 1980. A prodigious, almost unthinkable, amount of work had to be done to meet that deadline. On May 21, 1979, Turner formally announced the plan in Las Vegas to the convention of the National Cable Television Association. CNN, as it was originally designed, would resemble a working newsroom, avoiding the appearance of being packaged into polished program segments. Anchors would appear alongside producers, directors, editors, and even technicians.

In the summer, Turner found the building that would house his news channel. Formerly a Jewish country club near the campus of Georgia Tech, it was now deserted and in disarray, dirty and depressing. It had even become a home to derelicts, who were chased away. But Turner was drawn to its former ballrooms. They would make excellent studios. He could locate administrative offices on the second floor and the newsroom in the basement. Turner and Schonfeld then began the work of building a staff. Jim Kitchell, the general manager of news services at NBC, had spent twenty-nine years with the network, helping coordinate coverage of everything from the Kennedy assassination to the *Apollo 11* moon landing. Sam Zelman came from CBS; Bill MacPhail left retirement after almost nineteen years with CBS Sports. Ted Kavanau and Burt Reinhardt joined as key news executives. Kitchell became CNN's vice president for production and operations. Zelman became a vice president for news and executive producer. MacPhail headed CNN sports. Ted Kavanaugh was in charge of personnel. Reinhardt was named president of the network. In April, one major hurdle was cleared when the FCC ruled that CNN could lease space on RCA's SATCOM 1 satellite.

"We're gonna cover national news," Schonfeld told a colleague, "as if we were handling local stories. We'll report the big stuff out of Washington on the basis that these things really affect our viewers' ordinary lives. We're not gonna try to prove how smart we are. As a result, they won't feel like they need a Ph.D. to understand it."[9]

Schonfeld began to plan the broadcast day for CNN. An early problem in the planning stage was how to fill a twenty-four-hour news hole with short stories. A two-hour nightly report, from 8:00 to 10:00 P.M., would be the centerpiece of the day. It was decided that much of the news would be recycled, with an attempt to add a new angle in later newscasts during the day.

Other managers remained concerned with the cost of the whole enterprise. Although superstation WTBS, which by now was carried in millions of homes, was the source of much of the capital needed for CNN, the company still needed to borrow in order to get under way; Turner even pledged his collection of solid gold South African coins as collateral.

By May 1980, 16 million homes across the United States were wired for cable. But CNN, it appeared, would be able to be seen in only 1.7 million. At 6:00 P.M. on Sunday, June 1, 1980, CNN finally came to life. David Walker and Lois Hart were the anchors, and the first story concerned the shooting of civil rights leader Vernon Jordan in Indiana. The second hour consisted almost entirely of sports.[10] On paper at least, CNN began with a fully developed weekday schedule, beginning at 6:00 A.M. with a two-hour block of news, sports, and weather. Two- and four-hour blocks were programmed through the day, with a half hour of financial news at 7:00 P.M., a two-hour prime-time newscast at 8:00 P.M., a call-in show at 10, sports at 11, and entertainment news at 1:00 A.M.

The early days were filled with glitches, technical and otherwise. CNN struggled to compete at the Republican National Convention in mid-July and again on election night, November 4, with a broadcast anchored by Bernard Shaw. Daniel Schorr was sent to West Germany to cover the pending release of the American hostages in Iran. Covering the news cost money.

On March 30, 1981, CNN reporters and producers were on hand to cover the shooting of President Reagan at the Washington Hilton. Bernard Shaw broke the story on the air, beating the other networks by four minutes. Even so, CNN still had not earned the reputation of a professional news outfit among its competitors. They derided it as the "Chicken Noodle Network." Nonetheless, in 1982, Turner introduced CNN2, later known as "CNN Headline News," and made it available through syndication to over-the-air broadcast outlets. That year, Turner made the cover of *Time*, and in 1985, CNN reported its first net profit of $20 million. By then, he had invested more than $77 million in it.[11] In 1987, CNN moved into striking new quarters in downtown Atlanta. CNN probably reached journalistic maturity while covering a Sino-Soviet summit in Beijing in May 1989. Bernard Shaw anchored the coverage, supported by four correspondents and a crew of forty. The live coverage from Tiananmen Square marked a watershed for CNN. Covering massive, unexpected protests, Shaw pledged to stay on the air "until the Chinese authorities pull the plug on us." This is a portion of an on-air exchange between Shaw, Moscow bureau chief Steve Hurst, and Tokyo bureau chief John Lewis, all in Beijing:

> SHAW: Hold on, just a second . . . a Reuters bulletin out of Beijing is that martial law has been imposed . . . this is very sketchy. The lead says that martial law has been imposed on portions of Beijing. . . . We have five minutes on the satellite or the bird, as we call it. Things that are rushing through all of our minds—one thing, to all of our families and all of our friends watching anywhere in the world, are we endangered? No. . . .
>
> If you're wondering how CNN has been able to bring you this extraordinary story . . . we brought in our own flyaway gear, about eighteen oversized suitcases with our satellite gear. . . . We unpacked our transmission equipment and our dish. So whatever you've seen in the way of pictures and, indeed, in the way of words, came from our microwave units at Tiananmen Square bounced right here to the hotel, through the control room on one of the upper floors—I won't mention the floor for protective reasons—back down through cables, up on the CNN satellite dish, up on the satellite, and to you across the world . . . and I have to say this, for those cable stations that want to cut away, and I can't believe that any of you would want to cut away, you're gonna risk the anger and angst of all your viewers if you do . . . we have about two and a half minutes left on the satellite. . . .
>
> HURST: How in the world the government let us keep reporting out of Tiananmen Square with all our paraphernalia, watching what was going on? . . . why they didn't shut us down right from the very beginning when it was clear that this was out of hand. . . .
>
> LEWIS: It is just unbelievable to me that we were allowed to continue to do what we were doing for so long. . . . They can stop us, but I don't know how they're going to stop these hundreds of thousands or million or so people in the streets right now.[12]

The live pictures continued until CNN was, indeed, thrown off the air. CNN's coverage was widely praised.[13] In February 1990, CNN's coverage of the first missile attack on Baghdad during the Gulf War was similarly praised. Correspondents Peter Arnett and John Holliman and anchor Bernard Shaw crouched at the window of their darkened hotel room and "provided an exclusive—and riveting—description of the attack," according to *The New Republic.* "And as the night progressed, CNN's ratings exploded to twenty times normal. Eleven and a half million homes tuned to the network, and more were watching its feed on their local stations."[14]

CNN Evolves

The O.J. Simpson case changed almost everything about CNN. Before the double-murder case, CNN's most popular program was *Larry King Live*, with an audience of about 1 million. Prime-time news was watched by about 400,000 people—less than half a rating point. The Simpson story resulted in schedule changes to accommodate breaking events in the case, new programs to discuss legal strategies and the day's events, and a sharp upsurge in viewership. The Simpson story gave an insight into how CNN would operate in the future: with a modest audience in normal times, with at least four or five times that audience when something of major importance was happening.

By the year 2000, CNN comprised six cable networks: CNN/U.S., CNN Headline News, CNN International (regionalized into four separately programmed channels: Europe/Middle East/Africa; Asia Pacific; Latin America, and International U.S.), CNNfn (which provided business news, but would be gone within a short time, defeated by rival CNBC), CNN/Sports Illustrated, and CNN en Español. The group's networks and services combined were available to more than 1 billion people in 212 countries and territories, with 37 bureaus worldwide and more than 800 broadcast affiliates. CNN was not without its critics, however. CNN may well have broadcast "more live stories from more places" than any other network—the stated goal of executive vice president for news Ed Turner (no relation to Ted)—but it never approached the all-live feeling that Ted Turner wanted it to have when he first thought about CNN.[15] Media critic Tom Rosenstiel wrote in 1994 that the network had not "made much of itself":

> In certain respects, the network has even had a pernicious effect on the rest of journalism: It has accelerated the loss of control news organizations have over content, which in turn has bred a rush to sensationalism and an emphasis on punditry and interpretation at the expense of old-fashioned reporting. . . . And too much of its programming is tired and unimaginative television.[16]

Despite the naysayers, CNN has become a powerful global presence. It has about 4,000 employees and broadcasts in nine languages over the Internet, radio, and television.

In 1996, Turner Broadcasting merged with Time Warner to form the world's largest media company. In January 2000, Turner and Time Warner agreed to merge with America Online to create the leviathan AOL Time Warner.

MSNBC

A joint venture of NBC and Microsoft, MSNBC was launched in July 1996. Its "look" was sleek and futuristic, meant to reflect a new-technology orientation. At the beginning, it was programmed to be different from CNN. So, although each day's programming contained several traditional news segments each hour, a good deal of the time was devoted to talk between anchors, correspondents in the field, and in-studio contributors—experts or commentators with varying affiliations.[17] The set was a striking departure from the sober look of CNN. The news stage in Secaucus, New Jersey, resembles the interior of a brick warehouse that has been remodeled—the visual equivalent of the popular notion of what a high-tech start-up firm in Silicon Valley or Seattle might look like: "The furniture and a stairway are industrial-strength stainless steel. There is a commercial-sized espresso machine behind the anchor desk. A wall-sized photograph of the continents is enshrouded by Plexiglass."[18]

The look was intended to be "hip," urban, youthful. The signature program was *The News with Brian Williams*, an hour-long newscast targeted at younger viewers. However, experiments with attracting a different, younger demographic with such programs as a nightly Internet show called *The Site* did not work. By 2000, ratings showed that MSNBC had made some gains among the twenty-five- to forty-four-year-old segment of the audience. The MSNBC vice president of research, Robin Garfield, said the network was beginning to consistently beat CNN among first-time viewers: "MSNBC has been able to continually reinvent itself with what we find people are watching. We're embracing other definitions of news," she said.[19]

The vagueness of that description was mirrored in the MSNBC product. The network has yet to become the digitally blended medium—television married to the Internet—that it was promoted to be. The network's Web site announces that the interactive nature of MSNBC allows viewers to:

> —Design your own personal front page to display only headlines and information that interests you—including current stock quotes and sports scores.
> —Select the MSNBC local station in your town and read your local news.

—Join other readers in a chat session for a timely discussion.
—Send us your opinions about current events, and we may publish them![20]

The Internet-cable-broadcast linkup has been slow in developing and receives less attention now than when the network premiered. But its ratings continued to show some progress, especially with a 37 percent increase in viewers aged twenty-five to fifty-four in a four-month period in 1999 and 2000. From the fall of 1999 to the fall of 2000, MSNBC gained 15 percent in total audience, and CNN lost 28 percent, falling to just over 250,000 households. More ominously for both of them, Fox News Channel gained 22 percent.[21]

Fox News Channel

The most controversial of the all-news channels is without doubt Fox, which entered the field in 1996 with a stated political mission: to offset the perceived liberal bias of the major networks and CNN with "fair and balanced" coverage. The company, based at 48th Street and Sixth Avenue in New York City, was the vision of Australian media magnate and conservative icon, Rupert Murdoch. "Only Murdoch could have taken a serious run at Ted Turner's stranglehold on cable news," reported the *New York Times Magazine* in 2001. "The channel has become a major player in Murdoch's global empire of right-leaning media outlets, which include *The New York Post*, *The Weekly Standard*, and *The Times of London*."[22]

At the outset, the Fox News Channel (FNC) faced major hurdles: a staff one-fifth the size of CNN's, a budget one-tenth as large. Roger Ailes, a former Republican political consultant and one-time producer of *The Mike Douglas Show*, is the chairman of FNC, a reputed master at television "packaging." The senior vice president for news is John Moody, a veteran journalist with years of experience at United Press International and *Time*. Together they fashioned an all-news network that has the tone of entertainment programming; it is *meant* to be interesting (and if that means infuriating, so much the better).

Its daytime program mixes hard news with viewer phone calls and informal chat. *Special Report with Brit Hume* is the network's flagship newscast at 6 P.M., followed by a three-hour block of opinion programs, clearly conservative in tone and tenor, including *Hannity and Colmes* (Alan Colmes is the moderate paired with fierce conservative Sean Hannity) and *The O'Reilly Factor*, with pugnacious host Bill O'Reilly.

Roger Ailes bristles at the suggestion that Fox is "conservative": "There are more conservatives on Fox," he says. "But we are not a conservative network. That disparity says far more about the competition."[23] When FNC

113

began, Ailes instructed reporters and editors to "tell both sides of every story and take stories to the 'next level' of information." He says his news is not tabloid, and, furthermore, there is no meaningful distinction between mainstream news and tabloid: "News is what people are interested in. You can watch 'Dateline NBC' and, arguably, every one of those stories was done by 'A Current Affair' five years ago. We're just getting the same girls to dance around shinier poles."[24]

Liberal critics disagree strenuously. *Extra!*, a publication of the "media watch group" FAIR, calls Fox "the most biased name in news." In August 2001, almost an entire issue of the magazine took on the claim of "fair and balanced" reporting on FNC. It found those pundits on Fox who were identified as "liberal" to be halfhearted and ineffective counterparts to their conservative colleagues. On the Brit Hume newscast over a period of nineteen weeks, *Extra!* reported, Fox's sources were "slanted":

> On "Special Report" [with Brit Hume] 65 of the 92 guests were avowed conservatives—that is, conservatives outnumbered representatives of all other points of view, including non-political guests, by a factor of more than two to one. . . . Of the 56 partisan guests on "Special Report" between January and May, 50 were Republicans and six were Democrats—a greater than eight to one imbalance."[25]

In 1997, *New York* magazine quoted the Washington bureau chief of Fox, Kim Hume, as follows:

> "In the D.C. bureau [at ABC] we always had to worry what the lead story would be in the *New York Times*, and God forbid if we didn't have that story. Now we don't care if we have that story." Stories favored by the journalistic establishment, Kim Hume says, are "all mushy, like AIDS, or all silly, like Head Start. They want to give publicity to people they think are doing good."

Extra! concludes that

> The difference between [CNN and Fox] is that while such conservative-friendly fare airs on CNN *some* of the time, Fox has oriented its whole network around it. Contrary to what Ailes and other right-wing media critics say, the agenda of CNN and its fellow mainstream outlets is not liberal or conservative, but staunchly centrist. The perspectives they value most are those in the bipartisan establishment middle, the same views that make up the mainstream corporate consensus that media publishers and executives are themselves a part of.[26]

By 2001, Fox News Channel had stunned many observers by taking a ratings lead over CNN and even more so over MSNBC. In the desired demographic of adults between the ages of twenty-five and fifty-four, Fox viewership had increased by more than 400 percent in three years, while CNN's declined by 28 percent. In only its fifth year of existence, Fox News Channel was making a profit and was said to be worth an estimated $3 billion.[27] It had three of the five top cable-news programs in prime time, led by *The O'Reilly Factor*. In the 65 million households where CNN and Fox compete in prime time alone, Fox was winning by 30 percent.[28]

Arguably, Fox had followed a more personality-driven path to its success. Bill O'Reilly, a former *Inside Edition* anchor and a get-tough host on the air, had become the network's top celebrity and the author of a national best-seller. CNN's media critic, Howard Kurtz, was quoted as saying that FNC was not biased: "I think by and large that Fox's daily news, as opposed to their nighttime shouting-heads programming, is reasonably straight and balanced."[29] But Fox's coverage of the 2000 presidential election confirmed for many viewers their belief that Fox had tilted over backward to make possible a George Bush victory. On election night, Fox called a Bush victory, and on November 26, when Florida's secretary of state Katherine Harris ruled in Bush's favor in the fight over a recount, Fox used the logo "Florida Decision" while CNN and MSNBC were noncommital in their use of "Battle for the White House" logos. The involvement of a Bush cousin, John Ellis, in calling the election for Bush on Fox on election night left many viewers uneasy about the honesty and reliability of what was once third in the line of all-news channels.

CNN Responds

CNN was still profitable, and it had staked out the all-news territory first. It had also changed American expectations of news coverage. Mary Tillotson, who worked for CNN in Washington and in Atlanta for almost two decades, says Reese Schonfeld and Ted Turner were visionaries. "They truly believed that there was more than 22 minutes of news to be told to the American public each night and that it was a great shame that that's all they heard":

> I think CNN has broadened America's ability to talk to itself. I think the most singular impact it has had has been at persuading the other networks to do a great deal more live. From live stand-ups at the White House to live stand-ups from war zones to live coverage of O.J. Simpson. I am of the theory that it's very good for the people to see whatever's going on in the government—whether it's Clarence Thomas' hearings on his Supreme Court nomination or Congressional debate on the Gulf War.[30]

CNN's commitment to international news remained intact, and, according to author William Shawcross, it was at the time of the Gulf War "the most influential network in the world. Throughout the world, diplomats, politicians, and statesmen would watch CNN to know what was happening everywhere else. [President George Herbert Walker] Bush, Saddam [Hussein] and [Mikhail] Gorbachev were all known to watch it."[31]

After CNN and the rest of Turner Broadcasting were merged with Time Warner, then merged with AOL in January 2001, Ted Turner was maneuvered out of his role as vice chairman of the media giant. He no longer had managerial control over the Turner Broadcasting division of AOL Time Warner, which included CNN, TNT, Turner Classic Movies, the TBS Superstation, the Cartoon Network, the Atlanta Braves baseball team, the Atlanta Hawks basketball team, the Atlanta Thrashers hockey team, and Time Warner's Home Box Office.[32] The new management watched the ascent of the Fox News Channel with dismay. Rick Kaplan resigned as president of CNN's U.S. operations. The former managing editor of *Time* magazine, Walter Isaacson, became the top news executive for CNN. With Isaacson at the helm and Turner out of the picture, CNN seemed at the end of an era.

— 9 —

Celebrity News

We live in an age of celebrity journalism. There never have been more information outlets producing more stories about the rich, famous, and infamous. News-magazine journalism and tabloid television have both fed on celebrity news, celebrity profiles, and celebrity scandals to sustain audience interest. Our entertainment stars have never been more recognized and scrutinized, and our political leaders never more anonymous—at least in the era of television. The 1970s, 1980s, and 1990s were each progressively more concerned with fame and celebrity. This chapter begins, accordingly, in Hollywood.

Doing Celebrity Journalism: The Case of *Entertainment Tonight*

To see the broadcast fixation with celebrity news at its peak in 1995, I visited the set and offices of *Entertainment Tonight* (*ET*), a syndicated program produced by Paramount Pictures, owned by Viacom, while the most-covered celebrity story of all time, the murder case of O.J. Simpson, was still in the headlines. The producer of *ET* then was Jim Van Messel. It is now Linda Bell, the former producer of *Hard Copy*, a syndicated tabloid news show, who refused multiple requests for an interview. In any event, no story—certainly no other Hollywood story—has reached the frenzied heights, or depths, of the Simpson case, but there is much that has not changed about *Entertainment Tonight* in the years since.

The work day begins early at the offices of *Entertainment Tonight*. By 7:00 A.M., most of the day's staff has arrived at Hollywood's Paramount

Pictures. (The program is owned by Paramount, which is in turn owned by Viacom.) The staff includes almost 140 people based in Los Angeles, about 20 people who work in New York, 4 in Nashville, 2 each in Washington and Chicago, and 1 full-time staff reporter in Las Vegas, 1 in San Francisco, and 1 in London. The program also employs freelance journalists full-time in Boston, Minneapolis, Dallas, Denver, and Toronto. At midday the half-hour program will be taped and sent by satellite to more than 170 stations all over the country.

The cluttered offices at Paramount reflect little of the storied history of the studio. Motion pictures are infrequently produced on the lot at the intersection of Melrose Avenue and Gower Street, although occasional "pickups," individual scenes to be inserted in television or theatrical movies, are filmed on the lot. Instead, the studios are now home to a number of syndicated and network television programs, including the popular NBC comedy *Frasier*.

A steady rain falls outside. The city and the state are waterlogged, in the midst of the worst storm in at least ten years. Before the day is out, the Pacific Coast Highway will be closed, and more than twenty people will be evacuated from flooded rivers and canyons. It is a gloomy day, and the furnishings of the studio do little to brighten the mood. The Paramount lot incorporates buildings that once constituted RKO as well as Paramount. Once, *Sunset Boulevard* and *Citizen Kane* and hundreds more films were made here, but now the order of the day is news *about* movies and the rest of show business.

Tomorrow, the torrential rains will produce a lead story for the program, a set of reports on weather-related production delays facing film and television projects in southern and northern California. Today's program will lead with the second part of an exclusive interview with O.J. Simpson's defense attorney, Johnnie Cochran. The interviews, conducted by coanchor John Tesh, were taped at Cochran's home. The lawyer volunteered to talk with *Entertainment Tonight*, executive producer Jim Van Messel says, because Cochran believed that the *ET* coverage of pretrial events had been the "fairest" of any medium.[1]

Is celebrity-based news such as that offered by *ET* news or entertainment? At some point, the question itself becomes moot. Van Messel, who is fifty, formerly a local news director for stations in San Francisco, New York City, and Washington, D.C., defends the journalistic practices and standards of his program:

> The journalistic standards that we have are no different than the standards that I was involved in for 20 years before I came here. . . . We don't compromise

any journalistic principles when we do our job. Now the focus has to do with celebrity, with Hollywood . . . with television and the media, but how we cover it and how we present it are no different than if we were a news program on one of the networks.[2]

But is the content of the show primarily news or primarily entertainment? Van Messel suggests that the question can't be answered: "I don't know what a news show is, and I don't think that you do, either. I don't know what an entertainment show is, and I don't know that you do, either. And I mean 'you' figuratively."[3]

Tonight's program[4] will lead with a comparatively hard-edged story, the Cochran interview, almost seven minutes long. But the rest of the program will preview—or promote, depending upon your point of view—upcoming movies and television programs. Four stories will feature performers talking about their latest projects—two movies and two new television series. An *Entertainment Tonight* segment called "Coming Attractions" features journalism about other entertainment journalism: there are reports on stories in *Vanity Fair* (on actor Brad Pitt), *Entertainment Weekly* (on wines made and marketed by celebrities), and *US* magazine (a feature on an MTV personality).

Entertainment Tonight has long had its vocal critics as well as its supporters. Although *Variety* once praised *ET* as "the granddaddy of all magazine strips" for its "brighter look and provocative stories," *Time* magazine charged in 1994 that the show had become little more than "an arm of the Hollywood publicity machine": "It fills the air time with goggle-eyed 'behind-the-scenes' visits to Hollywood sets, fawning interviews with stars indistinguishable from advertising. Sometimes it *is* advertising."[5] Van Messel says the *Time* article "incensed" him, largely because Time-Warner, Inc., then the corporate owner of *Time*, had its own program to publicize, *Extra—The Entertainment Magazine*, and because *Time*'s reporter never bothered to interview him.[6] Van Messel rejects the allegation that *ET* has presented advertising in the guise of journalism, but he does say that the two are to some degree commingled on his program:

> I think there's a form of advertising in all reality-based programs. . . . I like to have things on our show that are actionable for our audience, where [viewers] can watch something if they want to, can see this film if they'd like to. Is that a positive thing for the [particular project that's being reported upon]? Yes, it probably is. We do review movies. Leonard Maltin does say "Don't go see this film." But why would we do a feature on a television program and say, "Don't go see this thing. We were there and it's awful." Why would we spend the time showing you only to tell you to stay away from it? That doesn't make any sense to me.[7]

119

According to Van Messel, *Entertainment Tonight* has managed to tap into the interests of mainstream America. "We've mainlined people in terms of giving them the information they want to know," he says, "and there's nothing wrong with that."[8] The program began in September 1981. He relates its considerable success, and its editorial persona, to that of *People* magazine (which debuted in March 1974) and *USA Today* (which was launched in September 1982).[9]

An Era of Celebrity Journalism

"Names make news" is a journalistic maxim that predates the current emphasis on news coverage of the rich and famous. Indeed, personality journalism is as old as journalism itself. But the placement of entertainment and lifestyle issues at the center of the "mainstream" news universe can be considered relatively new. Some observers trace its origins to the rise of gossip columnists in the 1920s and 1930s. Writers like Neal Gabler and Harold Brodkey view columnist and radio broadcaster Walter Winchell as the pivotal figure in that movement.[10] Brodkey writes that "the Luce magazines [which at the time included *Life*, *Time*, and *Fortune*] imitated Winchell's tactics and improved on them—a process that culminated later in the creation of *People*."[11]

In the 1970s, following the demise of *Life* magazine, Time, Inc. began to explore possibilities for the development of new magazines. The idea that became *People* magazine started with board chairman Hedley Donovan, who made the suggestion in the spring of 1973. The new publication's audience was envisioned as "young, urban, [predominantly] female, visually oriented, busy and with short attention spans."[12] Among its departments would be Sports, Children, and New Movies. Within the Time organization, however, the first dummy of *People* was met by some with disdain. It was labeled "journalistic popcorn" and even "sleazy and cheap."[13]

But sales of a test issue in eleven cities were brisk; the inaugural issue followed on March 4, 1974. *People* never actually struggled and eventually proved to be the most successful new magazine of the decade. By 1980, circulation had reached 2.5 million. The magazine's founding managing editor, Richard Stolley, later explained its success as the result of arriving in the midst of a prevailing "psychological, sociological climate":

> First, it was a great idea. Second, it had no competition. Third, there weren't any picture magazines around when *People* was born. *Life* and *Look* were both gone, leaving us a vacuum to fill. Finally, there was a psychological, sociological climate that worked for us. This was the real beginning of the Me Decade. We found out that people in the news were quite willing to talk to us

about themselves. They'd talk about lots of personal things—their sex lives, their money, their families, religion. They'd talk about things that a few years earlier wouldn't even have been brought up. The counterpart of the Me Decade was the You Decade, and that meant more and more curiosity about other people and their lives.[14]

Stolley sensed in the 1970s and early 1980s that personality was becoming an important vehicle for news within both print and broadcast journalism:

A lot of American magazines, especially the news magazines, had gotten away from the personality story; they'd become more issue-oriented. We intended to reverse that idea with *People*. We'd do issues, of course, but through personalities. I think the formula has worked and certainly has made an impact. More and more magazines and newspapers, and even TV, are now leaning toward personality journalism.[15]

Entertainment Tonight premiered in September 1981. Jim Van Messel says his program is a direct result of an increasing interest in celebrities. He calls it "a wave that started a hell of a lot farther from shore than you thought and got a lot bigger than you expected, and a lot of people have tried to get on that wave and have fallen off." Van Messel relates the emphasis on entertainment to the audience's pervasive desire for escape and a fascination with learning about famous people outside of the characters they play in film and on television.

Television and Celebrity News

The medium of television has from the beginning been in the business of creating celebrities: as known performers in its entertainment programs, as the subjects of personality-oriented news coverage, and in the form of television journalists who become stars themselves.

If Edward R. Murrow was one of the pioneers of broadcast journalism, he was also one of the pioneers of celebrity journalism. His Friday night interview program, *Person to Person*, which began in 1953, was paradoxically conceived as a half-hour visit by the correspondent to the homes of ordinary Americans—teachers or farmers or civil servants; the key point was that they would be unknown to the public. Within a few months, though, the idea had evolved instead into what Murrow biographer A.M. Sperber calls the "quintessential home tour of celebrities."[16] Network executives had rejected the idea of interviewing ordinary people. Instead, Lauren Bacall, Jayne Mansfield, Sophie Tucker, Marilyn Monroe, and Jerry Lewis are a representative list of the program's subjects. The show was enormously popular, and Murrow was reported to have earned more than $100,000 a year, at the time a great deal of money, for his work on *Person to Person* alone.[17]

Television's emphasis on news about celebrities was heightened by the arrival on the scene of morning programs such as *Today* and, considerably later, *Good Morning America* and *The CBS Morning News* (later called *CBS This Morning*). The *Today* show, which premiered on January 14, 1952, embodied a mixture of some attention to "serious" issues with subjects that were trivial, profane, or merely diverting. The combination became prototypical for broadcast journalism, especially for the evolution of every morning program and the later generation of television news magazines. *Today*, after all, was the show that featured J. Fred Muggs, a chimpanzee, as, in effect, Dave Garroway's cohost.

News was always important in the morning mix of program ingredients, but "variety" was as well. Early on, performers came on the programs and performed. Eventually, celebrities, politicians, and authors alike appeared regularly to promote their most recent ventures. Occasionally this constituted news, but often it did not; at some level, celebrity journalism and self-promotion have always been difficult to separate.

The current *Today* show, hosted by Katie Couric and Matt Lauer, is perhaps the one most devoted to hard news, especially in the first hour. There are no commercials in the first half hour, and the content could be described as all hard news. The program becomes noticeably different after the 8:30 mark, when the demographic shifts to an audience mix that is younger and considerably more female, and from 8:30 to 10:00, the stories are lighter and more home-oriented.

Good Morning America (*GMA*), produced for most of its history by the Entertainment Division of ABC Television, began broadcasting in 1975 with David Hartman, a former actor with most of his credits on television, as its host. While the differences between being in the news division (as are *Today* and *CBS This Morning*) or the entertainment division of a network can be overstated, *GMA* at the outset did in fact pay more attention to celebrity figures and entertainment issues.[18] In any event, all the morning programs are best thought of as hybrids of traditional broadcast news and celebrity journalism.

News about entertainment is a staple of the morning programs, and the competition to interview the most popular movie and television stars is intense. Each program would like to exclusively cover the opening of an important movie, for example. Staff producers may compete for an exclusive by guaranteeing the producers that a certain number of cast members—and perhaps the director of the film—will appear on consecutive days or, perhaps, on consecutive segments within one program.

One former executive producer of *Good Morning America*, Bob Reichblum, says there is no fixed proportion of entertainment stories in the *GMA* program mix. "The day that you start saying, 'I have to have one of these [stories] and three of those spells death,'" he says.[19] Still, Reichblum notes an effort in general to make the first hour of the program "a little bit harder," tied to breaking news stories, and the second hour somewhat lighter, with more time devoted to entertainment-related stories. Assistant and associate producers who work for the program as bookers of interview subjects deal every day with publicists. Reichblum says *Good Morning America* "will always receive pitches from movie companies, publishers, and public relations firms hired by companies that sell things." The producer says he would be foolish to ban information from at least being considered for the broadcast for the simple reason that interested parties are promoting it. The key, he says, is recognizing that the program's main client is the audience and its legitimate interests in new movies, toys, recipes, and other products.

In dealing with celebrities, what Reichblum says he tries most to avoid is predictability: "I keep saying we want to avoid the rented hotel room with the rented flowers and the three-minute interview." Yet movie stars often appear in taped interviews, although Reichblum says he insists on live, in-studio appearances whenever possible.[20]

Sources close to the production of the morning shows say there may at one time have been a significant difference in the programs based upon whether they were produced by the news or entertainment division of the network, but there is a general sense that the distinction is less meaningful today. One generalization that can be made is that all the morning programs have tended in the last decade to give more attention to show business. The difference between being a product of the entertainment division or the news division probably has had less to do with what was covered than with the amenities granted to out-of-town guests. Some news division-affiliated programs, such as *Today*, reportedly did not have budgets to allow for first-class airfare and extended hotel stays for stars and their families or retinues, while *Good Morning America* was able to provide such accommodations.

Several examples help demonstrate the complex and powerful role that television news programs play now in the promotion of celebrities and entertainment projects. In 1994, *Good Morning America* featured on four consecutive days segments that focused on a new movie, *The Paper*, directed by Ron Howard. Negotiations between *GMA* and the producers of the film began early in production, according to Roberta Dougherty, a senior producer for *GMA* in New York, when another *GMA* producer based in Hollywood alerted New York that "this was a big movie, [with the] intelligence of a Ron Howard and a good script."[21]

The Paper featured a number of major stars in its large cast—which included Michael Keaton, Glenn Close, Jason Robards, Randy Quaid, and Marisa Tomei. A report on the making of the movie appeared on *GMA*, and its producers in effect contracted with representatives of the film for coverage during its opening week on four consecutive programs. Among the segments were a live interview with director Howard and a taped interview with Michael Keaton.

GMA's Dougherty says the morning shows often compete for such coverage, and that *Today* and *Good Morning America* bid against each other to provide the best coverage (or, one might just as easily conclude, the best free advertising). "The *Today* show always outbids," she says. "They'll sometimes say nine or ten [episodes]. They seem to bid high for everything . . . lots of things that we don't think are worth it. Doing that makes you more of a hostage to the film company."[22]

Yet Dougherty will not say that *GMA* is itself ever hostage to a film company. (Incidentally, although generally well-received by critics, *The Paper* was a disappointment at the box office.) She compares negotiations with movie producers to competing for interviews with cabinet officials. In the case of the movie, *GMA*, she argues, made a news judgment about "the validity and worth" of the particular film. Negotiation with sources is a way of life for the program, she says, pointing out that in many respects dealing with entertainment figures is no different from dealing with politicians. "A member of Congress does not want to come on unless it suits his or her purposes. It's amazing the way Congress is trying to control your agenda."[23]

In general, for the author, politician, or actor who is engaged in promoting a new project, each appearance on a news program becomes part of a carefully orchestrated campaign aimed at the success of the project. Those appearances may be tied in with a multicity tour for signings at book stores and interviews with the local media. News at all levels becomes part of a well-timed process of promotion.

For example, in March 1995, Olympic champion diver Greg Louganis introduced an autobiography published by Random House called *Breaking the Surface*. The book contained the revelation that Louganis, perhaps the greatest diver in history, had AIDS. That fact was first made public in an exclusive interview with Barbara Walters on *20/20*. In short order, Louganis, previously an intensely private person, followed up the Walters interview with appearances on *Larry King Live* and with Oprah Winfrey. At the same time, Louganis launched a sixteen-city book tour that included more television appearances, book store signings, and appearances at fund-raising efforts to fight AIDS. A professor of popular culture, Neil Alperstein, observed during the Louganis media tour the fruits of a "commodity culture. . . . It's the nature of things," he says, "that not just everything is for sale, but everybody is for sale." By definition, celebrity journalism advances the objectives of the celebrity—commercial, political, and personal.[24]

In June 1995, television journalism was made part of one of the most elaborate and expensive promotional campaigns in music history. An entire hour of ABC's *PrimeTime Live* was devoted to an interview with singer Michael Jackson and his wife at the time, Lisa Marie Presley. The interview was accompanied by the airing of a music video from Jackson's first album in more than two years, set to be released the following week.

Diane Sawyer's *PrimeTime Live* interview was carefully used by Jackson and his recording company as both advertising and damage control. In 1993, the singer had faced allegations that he had sexually molested a thirteen-year-old boy. The charge was settled out of court for a sum rumored to be as much as $20 million. In December 1993, Jackson went on live television proclaiming to be innocent of all charges and speaking directly about his humiliation at the hands of police who had strip-searched him and photographed him naked. The next year, he married the daughter of Elvis Presley, Lisa Marie. Both appeared on the *PrimeTime Live* broadcast, and, according to Richard Harrington of the *Washington Post*, "Sawyer did not push on any issue and made two errors of fact."[25] Those errors were connecting the charges against Jackson to an extortion attempt and reporting that the case had been closed; neither assertion was true. On *PrimeTime Live*, Jackson's effort at image control and career rehabilitation went unchallenged before an audience of about 60 million viewers.

The interview with Jackson and his wife was promoted widely as an "exclusive" with the two personalities. It was not an especially unusual practice for such a story to be promoted that way; what *was* unusual was the lengthy teaser that appeared on *PrimeTime Live* the week before and, during their appearance on the one-hour program, the airing of a complete music video and a promotional clip for the accompanying album. If ABC News had been manipulated by the star for commercial purposes, the network had been a very willing partner.

The Journalist as Celebrity

In addition to relying on show business personalities as a source of program material, electronic journalism has a vested interest in the business of creating its own celebrities. The cultivation of Edward R. Murrow as a star led eventually to a focus on the news anchor as the embodiment of his or her network or local station.

At the networks, the first nightly anchors who became genuine national celebrities in their own right were Chet Huntley and David Brinkley of NBC. Paired first at the 1956 political conventions, the two proved a formidable team, especially with respect to their combined television persona. Huntley was ruggedly handsome and a superb news reader. By comparison, Brinkley was impish and given to irony. He wrote with wit, detachment, and in a conversational rhythm uniquely suited to his on-air delivery. Over time, NBC executives could not help but recognize the star power of Huntley–Brinkley and could not resist the opportunity to make them bigger stars. Documentaries were fashioned to give them greater exposure as well as to capitalize on their journalistic strengths. It was a model for the making of an anchor that CBS and ABC would learn well, although with varying degrees of success over the years.

In 1976, the premier celebrity journalist—in terms of her own notoriety, her longtime professional associations with show business, and a somewhat high-profile lifestyle—was Barbara Walters. After twelve years as a principal cast member of the *Today* show, she resigned to join ABC as cohost of the *Evening News* with Harry Reasoner. Her ABC salary, set at $1 million a year for five years, established a new benchmark for television anchors.

CBS anchor Walter Cronkite, speaking for the remaining traditionalists in television news, lamented the turn to high-priced talent. "The Barbara Walters news at first did shake me up," he told a group of CBS affiliates, referring to the bidding war that resulted in her unprecedented salary; "There was a first wave of nausea, the sickening sensation that we were going under, that all our efforts to hold network television aloof from show business had failed."[26] CBS News president Richard Salant was even more blunt: "I'm really depressed as hell. This isn't journalism—this is a minstrel show. Is Barbara Walters a journalist or is she Cher? In fact, maybe ABC will hire Cher next. If this kind of circus atmosphere continues, and I have to join in, I'll quit first." There was more than a touch of self-interest (as well as thinly disguised male chauvinism) in such comments; still, the tone of utter revulsion seems surprising now, almost entirely out of proportion. Television critic Ron Powers writes that "most people reacted as though a topless dancer had been appointed to the Supreme Court."[27]

In a sense, Walters never broke free of the criticism that, by either experience or inclination, she was not serious enough to be a national news anchor. To counter her detractors, she would cite meaningful interviews she had conducted with U.S. president Richard Nixon, secretary of state Henry Kissinger, Cuban dictator Fidel Castro, Nixon aide and Watergate figure H.R. Haldeman, and Nixon's vice president Spiro Agnew. She argued that she had never thought of herself as a performer and should not be considered one by others. Yet her new ABC coanchor, Harry Reasoner, apparently never accepted her as a journalist and was uncomfortable in her presence, nor was she taken seriously by many critics who disliked her particular way of dealing with newsmakers.

Her arrival at ABC did not appreciably improve the ratings of the *ABC Evening News*, which remained a distant third to CBS and NBC. On one of her prime-time interview specials, Walters asked President Carter and his wife whether they slept in the same bed. That interview ended with her request of the president—"Be good to us, be kind to us"—that, for many industry insiders and viewers, confirmed her status as a lightweight in the news business. In March 1977, *TV Guide* went so far as to publish an editorial calling for her resignation. Eventually, of course, things changed for the better: She found a home and a comfortable format on the news magazine program *20/20*; the entire environment in which national news was reported and presented changed, repositioning her in the mainstream—or even as an elder stateswoman; and her on-air manner no longer outraged anyone.

As a celebrity journalist, Barbara Walters was a product of the national networks and programs such as *Today* that were well-respected hybrids of news and entertainment. Geraldo Rivera, who is arguably at least as important a figure in the conjoining of journalism and show business, had an altogether different pedigree. He began in local news and went on to construct a career that defies categorization. At one time Rivera was identified as the sole author of "Trash TV." What he did in fact took a long time and was considerably more nuanced: he created Geraldo Rivera.

The story of Rivera's career really begins with that of a man named Al Primo, who was Rivera's news director at WABC-TV in New York. In 1967, Primo became the news director at KYW-TV in Philadelphia. He decided to promote his newscast as the product of a very distinctive team of reporters. They were to serve as surrogates for the viewers, or "eyewitnesses." They were treated as being almost as important as the anchors. To emphasize their involvement in the newscast, their daily filmed reports were presented by the reporters themselves appearing live in the studio, where they talked with the anchor about the stories they had covered that day.[28]

In 1968, Primo went to WABC-TV in New York, where he assembled a new team of reporters that included Rivera. On a multiethnic newscast, he was the representative Hispanic, but to leave it at that is an oversimplification. Rivera was raised on Long Island by a Jewish mother and Puerto Rican father. He had attended Brooklyn Law School and practiced as a storefront lawyer before choosing reporting as a career. From the beginning, he blended Latin looks and his own swagger with a savvy born out of knowing the

ABC correspondent Barbara Walters interviews Egyptian president Anwar Sadat in 1977. (*Copyright 2002 ABC Photography Archives*)

streets of New York. At WABC, he made a reputation as a "serious" journalist, particularly with an exposé of shameful practices at Willowbrook State School, a facility for the mentally retarded on Staten Island.

Rivera became the prototypical "action reporter," deeply involved in his stories (and making sure the audience was aware of that) and reveling in the role of public advocate. His work on *Eyewitness News* led first to a starring role in an ABC talk show called *Good Night America*. Rivera writes that *Good Night America* "made me the first of the late-night hipsters, a journalist/talk show host for the pre-Letterman, pre-'Saturday Night Live,' pre-MTV generation."[29] Rivera's autobiography, *Exposing Myself*, reveals that throughout his career he saw himself as many things: a street-tough adversary of evil elements in the city, not unlike the gang members he had once fought as a youth; a swashbuckling adventurer who could commute between social classes and continents; the spiritual heir to Edward R. Murrow, carrying on the legacy of investigative reporting for television; and, perhaps most compellingly, the journalist as rock star, a socially conscious celebrity who would serve and represent his generation.

Rivera's path would take him to *Good Morning America*, then to newsmaking, attention-getting work on *20/20*. His reporting was often controversial, because of both his methods (his version of the "ambush interview" was to chase a reluctant source for blocks at a full sprint) and his subjects (he did groundbreaking reporting on the facts and background of Elvis Presley's death, and he finally left *20/20* after a dispute over a story concerning Marilyn Monroe's relationships with John and Robert Kennedy). Sex, drugs, and rock-and-roll seemed to be his specialties as a reporter, but celebrity was his stock-in-trade. Before he had given a thought to becoming the host of a daytime talk show, Rivera had in some measure redefined the relationship between journalism and entertainment. By 1973, he writes, "I had invented myself as a journalist, as a reporter, and as a man."[30] Eventually, he would make millions of dollars as the host of an often outrageous talk show, then return to more "serious" work as the scholarly looking host of nightly programs on the cable channels CNBC and Fox News.

By the 1980s, the industry focus shifted to network anchors and became even more intense with the awkwardly handled retirement of CBS anchor Walter Cronkite and the bidding war for Dan Rather—and then Tom Brokaw—that ensued.[31] (Rather's desire to advance his own position led CBS executives to force Cronkite to leave the evening broadcast sooner than Cronkite at one point had wished.) Multimillion-dollar salaries confirmed the power of the anchors, and their contracts expanded the range of editorial control each had. Veteran producers were dismayed at the evolution of a system that placed celebrity anchors at the top of the news hierarchy. NBC's Reuven Frank, who had served as both a producer and a network news president, was one executive who expressed his concern:

> Producers are nothing more than chief operators today. The way the system used to work, the producer was the principal editor, deciding what stories would be assigned, who would do them, what would get used on the broadcast, and so on. Huntley and Brinkley never gave me any trouble and management left me alone. Then, in the seventies, management started to intervene. They would call the producer every day asking, "What are you covering? What do you have for tonight?" The function of management should be to criticize afterwards, and if they're not satisfied with the producer's work, they should replace him. Then, management started giving away editorial control to the talent. The anchors are running things today.[32]

The "talent" eventually would be sent to cover stories all over the globe, and not solely for journalistic reasons. Anchors became the personification of their news organizations, promoted as their networks' greatest strengths and ultimate sources of credibility. Roger Mudd, the veteran correspondent who lost the battle to succeed Walter Cronkite as anchor of the *CBS Evening News*, says change came in the 1980s, when news divisions had to pay their own way:

> That meant fewer news programs and more programs about the news. And finally it meant the corrosion of the wall that separates the news business from the show business, the slow surrender to the tabloids [and] their ever-falling standards of what constitutes news. How seriously should we regard a network whose leading anchorwoman [Diane Sawyer of CBS], a woman of intelligence and culture and perception, is paid more than $5 million a year and spends her time doing stories about date rape in the Los Angeles Police Department?[33]

Simultaneously, a select group of reporters also earned celebrity treatment and were accordingly lionized.

NBC News was probably the first network to actively promote its reporters as stars. The vehicle was coverage of the national political conventions during the Huntley–Brinkley years. Reporters assigned to the convention floor were in a key position to discover breaking news; an added benefit was that what happened to them was occasionally unpredictable. They might be ejected from the floor (as NBC's John Chancellor was in San Francisco in 1964) or literally shoved aside (as was Dan Rather at the 1968 Democratic convention in Chicago). Their work seemed to supply unusual insight for viewers about the process of gathering news.

60 Minutes was created on the foundation of reporters as stars. Don Hewitt encouraged his correspondents to place themselves at the center of their stories as protagonists and to develop a unique personal style. After a while a "Mike Wallace story" was clearly identifiable, as was a "Morley Safer" or a "Harry Reasoner" or an "Ed Bradley."[34] Each story was structured as a minidrama, often a morality play. Hewitt and his reporters became accustomed to the charge that *60 Minutes* was as much entertainment as journalism. Wallace offered this response to the show-business critique in his autobiography:

> A common criticism is that we are in show business, not in journalism. Some of that frankly smacks of journalistic elitism, the kind of attitude that frowns on any story that is not important with a capital I and serious with a capital S. To those who think that way, every time we do a celebrity profile or some other soft, back-of-the-book feature, we are being "trivial" and are "wasting" the precious air time that has been granted to *60 Minutes*. Nonsense. We are, after all, a magazine broadcast that is committed to a multi-subject format, and we have never pretended to be anything else.[35]

The Cultural Critique of Celebrity News

The coloration of journalism by entertainment- and celebrity-related topics has been a frequent target for critics of evolving news values and practices. More broadly, social critics have identified in journalism and other cultural artifacts—especially television—a numbing societal fascination with celebrity that reflects a culture steeped in shallowness, the elevation of the trivial, and an overweening absence of taste. Brodkey writes that one product of gossip-based journalism was the mass-marketing of celebrities:

> What happened to the notion of celebrity was paradoxical: there was a demystification, based on the mystique of success, but a success that anyone could have. This new social reality did not concern the most interesting lives but lives that anyone could live (depending on how well you were groomed and how good your publicist was).[36]

In *Amusing Ourselves to Death*, social critic Neil Postman makes the case that "Americans are the best entertained and quite likely the least well-informed people in the Western world," largely as a result of the content and quality of the country's broadcast journalism.[37] At the heart of television's failure to inform, he argues, lies "a type of discourse that abandons logic, reason, sequence, and rules of contradiction. In the parlance of theatre, it is known as vaudeville."[38] An emphasis on personality is magnified, according to Postman, by newscasts that are so truncated that stories and facts do not flow understandably. Instead of explanation, viewers are offered visual stimulation, bite-sized stories, and performers in the studio. He worries particularly that the newscaster's likeability and credibility are interrelated: "It is frightening to think that this may be so, that the perception of the truth of a report rests heavily on the acceptability of the newscaster."[39]

In his book *Carnival Culture*, James Twitchell views a society saturated with celebrity in which popular culture has virtually driven out everything else. He notes that the *Tyndall Report*, a newsletter that monitors the evening newscasts of the commercial networks, reports that the nightly newscasts spent an average of sixty-eight minutes a month on show business stories in 1990, up from thirty-eight minutes a month for both 1988 and 1989.[40] In addition, more than 25 percent of ABC's "Person of the Week" choices were from the world of entertainment.

> Showbiz even has its mythology carried in the fastest growing sector of the entertainment industry: information and gossip about showbiz. Called "enfotainment," this grist is the result of the surge of new delivery systems of entertainment in the 1980s: home video, cable, compact disks, and an audience eager to know not merely "what's on" but "what's in." We have television shows about television shows (*Entertainment Tonight*); television shows about movies (*Siskel & Ebert* [now *Ebert and Roeper at the Movies*] *Sneak Previews, Showbiz Today*); low-priced videocassette "magazines" sold at supermarket checkout stands (*Persona*), and even an entire cable network broadcasting puffery (*E!*). Throwaway print magazines about show business (*Premiere, Movieline*, and *Entertainment Weekly*) are dedicated to "what's on *right now*." *USA Today*, "McPaper," not only has an entire section dedicated to enfotainment but is itself an entire enfotainment approach to the news. *Time* and *Newsweek* have vastly expanded their show-business coverage as have national newspapers.[41]

The battle between entertainment and information—or between triviality and quality—cleaves all American media, according to Twitchell. It began as a conflict between the "gatekeeper of ideas" and the "merchandiser of printed pages" in book publishing in the eighteenth century, then reappeared in the mass-market publishing of the nineteenth century.[42] By the 1970s, commercial publishing was in the ascendancy, with sales figures determining the winners of publishing awards that once had been based on artistic merit. Gerald Howard describes a "fault line" that has divided the two classic functions of book publishing (and of mass communication in general): the "more vocally trumpeted mission" to instruct and uplift the reading public, and the goal of separating the consumer from his cash.[43]

At the least, news media reflect the values of the culture in which they operate. The major American news media are commercial enterprises that attempt to garner large audiences. Large audiences are, not surprisingly, attracted to celebrities and to stories about entertainment. But the celebrity-news nexus implies something more: that journalism invests entertainment with greater weight in the culture than it might otherwise receive, and that journalism accordingly shapes the values of a culture where celebrity is exalted. In the case of television, there are two particular problems with robust curiosity about and extensive coverage of entertainment. First, the coverage inevitably becomes self-reflexive, as Twitchell argues. Television is more and more about television. Much of the coverage of the O.J. Simpson trial was coverage of a television event, and much of the commentary concerned how the action played on television. The Lewinsky scandal was often about the coverage of the Lewinsky scandal, and the pattern was repeated in the Chandra Levy–Gary Condit story.

The second problem is inescapable: the gradual intermingling of news and self-promotion. Again, news figures in the O.J. Simpson case were able throughout the trial to exploit the media for their own gain and self-aggrandizement. Over time, the problem can become an acute one for the profession of news-gathering and for the society at large. When advertising and journalism are indistinguishable, how are we to define journalism—and how can it be trusted?

III

PUBLIC SERVICE IN
THE DIGITAL AGE

— 10 —

Local News

Is Local News Really That Bad?

In its issue of September 1993, *American Journalism Review* featured a main story with a stark question on the cover, presented in huge white-on-black letters: "Why Is Local TV News So Bad?" Inside, the cover story included the comments of ten television professionals, academics, and critics.[1] All but one, David Bartlett, then the president of the Radio-Television News Directors Association, were disdainful of local news.

The collective critique comprises a litany of the worst attributes of television news at the local level. The main points are familiar to most viewers. Far too much coverage of crime—"endless coverage of grisly, blood-spattered offenses that [feed] our national paranoia."[2] An emphasis on video that contains visual drama, even better a disaster, with no concern for its merit as news—crashes, fires, "hot" footage. Reporters who are ill-trained and do not cover beats. "No one regularly covering education, or the environment, or local government, or minorities, or public health."[3] The use of technology as a gimmick, so that live reports and helicopter-based coverage are all there for show. The endless self-promotion within the newscast, along with the use of cars and vans and satellites as billboards to advertise the product. Just plain silly conventions, such as the live stand-up report from city hall hours after that morning's news event and hours after everyone left the building and went home. Superficial coverage of just about everything except sports and weather, with no real attention given to the issues that underlie urban violence or poor schools—or good schools, for that matter. Not enough reporters to do justice to the news that is important. (In just about every city in the

United States, the local newspaper has about ten times the number of reporters covering the city as does a television station.) An unseemly attention to anchor appearance, coordination of clothing color with hair, makeup, and the set, theme music, and making the most money possible every day. No quality control and no real investigative reporting. Racial insensitivity, or worse, racist practices. Ishmael Reed, an author nominated for two National Book Awards, suggests that the television media, controlled by whites, are in the business of protecting whites as a group by portraying backs as overwhelmingly antisocial and out of the mainstream:

> What's wrong with local television news? It polarizes whites and blacks by racializing issues such as welfare, affirmative action, and crime. After reviewing local news programming, one almost has the feeling that the media consider the black community to be an enemy nation. But instead of attacking it with missiles, the media zap it with videotape. When reporting news about African Americans, reporters for local stations tend to wing it with their prejudices rather than go by the facts. And even when these reporters accurately present the facts, their stories are usually undermined by the accompanying visuals.[4]

Reed adds that the media constantly portray blacks as the victims of social problems that are more evident among whites. He points out that only 39 percent of welfare recipients are black and that the typical beneficiary of affirmative action programs is a white woman, but that the local television audience would have no reason to believe either fact.

In 1995, Max Frankel presented a similar list of local-news atrocities in the *New York Times Magazine*:

> [Local news] assails the mind but offers nothing much to think about—not even about crime, war, and disaster. No helpful assessments of the police or local hospital. Almost nothing about education except some school shooting. Nothing about housing except some landlord's venality. Nothing about traffic except some flaming collision. Much less anything reflective about politics, economics, foreign affairs.[5]

Frankel cites statistics that in a typical thirty-minute local newscast in 1995, sports and weather consumed more than six minutes. Commercials claimed between eight and ten minutes. And the news segments were dominated by news of crime and disaster, so-called "mayhem stories." Station KMGH-TV in Denver, which promises "No filler, no fluff, no contests," was judged by the Rocky Mountain Media Watch in Denver to have a fluff-to-news ratio of nearly 1 to 2.[6] The average local newscast on fifty stations in twenty-nine cities served up one minute of fluff to every three minutes of news. Half the time devoted to purely local news was given over to mayhem.

Can all this be true in 2002?

Paul Steinle of the University of Miami School of Communication suggests these criteria for evaluating local news:

1. Quality control. Does anyone fact-check copy before it goes on the air or critique weak stories after they are broadcast?

2. What are the standards for live remotes? Are live remotes as well-edited and well-written as taped field reports? Are remotes given extra time, because they are live, without regard to their news value?

3. Are stations hyping the news? Are promos and teasers promising much more than the stories deliver?

4. Do the anchors know the city, its people, and the area's power brokers? Do they know enough to guide viewers through an election night or a major disaster?

5. Where do news-coverage dollars flow? Is there really a local angle when stations pull stories off a satellite?

6. Do reporters report the news or spout speculation? Do reporters have enough time to research stories and ask questions? Can they confirm what *really* happened?

7. Does the assignment editor know the community? Did the editor work the streets as a reporter? Does the editor understand local interests and local mores?

8. Are stations production-driven or news-driven? Are stations more concerned about how a story looks than what it says?[7]

There are signs that the situation is improving, I believe. Some of the worst excesses appear to have been curbed in many markets. "Happy talk" on the air is less prevalent, and there is some hard evidence that crime is being covered less on many local newscasts. A number of cities have all-news channels, and there are some outstanding regional news channels, where the station is not chasing a narrow demographic dictated by advertisers.

The current president of the Radio-Television News Directors Association, Barbara Cochran, says the improvement in local television news in the last nine years (since the *American Journalism Review* cover story) has been significant.[8] More stations, she says, are doing in-depth reports of quality. There are more than a few examples of photojournalism at its finest. She admits that many stations lack adequate resources to cover the news, noting that local stations have now been given large blocks of air time to fill with news, but without a corresponding increase in the number of producers, editors, cinematographers, and reporters. She cites the outstanding work of many local news organizations.

Among the most honored are KING and KOMO in Seattle, both of which are known for producing excellent documentaries, WESH in Orlando, WBZ and WCVB in Boston, WFAA in Dallas, WRC in Washington, D.C., KUSA in Denver, and KARE in Minneapolis. KING and WFAA have outstanding on-line services as well. WFAA provides at its on-line site a law center for local issues and legal remedies, resources for job and career planning and for college admissions, a community calendar, home advice, places to go, and information about town meetings, how to adopt a pet, and where to report local problems. KING, an NBC affiliate, provides free Web sites for local nonprofit organizations, results of tests on children's toys for safety and durability, shopping guides, and ratings of the best things to see and do in the Seattle area. Perhaps it's only a start for the country as a whole, but there do seem to be models of excellence to turn to in many parts of America.

More local stations have time for news, in the late afternoon and evening, but especially in the morning, when one- and two-hour blocks of news precede the network's morning news show at 7:00 A.M. in many communities. Harry Fuller, former vice president and general manager of KPIX-TV in San Francisco, says local news early in the morning fits together well with busier lifestyles: "You can move around, you can be doing your hair, you can be shaving, you can be dressing, you can be looking for the wallet that you put somewhere last night—you can do all of that with the television on. So TV fits better into the continually more busy household environment that many middle-class Americans live in."[9]

Local news, though, is more closely monitored by ratings, and ratings more closely monitored by station management, than ever before, and that should be a cause for concern. Ratings have been used as the basis for decision-making at local news operations for years, and the importance of ratings is now greater, not lesser, than in the past. The careers of reporters, especially anchors, and certainly news directors rest with the ratings, which are now available for the previous day's programs. Ratings seem to dictate local news teams made up of an older, distinguished-looking male anchor; a younger, conventionally attractive, and perky female partner; a folksy weatherperson; and a rugged or funny sports reporter. Why should we see this mix literally all over the country? The ethnic and racial profile varies, but the template seems set in stone. Couldn't it be time to disregard the ratings, at least once? Then again, Jamie Malanowski, a features editor for several magazines, offers a different approach:

> Don't fiddle with the anchor talent. The classic anchor team (craggy veteran anchorguy; attractive, poised, perfect-second-wife-for-the-anchorguy anchorgal; jolly weather-fella; rugged sportsguy) along with the by-now classic derivations (cheerful weathergal; canny, knowledgeable sportsguy) has

been tested by time and found widely palatable. Why mess with it? Here's an easy test: If your local anchorperson can correctly pronounce Slobodan Milosevic, Mogadishu, and Robert Reich, he or she is a keeper.[10]

On a more serious note, Harry Fuller says that, to an extent, overnight ratings are often extremely useful. "I think overnights do give you a good message when a story breaks, and you see where people go for information when there's a new story in the market. Like if we were to have an earthquake of any size and people felt it, the next day's overnights would be a very good scorecard on who did the best job of responding."[11] But at the local level, ratings may be used too often to micromanage the content. Jill Campbell, who produced the 6:00 P.M. news on WJLA in Washington, D.C., says that "the ratings monster," in practice, is at work making news decisions all the time:

> If we lead the newscast with something and the ratings drop, we can tell in 15-minute increments [from overnight ratings]. If the ratings dropped down drastically at 5:15, then obviously we did something wrong and people weren't sticking around. [The managers] then come in the next day and tell us that what we did yesterday didn't work and they then decide what we can do to fix it.[12]

The ratings fell; therefore "we did something wrong." A reform movement called "civic journalism" is an effort to encourage wise individuals to penetrate this defective logic and replace it with a mind-set more in tune with public service and responsibility.

The Argument for "Civic Journalism"

Frustration with local news breeds both apathy and resentment, but it has also produced a movement to change the nature of local journalism in the United States. The reform movement to promote civic journalism began a little more than a decade ago. Professor Jay Rosen of the New York University School of Journalism was a catalyst in urging a reconsideration of what news, principally local news, had become and how it might be changed. The initiative was underwritten by a development grant from the Pew Charitable Trusts in 1992, which has funded projects across the country in the years since to implement civic journalism in local markets. The hands-on projects to redefine news and the role of citizens in the news process began in 1993.

Jan Schaffer, the executive director of the Pew Center for Civic Journalism, defines civic journalism as a process of involving citizens in news-gathering, production, and presentation in newspapers and on television stations as part of the larger goal of involving them in the maintenance and betterment of their communities. Instead of news that focuses on conflict and wrongdoing, the Center for Civic Journalism advocates news content that concentrates on "solutions, things that work, leaders, and catalysts for change."[13] It assumes that editors and news directors do not have the answers to all the questions about their communities and that they need help from citizens to learn the right questions to ask.[14]

Civic journalism, Schaffer says,

> is more than a set of tools. It is also a set of core values that guide how [reporters, editors, producers, and news directors] practice their craft, how they try to connect with their communities, and how they try to empower their readers and viewers. . . . The most important and most competitive thing local news organizations can do is to cover their communities well. In return, journalists get better stories. They diversify their reports with new voices, new opinions, and new kinds of leaders.[15]

In many communities, local television news is learning the lessons of civic journalism well. In Rochester, New York, WXXI collaborated with the local newspaper to present a series of live, two-hour, prime-time debates with the five mayoral candidates. Questions from citizens—about graffiti and noise ordinances and the problem of stray dogs—were included. Gary Walker, WXXI's vice president for news and public affairs, says, "The candidate who was trailing the pack, with no money for TV ads, eventually won the race. Rochester elected its first African-American mayor. And he credits the debates with his election."[16] In San Francisco, KQED held town hall meetings for a year as part of a community-wide attempt to determine the Bay Area's transportation needs and possible solutions to its problems, not relying solely on transportation agencies, pressure groups, or reporters' own instincts for their information.

In Madison, Wisconsin, WISC-TV teamed up with the *Wisconsin State Journal* in a five-year community project aimed at closing the racial achievement gap in schools. "Schools of Hope" has in fact narrowed that gap. Similar projects have been undertaken in Boise, Idaho; Tampa, Florida; and in the state of New Hampshire. On-line, local stations have created games for city planning, calculating real-estate taxes, and redistricting. "Gaming the News" has become a model for increasing local participation in important public issues.[17]

Civic journalism is not without its critics. Some news directors and editors reject the reliance on audience panels for news story ideas. Some bristle at what they consider the imposition of one institution's definition of news and the "proper" newsroom procedures. Some do not like the label "civic journalism," believing that it resonates with the sound of local boosterism. But given how much effort had gone in to making local news substantively weaker over the years, it seems difficult not to applaud a movement that clearly has had many positive outcomes. It also is apparent that the network news divisions might be advised to study and apply the techniques and values of civic journalism to their national coverage. Local news is probably where positive change will take place first, though, because it has much closer ties to a community, to civic leaders, and to advertisers, so pressure from the audience can be more direct and effective.

The Centrality of Community

For local television news to be of high quality and socially responsible, the news organization must have an active role in the life of the community. It is easy enough to write that, but exactly what does it mean? The debate within the news profession over civic journalism derives from differing understandings of how that role is defined and enacted. This brief discussion begins with an attempt to define "community."[18] Among the dozens of definitions of community in the sociological literature, several seem particularly suited to the multiple roles that local television news plays in the life of any locality.[19]

The community as geographic unit.[20] The community served by a local news outlet may be defined simply as a geographic "area of dominant influence." That is how the ratings companies define a broadcast market. The community is made up of those with access to the station's signal. But cable and satellite transmission have complicated the geography of television audiences; the signal is often available on cable systems hundreds of miles away.

The community as microcosm. The local audience may at times be regarded as a self-sufficient social system that reflects the larger society. For example, the problems of the elderly may be no different in one city than in another, but the general issue may serve as the springboard for local coverage.

The community as a sphere of practical knowledge. In the process of serving as a community "billboard," television news may be defining the community as a collectivity of people who need practical information and everyday guidance: weather reports, notices of traffic tie-ups, road closings, power outages, and tips for the weekend.

The community as an interdependent social system. The report of a traffic tie-up also underscores the ways in which a community is defined by its interrelatedness. Disasters—natural, political, and otherwise—perhaps make this point most clearly. The terrorist attacks of September 11, 2001, demonstrated this tragically not only in New York, Pennsylvania, and Washington, D.C., but all over America.[21]

143

The community as the object of close personal attachments. Stories that presume or encourage loyalty toward the community or its symbolic representatives (local sports teams are an obvious example) invoke strong ties "to the conventions and mores of a beloved place."[22] Care for the community does not have to mean the abridgement of objectivity. There are many examples of public-service journalism that do not require changing or abandoning traditional journalistic goals.

Within a single local television newscast, or even within a single story, implicit media definitions of community may vary. That diversity suggests the range of social and political functions television news may have at the local or community level. Understanding the ways in which a locality can be defined is a key to determining the communication needs of an area or municipality. Local media may find particular benefits by, in effect, creating needs and then fulfilling them. For station management, for example, cultivating loyalty to the community can be useful as a way of reinforcing loyalty to the station itself.

The "local" component of television news is changing. Mobile satellite transmission has extended areas of coverage, diffusing notions of who, and where, the audience is. The now-familiar practice of assigning local anchors and reporters to cover national and even international stories has "localized" stories ranging from the national political conventions to Afghanistan and the Middle East. Those developments, stirred by the enhanced profit potential of local news and innovations in the available technology, already have reshaped the content of local news and, with time, may contribute to a redefinition of its purpose. The members of a community, linked by bonds of common interest and close communication, are presumed to have responsibility for each other and for the maintenance of social order. Playing a vital role in the community is essential if local news is to remain relevant, if not a powerful force.

A Satellite Revolution in Local News

Spurred by the possibilities for the instantaneous dissemination of news by satellites, the relationship between the networks and their affiliates is a story of significant and startling change. The agencies that are reshaping news for most Americans form a puzzling list of mysterious names: News Channel, NewsOne, Newspath, NewsEdge, Newsource, NNS, ABNET.

Sound familiar? If not, welcome to the dynamic and little understood world of network television news in the 2002. The odds are that most viewers haven't been following the explosive, arcane growth sector that is called affiliate relations. It turns out that in the midst of declining audiences, a sharply reduced international presence, the end of the bureau system as we knew it, staff contraction and the power of infotainment, network news divisions were actually hard at work redefining themselves for their local affiliates.

It's been apparent to network executives for well over a decade that their flagship newscast at six-thirty or seven o'clock in the evening was destined to keep losing its audience. Increasingly, the American family gets home later, eats dinner more irregularly, and simply isn't in front of the television set that early. And, of course, there are many more alternatives to network news than there were in the past.

One response has been to experiment with a later news program, such as the nine o'clock evening news on MSNBC with Brian Williams, or a nine or ten o'clock news magazine program with the capability of covering the day's major story. But satellite technology has played perhaps the most important role in reshaping the relationship between network news and local stations. For more than fifteen years, ABC, CBS, NBC, and CNN have used satellites and the cooperation of willing affiliates to restructure a significant part of the news-gathering process.

Using satellites, networks make available hundreds of stories—both domestic and international—to their affiliates each day. An important breaking story will be provided to affiliate stations at 6 A.M. or at noon or at 4 P.M., well before the network newscast. The changes have been dramatic, even if little noticed. Reese Schonfeld, who helped found CNN with Ted Turner, has noted that as early as the 1980s, local stations were scooping the networks with CNN material.[23]

If nothing else, network hegemony has been diffused. Local stations decide earlier in the day which national and international stories to use, a role they once ceded to the network. In theory, local news producers can now act as gatekeepers for the entire range of national and international news. In reality, satellite news services have extended the reach of local newscasts in several demonstrable ways. In covering breaking news of distinct local interest, local stations around the country have been given more access to the resources of the networks and their affiliates. Similarly, the ability to cover regional stories has been bolstered substantially by network assistance. And viewers can now expect to see local newscasts that routinely include coverage, often live, of the top news story of the day in the country.

Moreover, it is possible now to make out the contours of the network news division of the future: servicing local affiliates throughout the news cycle with live and taped stories; less tied to nationally originated programming, even less to one evening newscast; electronic in form rather than bricks-and-mortar; more dependent on reciprocal exchanges of news and less on bureaus staffed with people.

At its most elemental level, networks provide a video wire service in the form of satellite feeds for their affiliates, but each network's service is layered and complex. In 1985, a network provided one daily feed of fifteen minutes or half an hour of video material, often about the president and sometimes made available a day late. Now that service might feed sixteen or eighteen hours of new material each day, from breaking news to sports highlights packages to features on health, business, and travel. Video made available by one affiliate can be distributed to all the other affiliates. Each network also makes available live reports staffed with network correspondents and production crews to local stations across the country throughout the news cycle, which now begins at 5 A.M. in the Eastern time zone and doesn't end until 11:30 P.M. on the West Coast; affiliate services also coordinates satellite time for stations' own live remote broadcasts and may offer technical assistance to local crews on location away from home.

Producers and editors live in a dizzying world of multitasking, servicing affiliates and other clients, deploying resources from their dedicated bureaus and broadcast partners (ABC alone has reciprocal arrangements with more than eighty international broadcast stations, networks and agencies), and providing live reports, sometimes for hundreds of affiliates, every day. ABC's vice president for news services, Don Dunphy Jr. (his late father was the most famous of all boxing announcers) explains that before the mid-1980s, a satellite feed service was impractical because so many stations could neither send nor receive material. Networks distributed filmed reports by long-distance telephone lines, but that was prohibitively expensive for individual stations. "Satellite news-gathering," he says, "was in its infancy. Conus had just started."[24] Conus Communications, owned by Hubbard Broadcasting Co., was the world's first statellite news-gathering organization, pioneered by Stanley S. Hubbard, whom most broadcasters consider a visionary. Conus deployed satellite trucks, which are in effect mobile sending and receiving stations that transmit on the KU-band. The satellite truck, Dunphy says, was the financial and technical breakthrough that made a satellite-linked news network possible. KU-band transmission was considerably less expensive than the $500,000 cost associated with a fixed satellite dish.

Changes in local news programming created the demand for more video and more coverage. When local stations began airing afternoon blocks of news that were as long as two or three hours, they found they had a pressing need for more content. That desire has continued to grow as the early morning time slot, from 5 A.M. to 7 A.M., has been filled around the country with local news programs. Jack Womack, executive vice president of CNN Newsource, says the affiliate services "have become fiercely competitive. [Local stations] want to have as many sources as they can. You just don't want to miss the picture."[25] CNN itself, with an unprecedented news hole and a large staff of reporters and videographers, accelerated the competition.

Joe Duke, director of marketing for Newspath, says "the ability to go live from distant places" changed the nature of local news broadcasts. "More stations started to go live, and that ratcheted up the competition. . . . Having a story that [involved] local residents in some distant place gave the station an enormous competitive advantage."[26] Duke has years of experience competing in local news. A former news director for CBS affiliates in Houston and New Orleans, he says local stations now demand thorough regional and national coverage: "If I'm an affiliate, I want Super Bowls, Final Fours, national political conventions, the Academy Awards. . . you name it. If the network makes sure that Chicago has everything it wants, it's going to make sure that Dayton has everything it wants, too."[27]

There are approximately 860 television stations in the United States that produce news programming. ABC, CBS, and NBC have about 200 affiliates each. Most of those 600 stations are affiliated also with CNN, which has a total of 677 affiliates. Fox Television has about 125 affiliates that produce news.

CBS started the first satellite feed service for affiliate stations, now called Newspath. The Fox service is called NewsEdge. NBC's is News Channel, and CNN's is Newsource.

National News Service (NNS), is a cooperative formed by ABC, CBS, and Fox. ABNET is an ABC consortium of affiliates that purchases and re-sells satellite time. NBC's News Channel facility may be the most state-of-the-art. It occupies a 10,000-square-foot studio that sits inconspicuously on the Billy Graham Parkway in Charlotte, North Carolina, between an impressive nest of satellite dishes and the local NBC affiliate, WCNC. Bob Horner is the president of News Channel. He began working in television news with jobs in Wyoming and Alabama. He then headed the CBS Atlanta bureau. After beginning the CBS news feed in the 1980s, Horner designed News Channel while he was a consultant to General Electric. He chose to locate it in Charlotte, mainly, he says, to avoid the expense of doing business in New York City. The result of his planning is a visually striking newsroom decorated in shades of red and gray, with circular desks facing a wall of close to a hundred television monitors. At one desk are regional producers who talk with the local stations several times a day. "Every NBC affiliate hears from one of our regional producers every day," Horner says.[28]

Regional producers for the Southeast worked with local affiliates in Florida to cover Dale Earnhardt's death at the Daytona 500 and routinely work with them to coordinate coverage of all space shuttle flights. Producers for the Northeast teamed with WNBC in New York to cover the verdict in the Sean "Puffy" Combs trial and worked with affiliates up and down the coast to cover a late winter nor'easter. Local affiliates in Des Moines and Omaha provided logistical, technical, and editorial support to cover a trail derailment in rural Iowa.[29]

Another News Channel desk handles "nonbreaking" or "specialty" stories such as medical, entertainment, or consumer items. A third desk coordinates live broadcasts for local stations. At the satellite desk, producers and engineers schedule satellite time for News Channel itself and for all NBC affiliates.

News Channel is the only stand-alone satellite-feed facility, but the other networks have very similar structures in place and staffs of between 80 and 120 people, including between six and twelve dedicated correspondents for coverage of breaking news.

All of the services offer live coverage in two forms, using a lexicon that has become standard in the world of satellite feeds. A "generic" story is a live feed aired at either thirty seconds or one minute after the top of the hour. It can be broadcast "as is" by any affiliate in the country. During a major breaking story, such as the Florida election aftermath, a generic story was offered to local stations at virtually every hour of the day. On one Sunday, a 6:00 P.M. story from Tallahassee was broadcast simultaneously on 114 NBC affiliates. (NBC has only recently had the ability to record how many stations use its live feeds.) News Channel's executive producer, Sharon Houston, points out that stations may tape live reports and air them later, in the process suggesting erroneously that the stories are being seen live. That practice, she says, is discouraged. But if the local station doesn't want to take a generic feed at the top of the hour, it is welcome to use the story later in the newscast or on a different news program. All generic stories are provided free for local stations.[30]

"Custom" stories, the second form of live coverage, refer to a variety of methods for serving individual stations and personalizing the product. On occasion, one affiliate will request a live feed on a story from, perhaps, Washington that has news value only in that local market. Or an affiliate might want a customized close attached to a widely distributed report of a major story ("Back to you, Jill and Robert . . . "). The local station can request cross-talk between the local anchor and the reporter on-scene. CNN's Jack Womack says the cable network's record for custom "tags" or story endings is ninety in one day by one correspondent for the same story. In that case, the tags were taped ahead of air time and fed to ninety stations individually.[31]

The affiliate services generally charge stations a fee for custom services, but overall they do not expect to make a profit from the business of offering satellite feeds. In theory, better news coverage for each station will improve their profitability and, accordingly, their value to the network. The networks do cultivate some for-profit clients. ABC's NewsOne, for example, provides video to the *Oprah Winfrey Show*, Black Entertainment Television, and several other cable clients.

Stories are sent 22,300 miles skyward to communication satellites throughout the day—it is estimated that the four major news services use twenty to forty different transponders (combination receiver-transmitters on each satellite) in the course of a news cycle. News Channel sends out about 200 items each day, CBS Newspath and ABC NewsOne about 300, and CNN about 400. Bob Horner says most of the 200 News Channel items are regionally based stories, followed by national breaking news, sports highlights, thirty to forty international items, and features. News Channel has a "Big Story" designation for the day's top news item and classifies stories with especially gripping visual images as "Hot Shots," which are frequently weather-related items such as hurricanes, mudslides, or active volcanos. Producers say breaking weather stories are among the most important domestically.[32]

While allowing that certain feature stories, such as health-related news, have many interested clients, Horner says "the vast majority of what we do" at News Channel is "hard news" that is "event-driven." He adds that the all-news cable channel MSNBC has provided significant air time so that there is a place where all the additional NBC coverage can be seen.[33]

While satellite news feed producers juggle breaking news and requests from affiliates throughout the day, reporters concentrate on serving a multitude of clients and sometimes cover a multitude of stories. Carla Wohl has been a reporter for ABC's NewsOne for four years after stints with stations in New Haven, Connecticut, and Los Angeles. Based now in Los Angeles, she may do versions of one story for as many as thirty or forty affiliates on the same day. In one week in March, she covered an earthquake in Seattle, a hearing in Hawaii on the crash of a Navy submarine with a Japanese boat, and a school shooting in Santee, California, outside San Diego. At the scene of a breaking story, she'll file a "generic" story live at one minute after the hour and then do a series of "custom" reports for specific stations, which may involve a stand-up report or cross-talk with a local anchor. "It can get very busy on big stories," she says. "But on the second day, you're busier. On the first day, all the stations take the generic feed at the top of the hour. But when the story moves down in the newscast on the second day, they want stories at many different times. You can do live shots almost one after the other for an hour and a half or two hours."[34] Wohl wears a dual earpiece that allows her to hear her producer tell her the names of the anchors of each local station, and she may also be watching a small portable television to see additional coverage of the story she's reporting on. "It's a very challenging job," she says, "because you don't always know what's going to be thrown at you. When it's constant you're just going, going, going on adrenaline. You have to be quick on your feet. That's the fun of it. It's exciting." She cites the postelection coverage in Tallahassee, Florida, as the most chaotic story she has covered: "It changed every two minutes and it lasted for weeks." In about a month, Wohl did more than 250 live reports for local stations.

The demand for live reports can be so great that there's precious little time for actual reporting: "Everybody wants you live," Wohl says, "and you have to be innovative to find out what's going on." She often has done reports for the BBC and stations in Canada and New Zealand. But she feels she knows scores of local anchors in the United States personally. "If it's New York," she says, "I know that it's Roz at 5:00 o'clock."[35]

In Washington, D.C., News Channel reporter Jim Hanchett describes this day as "ordinary." The feed service has a small news bureau on Capitol Hill. Today, he's covering a Senate committee hearing on the drug Ecstacy. After the hearing, he files a seventy-five-second report on tape at 5 in the afternoon. He also files a "generic" close, "Back to you," that can be used by any station. He then does about twenty "custom" closes that stations have requested and will pay for: "This is Jim Hanchett for News Four . . . This is Jim Hanchett for Action News Two . . . This is Jim Hanchett for News Eleven." At 5:30, he does two live custom stories, one for Richmond, Virginia, and another for Miami. He explains that "our stories give local stations the appearance of having their own guy in Washington. It brands their newscast, while giving national news more of a local feel."[36] An eight-year veteran of News Channel, Hanchett enjoys the work: "Generally we get sent to most of the major stories. If it's going well, if the technology's working, then it's rewarding. One of the frustrations is that we're tethered to a satellite truck. That allows us less time for reporting and fact-gathering than you would wish."[37]

Day-to-day news decisions at ABC's NewsOne are made by managing editor Geoff Sadow. He determines what will be covered and offered to affiliates. He says story selections "funnel through me. . . . Are we going to Tallahassee today to cover the Civil Rights Commission? To Southern California to cover the weather?" (The answer was yes on both counts.) "There is always breaking news somewhere. We've got to get people on a plane . . . get satellite trucks, deal with our bureaus and [regional] crews."[38] The same story may be covered by separate reporters for the affiliates, for the evening news, and for *Good Morning America*. Or NewsOne may supply material for all of them.

The head of CBS Newspath, John Frazee, has a professorial manner and is described by colleagues and competitors as a technical wizard. He joined the network in 1983 and has been vice president for news services since 1989. He describes the Newspath daily feed as "two-thirds news and one-third sports." He says 100 to 150 items come from regional operations and about 100 items are generated in Washington. He notes that the 300 items generated each day do not include the number of updated stories, which can add up to eight or nine by a single correspondent.[39]

NBC, working with another company based in Atlanta, Video Networks, Inc., is the first network to provide digital delivery of satellite news. Other news services require that affiliates roll videotape throughout the day to record incoming materials. NBC, on the other hand, is able to transmit stories and accompanying scripts to a computer server from which local producers can call up stories on their screens in the newsroom. In Charlotte, Sharon Houston demonstrates at her computer: "If I'm looking for the Supreme Court story, I click there and it comes to my desktop. Script and video are there. I decide if I want to use that or not." Horner proudly calls the NBC digital delivery system, called Video on Demand News Tracker, a real "game-changer," and the other networks plan to implement similar systems as soon as they can.

NBC's News Channel is investigating ways to incorporate the Internet into its daily feeds. "Video news mail," Sharon Houston says, "is a good digital step that would help us cover much more ground," enabling News Channel to distribute even more content.[40] CNN's Jack Womack says that, technologically, "the bar has been raised immensely. We have to do better than the other guys." He, too, is interested in Internet applications, along with video on demand and the uses of two-way fiber optic cable. Recently, CNN Newsource announced an alliance with Internet Broadcasting Systems, Inc., a network of local Web channels—Internet sites that combine local television news and information with a variety of Internet services. In all, CNN offers affiliates more than half a dozen services, ranging from Marketsource (custom and generic live shots from the floor of the New York Stock Exchange) to Guestsource (custom interviews by local anchors with newsmakers and recognized authorities that are arranged by CNN staffers) to Imagesource (local use of archived stock footage). One unusual role for the satellite-feed services is providing local news stories that are tied to the network's entertainment programming. The current crop of reality programs has spurred the use of such tie-ins: profiles of local participants in *Survivor* on CBS or *Who Wants to Be a Millionaire* on ABC were offered up by Newspath and NewsOne.

If there is a substantive downside to satellite-feed services, it may be that they facilitate saturation coverage of the story of the moment. Although such coverage of the Florida recount was clearly justified (and CBS Newspath provided more than 1,000 live stories in the month after the election), coverage of the O.J. Simpson case probably represents technological and journalistic overkill. NBC's News Channel produced an astounding 15,000 live stories during the entire course of the Simpson saga. News Channel reporter Jim Hanchett says, at least half-seriously, "I probably did 5,000 live shots myself."

Womack, Horner, Frazee, and Dunphy agree that satellite news services are an important force in building affiliate loyalty; beyond that, Dunphy says, in an era of network cutbacks in news budgets and personnel, affiliate services "have become the main news-gathering apparatus for breaking news."

Generally speaking, the affiliate feed services don't track which stories are used by which stations. And if affiliates turn down comparatively important stories to broadcast fluff, the news service doesn't have to provide a rationale for the choice. Nor does it have to directly worry about ratings. Producers and editors working for the news services appear to take pleasure in the focus on news for its own sake. NBC's Bob Horner speaks for all of them when he points to the enjoyment of "working with a staff motivated by coverage and content."

News managers believe that affiliate services, although operating up to now under the radar of national attention, play a vitally important role for their networks. Al Prieto, executive director of ABC NewsOne, says, "the importance of our service is that the local stations get material that they would never be able to get without spending much more money. . . . Their appetite now for news material is really insatiable."[41] Indeed, a seismic shift in U.S. television news has been playing out for a number of years. As local stations gained the ability to receive more news material from networks, local news expanded to an hour, then to ninety minutes, then in many markets to two and even three hours. Reese Schonfeld, formerly of CNN, argues that "network news got softer and softer" as a result.[42] The satellite revolution in local news is part of an economically and technologically driven revolution that may make local news more national and national news more local. The revolution is perhaps just starting.

An Insider's Look at the Newsroom

In the fall of 2001, the Public Broadcasting Service, specifically Thirteen/WNET in New York and Lumiere Productions, presented a groundbreaking documentary about local news, presented in five hour-long segments on PBS stations. Lumiere Productions is a highly regarded producer of documentaries on race, politics, history, and the media. *Local News* was a cinéma vérité treatment of what went on over a period of months as station WCNC-TV in Charlotte, North Carolina, faced a series of challenges inside the newsroom, in the community, and on the streets where its reporters worked.

The production team had almost total access to the station's news operation. Meetings concerning personnel and budget decisions were off-limits, but virtually everything else was open to the documentary filmmakers. Filming began in April 1999. The story of WCNC is the story of a station trying to catch up with the competition. In third place in its market, much of what it does or thinks about doing is related to the effort to get better ratings. Good people work at a station that is struggling to improve ratings and to serve its community. Often, the insider's view is not a pretty picture.

We are given an unprecedented, behind-the-scenes look at a station with a newly hired news director and a new owner, A.H. Belo, Inc. The news director, Keith Connors, is confronted almost immediately in Episode One with a conflict between ratings and journalistic ethics. By urging caution in the coverage of a story about bomb threats rippling through Charlotte's schools, he loses a big story but, he thinks, begins a process of building public trust. There is another ratings dilemma when several white families sue to overturn the city's 1971 school busing plan. Reporters and producers debate about how much trial coverage is appropriate—and how much will result in the loss of viewers. In the same episode, an African-American producer resigns, confiding to the camera that she believes the station is prejudiced, especially in its hiring and promotion practices.

In subsequent episodes, an African-American reporter for the station is fired, either for salary considerations or because of her age or because her homespun image is wrong for the new management. A public protest follows, with picketing and a lawsuit, and station morale nosedives. An attractive white female anchor is demoted to reporter when audience research shows she is not popular with female viewers. In the midst of the school-busing case, an important newscast falls apart when technical miscues undo a very hard day's work. News director Connors takes responsibility openly for the entire mess before the staff. The series ends on New Year's Eve. Connors is clearly chastened by his experience, and Belo executives are not happy with the news department's performance. A printed viewer's guide poses the questions: "Is WCNC's experiment the shining hope for local TV news? Or is it an impossible dream?"[43] The series has been dramatic and often painful to watch. The lesson most boldly etched over five hours is that it is very hard to do good journalism, civic or otherwise, at a local television station.

— 11 —

Network News and the New Environment

The Declining Audience

The evolution of American television and the changing nature of its audience have followed a pattern typical of the various media in societies as they move from a preindustrial phase, when the population is characterized by a low rate of literacy and small audiences that are comparatively well-educated and wealthy in relation to the vast majority of others (an "elite" audience, to use the label of the research literature), to the postindustrial climate often labeled "the information age," when technology is advanced and the population is comparatively well-off and well educated, with enough disposable income to pay for the use of multiple media outlets. The newspaper in colonial America, for example, was written for small numbers of educated people and generally served political or commercial purposes. True mass media were not possible before the Industrial Revolution. The American newspaper of the mid-nineteenth century came about as the result of greater literacy, but owed just as much to the railroads that transported newsprint across the continent, high-speed presses that were capable of circulations in the tens, then hundreds of thousands, and an advertising and circulation base that conferred economic viability on the entire enterprise. In this phase of newspaper development, the goal for publishers was clear: increase readership, sell more papers, and print news and information with the broadest appeal. From the mid-nineteenth century to the 1960s, that was more or less the formula for success for most newspapers and magazines.

American magazines, though, entered a third phase with the failure of the general-interest, mass-circulation magazine. *Life, Look,* the *Saturday Evening Post, Collier's*—the benchmark publications of an industry—failed because they could not support themselves financially. And the new formula for magazines became, instead, targeted readerships, targeted advertising, and market segmentation. Magazines would need to be molded to suit special-interest audiences—for business or hunting and fishing or entertainment or simply for young women and their interests. Competition was no longer for the largest audience, but for the right audience. Circulation had peaked years before. Now it was not how many people read, but who read that made the difference.

For magazines, the point of demarcation was the late 1950s and the early 1960s. In radio, the huge networks began losing steam in the 1970s. Even before then, however, music had been stratified so that each format dictated a particular demographic that a sales force turned around and marketed to advertisers. "Middle-of-the-road" music meant no rock 'n' roll, which for all practical purposes meant no teenagers, which meant no advertising for blue jeans and sneakers, which pretty soon became athletic shoes anyway. "Top 40" meant no Sinatra, no Broadway show tunes, and no commercials for life insurance. What was happening made economic sense to be sure, but it made societal sense as well. The media, armed with a multiplicity of approaches (we can call them "channels," of course), were capable of organizing the marketplace. Golfers could congregate at *Golf Digest*, possibly improve their iron play, and replace that sand wedge that never seemed to work. Now they can practice swinging the new club while watching the Golf Channel. Older Americans with traditional habits and values, neither yuppies nor regulars at power lunches, could lend an ear to radio commentator Paul Harvey. People who were interested in an around-the-world trip could get details in the Stanford or Princeton alumni magazines. Military families trying to make ends meet, on the other hand, could get useful tips from a large number of magazines always available near the base where they were stationed.

In television, dramatic change came a good deal more slowly. Indeed, the change is still taking place. Beginning in the 1970s, cable television became more available throughout the country. The measure called "cable penetration," which meant the percentage of homes wired for cable, was a guide to the erosion of network audiences. At first, cable penetration was slow, and the audience for network programs gradually, but inexorably, grew smaller. In the 1980s, as the first all-news channel premiered, the video-rental industry was sorting itself out (and, not coincidentally, the VHS format triumphed over Beta), providing the possibility of counter-programming on demand within one's own home. Meanwhile, other cable channels became more proficient at covering sports and providing commercial-free movies and the programming of several prior generations of situation comedies. In the 1990s, special-interest television flowered as home decorating, the environment, medicine, classic sports, science, World War II, science fiction, animal life, black entertainment, comedy, art-house movies, and many more specialized subjects found enough interest to sustain a channel dedicated to each niche audience and also able to make a profit. In the early 1990s, NBC executive Andy Lack told a private meeting of network news employees that the future of network news endeavors resembled a truck going downhill with no brakes, out of control and gaining speed as it approached a destination that no one, not one single industry expert in the world, could reliably predict.[1] The metaphorical truck, Lack did not need to point out, was dropping off more and more viewers as it descended, gathering speed, and no expert could predict how many viewers or what kind of viewers would be able to hold on or even might want to.

What could the networks do? The size of the audience for the three evening newscasts was down about 40 percent as the twenty-first century dawned. Network entertainment shows in prime time once were canceled if ratings fell below the high teens. Now a rating of 10 might be more than acceptable. (Keep in mind, however, that because of population growth, a rating point today represents many more homes than it did in the mid-1970s.) Some observers proclaimed as early as the 1960s that channel diversity—what became the age of cable and the cassette—would spell the end of network television. Perhaps surprisingly, they were wrong, even with the advent of new technologies and new sources of information.

The Internet, the one innovation that the futurists and engineers and sociologists had never predicted, meant that the audience had control of the content. The viewer programmed for himself or herself. An hour's worth of college lacrosse statistics? It's there, on-line. Fifteen reviews of the movie you're considering for tonight? No problem. Each woman her own editor. Each man his own news director. Could the networks compete?

The answer, at least for the time being, turned out to be yes, but the full explanation is not simple. No network saw a future in abandoning mass programming. The downside risk was enormous. CBS tried to launch a highbrow cable channel and gave up after losing $60 million. But eventually, and paradoxically, the networks realized that smaller could be bigger. The sitcom that had an audience of 25 million people in the 1970s generated substantial profits and was no doubt powerful, but in a fragmented television universe, the sitcom with 12 million viewers was not to be underestimated. Channel diversity ironically left the networks in some sense as important as they had been in the past because, in relative terms, they still drew the largest possible audiences.

When Media Giants Began to Roam the Earth

Still, there was no end in sight to the ongoing loss of audience members. Public corporations with a mandate to make more money each year could hardly be expected to accept declining profits every year of the foreseeable future, even if there were to be some profits for ten or twenty or forty years. To oversimplify the networks' financial history, neither NBC, ABC, Fox, the Warner Brothers (WB) and Paramount networks (UPN), nor CBS could devise a strategy for the future as a stand-alone television network. The impact and implications of new technology alone created massive uncertainty that required a coordinated and corporate approach. The networks needed to become more diversified themselves, and so they became spokes in a much larger wheel. After 1985, CBS was sold to Westinghouse, then to Viacom. NBC was purchased by General Electric, one of the two or three largest American corporations. ABC was purchased by Capital Cities Broadcasting, then by the Walt Disney Company. CNN became a part of AOL Time Warner.

Each media conglomerate hedged its bets in every direction. NBC became the leader in financial news on television with CNBC, which provided open-to-close coverage of the stock market, not to mention hours of comment and analysis beyond the day's trading. Together with the Dow Jones Company, the publisher of the *Wall Street Journal*, it produced CNBC International, allowing international investors the opportunity to get an up-close look at U.S. markets. NBC also joined Microsoft in the all-news channel MSNBC, at least opening the possibility of a digital future that melded broadcasting with innovations in computer software. General Electric expanded its nonmedia holdings and held its position as the most diversified company in the country with a major over-the-air network.

ABC, with the enormous power of Disney behind it, was part of a company that included ESPN, valued at more than $2 billion, extensive film, television, and radio properties, a major stake in music, games and toys, animation studios and technologies, the Internet, publishing, theater, sports, theme parks and resorts in America, Europe, and Asia, a virtual county in Florida where the largest single-site employer in America resides—Walt Disney World, employing more than 50,000 people in that part of Orange and Osceola Counties it calls its own (and where it has powers unlike any private entity in America, including police security and zoning with no governmental review). Disney leavens the mix with other media-related businesses operating all over the world.

CBS belonged to Viacom, with corporate partners including the Blockbuster video chain, local television stations, the globe-spanning MTV Networks, radio giant Infinity Broadcasting, the publisher Simon & Schuster, Black Entertainment Television (BET), and the Showtime cable network. Other media giants, such as News Corporation, built on a base of newspaper ownership in many parts of the world and added film, cable, Internet, and other media companies as they grew.

The media leviathans include half a dozen conglomerates—AOL Time Warner, News Corp., Disney, Viacom, Bertelsmann, General Electric, and perhaps a few others such as Sony and AT&T. The industry can be likened to a solar system with no sun. In the inner ring are the titanic companies. There is an outer ring of another six to eight companies that analysts believe will either be bought by or will buy enough assets to join the larger class of planets (perhaps Hearst, for example, or the Tribune Company, or Vivendi Universal). Then there is a third ring of more than a dozen valuable, but smaller or more focused, corporations (such as the Washington Post and the New York Times companies), all of which have the potential to merge or be merged.

Beyond returning profits to shareholders, the companies have somewhat different compositions and philosophies.[2] Each employs both vertical integration, defined as the control of a product from the raw-material stage to its sale, and horizontal integration, which is the ownership of companies, divisions, or affiliates that perform the same or similar functions or produce the same or similar products, such as news and entertainment. The Washington Post Company, for example, began as a classical case of vertical integration—timber holdings that produced pulp; paper-making machinery that converted pulp to newsprint; presses, reporters and editors to produce the *Washington Post* and *Newsweek* magazine. It became horizontally integrated with other media holdings, especially in broadcasting. To a considerable extent, Viacom and Disney are vertically integrated in the sense that books often become the raw material for movies, which in turn become the raw material for television, cable, and related retail products. Each of these companies also employs horizontal integration.

Each newspaper in Chicago owns a television station. The major networks own television stations in Chicago. In fact, there *isn't* a television station in Chicago that is not owned by a media conglomerate of some sort. For American media, specifically for television news outlets, the agglomeration of assets was a matter of financial necessity because of the declining audience base. According to a stock market analyst interviewed in the *New York Times*, "economic reality says that ABC, for instance, shouldn't be in the news business at all. CBS should just be doing '60 Minutes.'"[3] Wall Street analysts say ABC and CBS could make significantly more money if they completely eliminated their news divisions and kept only those programs that make sizable profits:

> ABC News, for instance, is estimated to have brought in $500 million of revenue last year [2001]. It spent nearly as much, however, and is estimated to have finished the year with less than $30 million of earnings before interest, taxes, depreciation and amortization [of assets]. . . . In times like these, a network news operation can seem a particularly bad business. News costs are high . . . [and] advertising revenues are low because of the struggling economy.[4]

From a business perspective, it seems that the evening newscasts are allowed to exist because of the financial help provided by *Today*, *Good Morning America*, CNBC, and MSNBC, no less than the revenues of *The West Wing* and *Survivor*. One media analyst for a New York brokerage says, "There is no legitimate business rationale for a stand-alone broadcast network news group. You need at least one of the two following approaches: either an extremely profitable prime-time franchise or a cable channel that fits well, like the NBC model."[5]

> The things that could conceivably stand in the way of the elimination [of regular network newscasts] are inertia and regulatory interests. Without network news, the thinking goes . . . , the parents of CBS, NBC, and ABC, respectively, could be criticized by politicians for not acting in the public interest, as their licenses require. That could bring added scrutiny or restrictions to their deal-making.[6]

CBS Television president Leslie Moonves was asked why news remained important given its costliness and failure to add to the bottom line. "If I wanted to put on Tonya Harding boxing," he responded, "it would do better than Dan Rather financially. Yes, profit is very important. We're part of Viacom and my job is to make a profit. But we still are a public trust."[7] The full commitment of the network to that public trust is under intense questioning, though, and some of it has come from Dan Rather, who has objected to the networks' use of tabloid material. "You have to remember, the tension existing between the corporation and the news division is not something new—it's a fact of life," said Robert A. Iger, the president of Disney. "The news division gets everything in terms of editorial independence. But not in terms of financial independence."[8]

160

Is Big Media Bad?

In several important books, media scholar Robert W. McChesney argues that the concentration of corporate control of American media has reached the point at which it is no longer possible to sustain a meaningful democracy.[9] Concentrated media power such as the oligopoly (meaning the control of a market by a few companies) that now exists is, he points out with an impressive amount of evidence, nonresponsive to the citizenry and, as a consequence, largely responsible for a marked decline in citizen participation in virtually all aspects of American public and civic life:

> Participatory self-government, or democracy, works best when at least three criteria are met. First, it helps when there are not significant disparities in wealth and property ownership across the society. Such disparities undermine the ability of citizens to act as equals. Second, it helps when there is a sense of community and a notion that an individual's well-being is determined to no small extent by the community's well-being. . . . Third, democracy requires that there be an effective system of political communication, broadly construed, that informs and engages the citizenry, drawing people meaningfully into the polity.[10]

In McChesney's view, private ownership of U.S. media has worked in such a way as to encourage a weak political culture that is characterized by depoliticization, individual apathy, and selfishness. McChesney relates the noninvolvement of U.S. citizens to the absence of a true "public sphere" for democratic discourse. The concept of the public sphere was articulated by European scholar Jurgen Habermas, somewhat idealistically, as a feature of democratic societies in the eighteenth and nineteenth centuries. The public sphere was independent of both state and business control, a space that allowed citizens to interact and debate the issues of the day.[11] McChesney endorses the return to a situation in which the public sphere has not lost its democratic capacities as the result of business control of any serious debate or airing of public issues.

So: Is Big Media bad for its audiences and for society at large? The question is devilishly complex and probably has no easy answers, but we can at least establish a framework for a discussion that may produce reasoned inquiries and, if necessary, social action to correct perceived inequities.

On one hand, the media conglomerates have the resources—and by that I mean the human capital—to produce media products of very high quality. The takeover of a locally owned newspaper by the Tribune Company or the *New York Times* has generally yielded a better newspaper. The worst newspapers in the country—and, of course, there is an argument over how anyone could make such a judgment without bias, but it will be made here anyway—generally have not been those owned by the conglomerates. Also, Disney, AOL Time Warner, and Viacom generally improve the properties they purchase. On the other hand, there is a key principle within the rationale for the First Amendment of the Constitution of the United States, the justification for free expression, that is absolute in its insistence on open access to the public forum. Supreme Court Justice Oliver Wendell Holmes made the argument succinctly when he said in a ruling that, in a democracy, two voices are better than one, three are better than two, four are better than three, and so on.[12] An oligopoly might be acceptable for U.S.-made automobiles. It might be acceptable for long-distance carriers, even though in both cases there hover about possibilities for collusive action and price manipulation. Still, one can argue easily that news is something altogether different. Are we to expect the truth if our only sources are three or four corporate behemoths? McChesney's answer is clear: no, we cannot.

To pose the question another way: Is it a source of concern, or should it be, that more than half of all books in the United States are sold by two companies, Borders and Barnes and Noble? For many consumers, the answer, at first blush, would be no. The two dominant booksellers are able to stock most books that readers would want and to price them reasonably. The two chains stock travel books, how-to books, children's books—they are the American supermarkets of publishing. But a case exists that, first, there are books that might not be marketable at Borders or Barnes and Noble. For such publications, the market power of the two companies is a formidable disincentive that keeps them and many other books from being published in the first place. As the small booksellers vanished in this country, the small presses that supplied their inventory also became less economically viable. In sum, the social good does not necessarily reside only in the books that I would want to read, or that the average consumer might want to read, but in the books that anyone would want to read—and write. Convenience, and discounted prices, have a social cost.

In Washington, U.S. congressman Bernie Sanders, an independent from Vermont, has begun a campaign against the concentration of corporate power that "controls the media." In April 2002, 600 citizens attended two town meetings in Vermont at which Sanders called corporate media control "one of the most important and least discussed issues facing our country."[13] Sanders contends that media ownership by massive conglomerates keeps many key issues out of the news:

> American workers now work the longest hours in any industrialized country. Where was the media discussion about the declining standard of living for millions of American workers? The United States is the only major nation that does not have a national health-care program guaranteeing health care to

all its people. Yet, with 41 million uninsured, and millions more under-insured, we spend twice per capita on health care than any other country. Heard any media discussions on that issue? We have many programs telling you how to get rich in the stock market. On the other hand, despite the fact that union workers earn 30 percent more than non-union workers for the same kind of job, there is no programming which speaks to how one can form a union, or the advantages of trade unionism. Our country has a $360 billion trade deficit, and has lost millions of good manufacturing jobs. Seen any good editorials or TV programming lately which speaks to the enormous problems with our trade policy?[14]

Does corporate ownership in effect censor the news? American society is probably too complex for an information conspiracy theory to be a sufficient explanation of how Big Media work. There are clear problems with the media oligopoly, however, and they can be stated as possible threats to the exercise of democracy and the free exchange of ideas. In the media systems of many other countries and in the regulation of American broadcast media, there is an implicit premise: the market will not provide everything we need, as individuals or as a society. Commercial television will not devote hours to the superb epic film *The Civil War* by Ken Burns, which appeared on PBS. Commercial media won't do justice to trade unionism or the systemic problem of health care or the declining standard of living, for whatever reason. (It may be the case that millions of people would rather watch *Survivor* instead.) Big Media poses these threats that need to be assessed and that deserve formal scrutiny:

1. Are conglomerates using their power to close off the entry of others, especially those less powerful, to the marketplace? Any collusion that restricts the free flow of information is dangerous.

2. Are voices outside the mainstream—especially voices that threaten the mainstream—being systematically excluded from our national conversation?

3. Do corporate goals result in the homogenization of opinion through the exclusion of dissonant voices?

4. Are there indisputable instances in which corporate control of media produces control of content because of the vested interests of ownership?

5. Is legislation needed to prevent the further accumulation of media power through several more rounds of mergers and acquisitions?

Congressman Sanders has staked out a clear position on these matters. He believes the threat has become a reality and that it is time to take corrective measures. Doing so will require a degree of national consensus about the problem that has yet to be created. But it is fair to say that the questions surrounding Big Media give us important issues to think about. More than that, citizens need to pay attention to the media marketplace and be active audiences rather than passive receivers of whatever the media conglomerates serve up.[15]

Market-Driven Journalism

No news operation, from *Time* magazine and CBS News to the college newspaper and the church newsletter, can dismiss the business elements of being an information provider. There is a limit to what can be spent and a need to maximize resources if one is to do the best job possible. Judgments about where reporters can be sent always are part of a cost-benefit analysis. However, "market-driven journalism" refers to something beyond that, to the undesirable filtering of news decisions through the prism of profit considerations. The phrase is meant itself as a warning that the public interest is not being served, and the warning and attendant concerns have produced an interesting literature.[16]

In the United States, news is a commodity, the end-product of a complicated industrial process in which large organizations produce and distribute information for purchase. Too much is at stake financially for news organizations to operate in the dark. What news is the most desired? What news will draw an audience? What news will generate reader and viewer loyalty, so that the customer comes back again? Television networks employ researchers to answer, as best they can, those questions and others like them. Local stations purchase research on how to select, report, and gather news profitably.[17] News about welfare reform doesn't sell. And there isn't much of it to watch on television. News about how to lose weight and how to stay healthy with just a little exercise is in demand in every key demographic. And news about health has never been so popular or so available. News about Indonesia, volatile politically, the fourth most populous country in the world, has no constituency here at home. Americans have trouble locating it on a map, along with El Salvador, Libya, Bagdad, or Beijing. Television may educate, but viewers receive a selective education.

Buffeted by market forces, electronic journalism in America has spent so much time packaging news to make it appetizing that it has lost much of its nutritional value. That is apparent not just in the most obvious examples. It is true that episodic instances of crime with no large social significance are overcovered, that the world outside our borders is undercovered, that elections are about more than who wins, and that good pictures make good television. But the marketplace has produced a preference for sound-bite journalism that tells us very little about the world at our doorsteps. We may be able to judge schools on the basis of test scores, but we know very little about what is being taught; whether the school environment is indeed safe; whether teachers and principals are effectively trained and responsive to the telephone calls of parents; whether there are policies for handling playground bullies; whether schools practice community outreach in any meaningful way.

McChesney makes an excellent point when he describes how American news media took the "public affairs" out of "news and public affairs," historically what television journalism prided itself on as its public-service contribution.[18] Where on television is real community discourse on issues that matter? The market-driven forms of journalism may on occasion mean that an advertiser gets preferential treatment on the air or in the press. The media company may use its own programs to reflect favorably on itself. But, with respect to television, market-driven journalism is most serious when it means less time for news (the time available on evening newscasts for news is down by at least four minutes over the last two decades—four minutes now given over to promos, teasers, and more commercials) and when it keeps information off the air because, no matter how important, audience research indicates that some news is nonmarketable or at least less marketable than desired. Media critic Ben Bagdikian summarizes the impact of market power as follows:

> The problem is not one of universal evil among the corporations or their leaders. Nor is it a general practice of constant suppression and close monitoring of the content of their media companies. There is, in the output of the dominant fifty [media companies], a rich mixture of news and ideas. But there are also limits, limits that do not exist in most other democratic countries with private enterprise media. The limits are felt on open discussion of the system that supports giantism in corporate life and of other values that have been enshrined under the inaccurate label "free enterprise."[19]

1976 versus 1996

To assess the changes in network news, I content-analyzed the evening news on ABC, CBS, and NBC during two weeks twenty years apart. The first week was that of April 15, 1976. The corresponding week twenty years later was the week of April 19, 1996. The content comparison appears in Table 11.1.

The 1996 newscasts were focused on both hard news and features. The most-covered story was the bombing of the federal building in Oklahoma City, with thirty-four stories accounting for 18 percent of the total number of stories. Second was the conflict between Israel and Lebanon, with sixteen stories and 8.5 percent. Third were stories about the Unabomber at

CNN's chief international correspondent, Christiane Amanpour, had a high profile as a reporter in such dangerous places as Rwanda, Bosnia-Herzegovina, and Afghanistan. *(Courtesy of Photofest, New York)*

Table 11.1

An Analysis of Nightly News Coverage for the Week of April 15, 1976, Compared with the Same Week in 1996

	1976	Percentage	1996	Percentage	Change**
Total Stories	251	n/a	191	n/a	−60
Average per newscast	16.7	n/a	12.7	n/a	−4
Election news	33	13	1	0.5	−962
Other politics	40	16	15	8	−50
Foreign affairs	19	7.5	14	7	−0.07
Economics	18	7	20	10.5	50
Arts and culture	33	13	1	0.5	−962
Science	5	2	18	9.5	375
Lifestyle	18	7	20	10.5	50
Other national	32	13	74	40	207
Other regional	40	16	15	8	−50
Other international	54	21.5	35	18	−16.30
Features	29	11.5	44	23	−100
Foreign correspondence*	24	20	23	23	15
D.C.-based stories*	21	8.5	7	3.5	−58.80

*Not a topic used in the content analysis of the newscasts (some stories were double-coded so that the total exceeds 100 percent).
**Growth or decline of a particular topic as a percentage of the newscasts.

eight and 5 percent. Regional stories, such as a worker's strike in San Francisco and a hot-air balloon crash in Arizona, were defined as short-lived stories having little impact on the nation as a whole. The three networks were, in the main, similar in their choice of subject matter. In 1996, NBC had the fewest international stories of the three networks, and half as many international stories as it had in 1976. NBC had the largest number of feature stories in 1996, an average of three per newscast.

The three networks aired 25 percent fewer stories in 1996 than in 1976. The number of features doubled in twenty years, and the number of health-and-science stories grew significantly. The author's interpretation of these measures is that news became more viewer-friendly. There was considerably more human interest and more lifestyle-related "news you can use." This comparison does not, however, support the assertion that news became necessarily more trivial or diverting.

The Future of Network News

There is no compelling reason to write the obituary of the network news divisions or, for that matter, of the nightly evening newscasts. ABC, CBS, and NBC earn a profit on their news operations, even with a declining audience. Interestingly, the three networks, with the addition of Fox, will lose more than $600 million on their sports divisions in 2002, according to reports.[20] If this isn't a time to mourn the passing of network news, though, it's not a time to celebrate, either. So many of the changes in the news environment in the last twenty-five years have taken the networks farther and farther away from the goals of public service and accountability. The pioneers of American broadcasting were owner/proprietors who had a clear notion that public service was part of the social pact that allowed them to broadcast. William S. Paley and Frank Stanton at CBS, David Sarnoff at NBC, and, beginning in 1953, Leonard Goldenson at ABC wanted to have strong news divisions and did not view news as one more opportunity to make money.[21] When control passed to larger corporations, news divisions became answerable to corporate heads who treated them as essentially no different than any other division of General Electric or Viacom or Disney. The bottom line was what mattered.

Ed Fouhy, a distinguished news executive at all three networks through the 1960s, 1970s, and 1980s, says the diminished importance of television news to its own proprietors is related to two other phenomena: first, the failure of television journalists and news managers at each of the networks to communicate the core values of service, accuracy, and objectivity—indeed, the unshakable importance of news itself—to their corporate bosses; and second, the reality that television news was fortunate in the 1960s and 1970s to be reporting huge, developing stories of great importance—civil rights, Vietnam, to a degree the space program— that were perfect for the medium of television. In the absence of such stories, it became easier to forget how powerful the medium could be.[22] In the 1970s, Ed Fouhy was the head of the CBS Washington bureau, and he had about twice as many reporters as the bureau does today. The networks today "do almost no reporting," he says. "When was the last time you saw a network correspondent break a story?" Fouhy says that he finds all the economic forces at work in network news "quite negative" and that he has never been so pessimistic about the future of TV news as he is today.

> The tragedy to me is not so much for the people [in television news] and the corporations, although those are certainly sad stories. The tragedy is for the country. Because if history is any guide at all, it is true that we will face another national calamity like Vietnam or like civil rights, and we won't have the ability to knit ourselves together and to reach a consensus over time because there won't be the kind of national attention to the news that there was during those events.[23]

The "Lessons" of 9/11/01

It has become hackneyed now to say that America learned some hard lessons from the terror attacks on New York and Washington. There were, indeed, painful and important lessons. We learned that the world is a more dangerous place than we thought. We learned that our own cities are not immune from death and horror originating in mysterious places on the other side of the globe. We learned the limits of our technology and of our intelligence agencies. We learned the precariousness of our national and personal security.

In the days and months after the World Trade Center attack, we were reminded that journalism, especially television news, was again a powerful national force in a time of crisis. The networks' news divisions seemed to wake from a twenty-year slumber, jolted into a new sense of responsibility to the audience. In those first days, there was always time on the air for more details about the assault and the nation's response. Commercials were not run until the time was deemed appropriate, at least four days after the attack on the four major networks. Professional journalism publications deservedly applauded the brave actions of reporters faced with danger and unimaginable scenes of human suffering here at home.[24]

We were told that American journalism, even television journalism, had shaken off the cobwebs of frivolity and fluff. One newspaper story was headlined "Serious Agenda, Serious Interest." "Most news organizations rose to the challenge," the *Baltimore Sun* reported, "providing an enormous amount of coverage of Afghanistan and post-Sept. 11 events." [25] Andrew Kohut, director of the Pew Research Center for the People and the Press, said that for the first time in fifteen years, the public image of journalists had improved. Polling conducted from mid-September through November 2001 showed that a significant number of people, between 50 and 75 percent of those surveyed, saw the press as professional, moral, patriotic, and compassionate. Kohut noted that these results reversed a pattern of declining regard for U.S. journalists:

> Much of the decline in perception of the press in terms of its values occurred during the Clinton/Lewinsky scandal years. That's when the American public began to doubt not only the press's performance and how it does its job, but began to doubt its values. This survey shows some considerable rebounding, at least for now, on these measures.[26]

But the rebound in measures of popular approval has obscured some truths about television's capabilities and inclinations in 2002. First, some general statements about American television news apply to this particular disaster:

169

- When the United States is attacked or suffers a true calamity, at the very least the major networks will respond in a pro-American fashion.
- Supreme crises historically have brought out the best in the American news media, although there have been a few exceptions.
- In moments of national duress, television news has the power to reassure viewers and provide solace to the country and its citizens.

The events of September 11 reinforced these truths and apparently helped change the opinion of many Americans about the news media. In the aftermath, many analyses concluded that the terrorist attacks marked the end of television news' flirtation with matters of little substance.

I don't suggest that we should worry because things have more or less returned to normal; that's to be expected, on television, in our homes, and in much of our daily life. Consider instead what television news could not or would not do with respect to this one huge cluster of stories, as well as the ways in which the news media performed admirably.

The commercial networks and the all-news channels as well were slow off the mark in covering breaking news on the actual day of attack. NBC News, for example, was extraordinarily slow in getting reporters anywhere near the Twin Towers. Despite the assumed advantages of covering a story in a city where the network has headquarters—and an owned-and-operated affiliate, WNBC, with reporters, vans, videographers, and helicopters on call—only two reporters, not well informed by any means, did most of the live reporting from an admittedly dangerous and chaotic scene. The networks all took too much time to knock down the erroneous story of a bomb at the State Department. ABC, NBC, and CBS hit full stride, it appeared to me, only when their formidable teams of news magazine producers and reporters could tell the heartbreaking, up-close feature stories of what really had happened to individuals caught up in the fury.

On September 11, the pictorial quality of television news-gathering was stunning until it became mind-numbing. It was mind-numbing until the unthinking repetition of the same images became both banal and unbearable to watch. My students at the University of Maryland asked me over and over why the networks kept replaying the same horrible visuals. Many of them were simply unable to watch the coverage after a few minutes. After numerous complaints, ABC News decided to no longer use video of the attack, the resulting fireball, or the collapse of the Twin Towers. "It's probably the most powerful image of our time," said ABC News president David Westin. "I was concerned that it was becoming almost like wallpaper. There's a temptation in television to go to the most powerful image. But it was playing a lot. I was concerned not only for adults but for children."[27] Electronic journalism was no more valiant, and no more socially responsible, on September 11 than when President John F. Kennedy was assassinated, when the space shuttle *Challenger* exploded, or in May 1989 in Tiananmen Square in Beijing. Deputy executive editor Gloria Cooper of the *Columbia Journalism Review* had only words of praise for her colleagues who covered the horror: "The nation's news media conducted themselves with the courage, honesty, grace, and dedication a free society deserves. In that tragic emergency, America's journalists knew what they needed to do. And, for the record, they did it."[28] With time to reflect, perhaps Ms. Cooper has reconsidered her words. All the anchors were excellent, but wasn't something missing in the coverage? Anything? Was the banner headline in the San Francisco Examiner ("Bastards!") a "lesson" for journalism students?[29] If so, what exactly should it teach them? More to the point, how much did we know then, or do we know today, about Osama bin Laden? Were you surprised that the White House, the Capitol, and the Pentagon were so poorly protected? Was anyone at the networks surprised?

The television coverage of the war in Afghanistan was significant for several reasons, one of which was an important advance in technology. Correspondents from all the American networks, as well as reporters for the British Broadcasting Corporation and Associated Press Television, used lightweight and relatively inexpensive videophones to transmit their stories from remote war locales. The videophones send about twenty frames per second, a grainy, halting image but a usable one. David Verdi, executive director of news for NBC, says the $7,500 phones can be set up or dismantled in minutes. "The biggest leap for us," he says, "is that we can now go to the story and broadcast from there, without having to leave and find a way to get the material out."[30] Using the phones, reporters can broadcast to a satellite virtually undetected in the midst of a wartime theater of action.[31] The question remained, of course, whether news coverage in general would change as the result of the terrorist attacks, whether new, mobile technologies would encourage more international news. The chairman of CNN, Walter Isaacson, said shortly after the attack that, some time earlier, television news had lost its way. "I think this has been a wake-up call to the public and to all of us in the news business that there are certain things that matter more than the latest trivial thing that can cause a ratings boost," he told the *New York Times*. "It's helped all of us regain our focus."[32] But Paul Friedman, executive vice president of ABC News, was not so sure. "I don't know that the current interest [in international news] will continue much beyond this story, no matter how long it lasts."[33]

David Sarnoff (left), visionary, radio pioneer, and head of NBC, with former President Herbert Hoover, who designed federal regulation of the airwaves as secretary of commerce in the 1920s. *(NBC/Broadcast Pioneers Library of American Broadcasting, University of Maryland—College Park)*

— 12 —

Electronic Journalism and the Public Interest

The Public-Service Model of Broadcasting

Great Britain established the model for state-sponsored or state-controlled, public-interest broadcasting in virtually all Western democracies with the notable exception of the United States. Decisions were made early in the development of British radio, and then television, to utilize the broadcast media for goals of individual and social improvement. This often has been called a public-enlightenment approach to the media by government, in which the media perform a role akin to that of a missionary. This may have a paternalistic, Big Brother sound in the United States in the twenty-first century, but, even considering the addition of commercial broadcast outlets in Europe and many revisions in the execution of public-service broadcasting, the house is sturdy and still stands. In much of the democratic world, broadcasting is still considered a public trust. As an example, the British Broadcasting Corporation offers extensive news coverage, with a corps of correspondents based around the world, and a wide range of cultural programs; no commercial sponsorship or advertising; and free time offered to political parties and candidates during election campaigns.

The history of British regulation of broadcasting dates to 1922, when a group of major wireless manufacturers, including the Marconi Company and General Electric, formed the British Broadcasting Company. John Reith was appointed its first general manager. The next year, the government appointed the first of many commissions to inquire into broadcasting and how it should be financed, managed, and supervised. A committee under the chairmanship of Sir Frederick Sykes interviewed thirty-two witnesses and received information on radio in the United States, Canada, and Australia. It considered advertising as a means of financing broadcasting, but decided instead to retain the system of issuing a licensing fee on the use of radio receivers.[1]

John Reith (later Lord Reith) was convinced that radio—and later television—had great potential as instruments for information, entertainment, and education. He insisted that broadcasters act in the public interest, with a strong sense of social responsibility. Broadcasting in Britain became a monopoly, financed by the license fee paid by the public and provided by an independent public authority. On television, the original service grew to BBCI, BBCII, and regional stations. In radio, there eventually would be several national channels, regional networks, and more than forty local stations. The BBC is independent of government control of editorial and management processes, but cannot promote its own views through editorials.[2]

Between 1955 and 1990, an independent sector of the broadcasting industry, with programming supported mainly by advertising and sponsorship, was established by the Independent Broadcasting Authority (IBA), which was replaced in 1991 by the Independent Television Commission (ITC) and the Radio Authority. Independent television includes Channel 3, made up of regional licensees (such as Granada, Scottish, and Anglia Television), and the comparatively experimental and innovative Channel 4, set up in 1982.[3]

Other European Broadcast Systems

In Western Europe, most governments followed the British example with some modification. Governments owned the transmitters, land lines, and other equipment. In Italy, Belgium, Sweden, and Norway, radio was, as in the U.K., administered by autonomous public entities answerable to the parliament or government for budgets. In Portugal and Spain, private commercial companies ran the system. The Netherlands gave responsibility for programming to independent, private broadcasting societies coordinated by a public corporation. In France, broadcasting was a function of the central government and was administered by civil servants.[4] German broadcasting was from the outset considerably more decentralized. Most European broadcast systems now have a public-interest base with a growing number of commercial program sources—a dual system of public and private broadcasting.

The New Regulatory Climate

In the United States, Ronald Reagan became president in 1980 with a clear mandate to deregulate American industry to the greatest extent feasible. There was, in fact, a blueprint for deregulation at the center of the Republican Party policy apparatus; it had been provided by the conservative Heritage Foundation, which targeted the communication industries for "comprehensive deregulation." The foundation's *Mandate for Leadership* argued that "regulation threatens to destroy the private competitive free market economy it was originally designed to protect."[5] The law that regulated communication in the United States was still the Communications Act of 1934, forty-six years old at the beginning of Reagan's first term and written in a different world, in which no one had a TV set (much less cable television), a computer, or a cordless phone.

Deregulation of the media meant creating a new framework for all of telecommunication, in the widest application of that word. Apart from broadcasting, and apart from the pervasive influence that large media companies might wield, there was a set of difficult and in some cases technical issues to resolve. During the two Reagan terms, the Federal Communications Commission, under the leadership of the extremely probusiness chairman, Mark Fowler, took a lead role in changing the regulatory environment from one that was concerned with ensuring fairness to one that focused on economic efficiency.[6] In a coauthored article in a 1982 law review, Fowler stated his objective with not a single frill. "Our thesis," Fowler and Brenner said bluntly, "is that the perception of broadcasters as community trustees should be replaced by a view of broadcasters as marketplace participants. Communications policy should be directed toward maximizing the services the public desires. . . . The public's interest, then, defines the public interest."[7] The FCC began the process of deregulating broadcasting, with one free-market measure after another.

But comprehensive legislation would take more time—until 1996, to be precise. At the outset, Congressional Democrats blocked comprehensive reform; nonetheless, any new law would have to deal with a number of very tough issues, to which there were many involved parties. Broadcasting was just part of a huge patchwork that included satellite transmission, long-distance service, and the digitizing of information processing. It included the role of the so-called Baby Bells, the regional companies spun out from AT&T. The regional Bells wanted to be able to produce content as well as distributing it. The regulations for long-distance telephone service would need to be significantly revised. And by the 1990s, the future was clearly digital. Lawmakers faced the question of standards for digital radio, television, and more: what would they be, and when could they be implemented, once decided upon? By February 8, 1996, when President Bill Clinton signed into law the Telecommunications Act of 1996, the law it replaced was almost sixty-two years old. What had happened in communication in those sixty-two years is just short of unfathomable—a technological, social, and cultural revolution.

The new legislation rewrote the basic law that governs communication from top to bottom. Its implications are so far-reaching that many of them have yet to receive the attention that undoubtedly will ensue. The old law was, in its day, the result of a compact between government and business.[8] The new law emerged as a compact between Big Government and Big Business. The outcome was a promarket document that invoked the public interest while relaxing public-interest standards.

Public-service advocates were more than distressed when the law gave broadcasters greater powers of concentration and cross-ownership, and much greater security in the holding of their licenses. Communication scholar Patricia Aufderheide called the legislation a set of "gift boxes" to the media industries:

> [The 1996 Telecommunications Act] maintains [broadcasters'] public trustee obligations but does not specify or extend them. . . . Broadcasters successfully maintained the privileges of an old order—preservation of monopoly control over spectrum—while claiming to be potential players in a competitive environment.[9]

The law places the future of digital television in the hands of broadcasters. It substantially reduces limits on ownership. In radio, it allows one owner as many as half the stations in a single market. In television, a single owner may buy stations that reach up to 35 percent of the national audience. (At one time, not that far distant, a company could own only five VHF stations.) In the fifty largest markets, it is now legal to own more than one TV station. It is also legal to own a TV station and a cable system in the same place. The 1996 law extends license renewals to every eight years (it had been five for television and seven for radio). The law virtually invites mergers by removing the regulatory barriers to multiple and cross-ownership. In a strange way, it was as if the 1934 experience had been reenacted. The public "owns" the airwaves, but again that ownership is in theory only. The practical truth is that the system is as private as ever, given new opportunities to enhance its financial and cultural might. The new law is simply put, a triumph for commercial interests.

The Internet

The Internet is already changing the nature of communication, and it has been viewed by some scholars as the democratizing medium of the future. Its implications for society and for journalism remain unclear, nonetheless. As this is written, the Internet makes available to its users a great deal of opinion, or opinion presented as fact, with much less information that is arrived at independently or reliably. There are few sites on the Internet where one can can find actual reporting, and much of the news that appears on mainstream sites is from the Associated Press or at Web sites maintained by newspapers. So the notion that the new medium will add voices to our national and global dialogue may be true; to date, it has added much less in the way of journalism.

Nicholas Negroponte of the Massachusetts Institute of Technology is an outspoken proponent of the digital future that awaits us. "The Internet is wildly underestimated," he states. "It will grow to be the enabling technology of all media—TV, radio, magazines, and so on."[10] His argument extends to the idea that the Internet will be enabling for individuals most of all, allowing them avenues of access to the public arena that may undermine corporate and commercial control of the future.[11] The questions of corporate ownership of the Internet, or at least ownership of the portals that are the most frequently used, has yet to be resolved definitively. But for other observers, the signs are ominous.

The Internet was created by the U.S. government in the 1960s as a project to share computing power through the Department of Defense. The network was soon opened to university programmers and computer industry engineers. Tim Berners-Lee, inventor of the protocols still in use, named his project the World Wide Web when there were only three connections to it. Ellen Ulman, a writer and former computer programmer, believes that the public Internet is already gone: "By 1994, the Internet had become a sales medium, its ownership ceded by default to commercial interests."[12] She notes that AOL, with already inordinate control, sells off "every square pixel of the screen" for profit. The relationships that bind the Web together, she contends, comprise "the whole range of product-placement and payola that determines the content of a Web page, the new and invisible techno-middlemen hiding in the code."[13]

McChesney echoes that theme in his insistence that corporate giants have already laid claim to the web:

> As an Internet stock manager put it in 1998, Internet company stock prices were "driven up by speculation about who will be the next company to get

snapped up by a much bigger company from another medium as a way of buying their way on to the Internet." . . . What should be clear is that this "market system" may work in the sense that goods and services are produced and consumed, but it is by no means fair in any social or political or ethical sense of the term. Existing corporations have tremendous advantages over start-up firms. They use their power to limit the ability of new firms to enter the fray, to limit output and keep prices higher. . . . A tremendous amount of talent simply never gets an opportunity to develop and contribute to the economy. It is unremarkable that "self-made" billionaires like Bill Gates [Microsoft], Ted Turner, Michael Eisner [Disney], Rupert Murdoch, and Sumner Redstone [Viacom] all come from privileged backgrounds.[14]

There are other perspectives, of course. Web sites for newspapers and magazines often encourage public response to questions of policy or seek comment about professional journalistic practices. Many writers have their e-mail addresses posted in print, making possible a form of two-way communication that is much more direct and effective than letter-writing. Scholars Jay Blumler and Michael Gurevitch view the present moment as "analogous to the early days of policy-making for radio. . . . The corresponding challenge today is to fashion and apply," they write, a public service role for the Internet and other online services. They find that it may be possible to create a public, well-supported, and vigorous "civic commons" in cyberspace. Such a public space might be created by "eliciting, gathering, and coordinating" citizens' reactions to and deliberations about matters of public concern.[15]

A Checkered History of Public Service

The relationship between U.S. broadcast news and the concept of public service has been problematic since the early days of radio. In the 1920s, radio was viewed as a technological wonder that offered public service almost *regardless* of what its programming actually was. It was a service to the audience to have the opportunity to be exposed to live popular and classical music, to have advance reports of forbidding weather, to listen to lectures on grooming and success, to hear the live broadcasts of Jack Benny and Bob Hope. The dictum that entertainment was one thing and news another—that news was an expression of a community-oriented service ethic and entertainment an engine to make money—simply did not apply. That networks with a clear profit motive took charge of the development of the broadcast media cannot be disputed. It neither can be viewed as the tainted early history of American media. That argument only makes sense in retrospect. To the listening public in the 1920s and 1930s, entertainment itself was the essence of public service.

178

As television became a national force, news and public affairs were sources of corporate prestige and personal pride. Executives at Edward R. Murrow's CBS knew that his most controversial (and historic) broadcasts were, if anything, losing money for the network. But the CBS chairman, William S. Paley, and the network president, Frank Stanton, at least for a while took pride in the courage they expressed by allowing Murrow's team to take controversial positions on domestic and international issues. They were less sanguine about the backlash from offended public officials who threatened the network in the aftermath of a Murrow–Friendly exposé. Their initial pride reflected the strength of a powerful, and socially responsible, institution. Their subsequent distaste for making powerful enemies reflected a reality of much longer duration. At its height, NBC News took considerable pride in its mastery of convention coverage, its leadership in the evening news, and its corps of widely respected correspondents posted around the world.

For the networks, the imposed expectation of public service was burdensome insofar as it meant no return on investment capital to shareholders, but for a very long time it was not perceived as an onerous burden. As Fred Friendly told Paley after the McCarthy broadcast, dealing with criticism "goes with the job" if a network is to meet its public-service obligations.

By the 1960s, the ground had begun to shift under Fred Friendly's feet. He learned, as a generation of journalists would learn alongside him, that controversy would prove to be more trouble to the networks than journalistic enterprise warranted. Why was that the case? The answers are numerous. The structure of broadcast regulation did not reward daring or controversial journalism; instead, measures such as the equal-time provision of the communications act punished any pointed form of editorializing (allowing wide latitude for broadcast editorials on the importance of civic involvement, the joys of a first snowfall, the duty of going to the polls, and the hope that elected representatives would be honest) and enforced "balanced" coverage. Some critics of the American media system charge, not without justification, that the balance enforced by the FCC in effect neutered journalism by depriving it of *any* point of view. There is an associated argument that "objectivity" is another institutional dodge, a strategy or ritual that exists most of all to protect the news organization from any parties— the government, newsmakers, the audience—that have the potential to harm it.[16] Moreover, enforcement of the public-service expectations of stations was, depending upon one's view, superficial or timid or libertarian. It was pretty much hands-off, in whichever case, so that there was little risk in sticking to conventional programming.

Regulation came at the level of stations, not networks; programming, which was what was supposed to be "in the public interest, convenience, and necessity," came from the networks. The networks themselves aired programs that would appeal to the largest audience, an approach that became known as the theory of airing the "least objectionable" material. Network and station success, measured in terms of the size and demographic makeup of the audience, was quantifiable through the use of ratings, which told executives how good a month, a week, or a day they had had in their competition with others, and eventually would be honed to the point of telling which story in a newscast lost viewers or gained them. In that calculus, there was little room for measurements of quality, public service, or societal good.

Television networks and stations operate like virtually all other institutions in trying to reduce uncertainty. A network that placed itself completely at the mercy of breaking news and had no regular programming at all is, almost by definition, an economic disaster waiting to happen (a lesson that CNN soon learned, thwarting the original intention of going live anywhere at any time and keeping regular programs to a minimum). So the news divisions, and later the all-news networks, routinized the news, covering predictable stories rather than reinventing the wheel each day. Entertainment programming was based on earlier programs, or earlier genres, that had been successful. The successful television Western led to a season full of them; decades later, the specific programs had changed, but not the mindset that produced them. Reality-based contests that cruelly pitted contestants against one another were an innovation; then, it seemed, they constituted much of prime time. Experimental broadcasting was, from a business point of view, a contradiction in terms. You copied what worked.

Amid the patterns of institutional behavior, two sets of changes, each gradual but fundamental, altered what public service could and would mean. First, networks and stations realized, news could be a so-called profit center in itself. Second, technology produced diversity: a multiplicity of channels on cable television and pay-per-view along with independent local stations that meant ultimately shrinking revenues for traditional, over-the-air broadcasting. Author and journalist Haynes Johnson notes that news of scandal was the natural outcome of an intensely competitive news environment:

> You have shrinking markets, declining audiences, fragmentation across the board, and a commercial fight to survive by appealing to a more prurient, scandal-ridden audience. People love scandal. They always have. There's nothing new about that in our business. People want to know about the foibles of the great, the powerful, and the mighty. Sensation and scandal are always going to be easier to cover, and you're going to get an audience. When the

networks had a lock on what Americans were seeing, they brought to that time a different standard on what was news. It was far more of a public-service-driven standard.[17]

Johnson adds that the public has largely forgotten, or ignored, the difference between print and broadcast media:

> One continually forgets in our country that they are the *public* [emphasis his] airwaves. We own them. And we license them to independent entrepreneurs who make a profit. But they were supposed to be a public-service venue. We, the public, are giving you the right to use these airwaves that we own to give us entertainment, sports, and news, but there has to be a public-service context. Sadly, that's almost gone now.[18]

One measure of the fading commitment to public service was the 2002 pursuit by ABC of CBS comedian David Letterman, who was renegotiating his contract. ABC executives made no secret of their desire to have Letterman supplant Ted Koppel and the much-honored *Nightline* in the Monday-through-Friday 11:30 time slot. (Letterman's ratings were not higher than those of *Nightline*, but his program was thirty minutes longer and his audience was far younger, thus more desirable.) ABC luminaries, including Sam Donaldson, Diane Sawyer, and Barbara Walters, openly questioned the values of a news division that could not hold onto *Nightline*, the "jewel in the crown" of ABC News, a program that had been on the air and made news for more than twenty years. Koppel himself wrote an editorial in the *New York Times* questioning the values of an ABC programming executive who had commented that *Nightline* was irrelevant. The signature Koppel program ultimately stayed on the air, but not because of internal pressure from Koppel or anyone else at ABC News. Letterman simply decided to stay where he was. ABC officially never took a position that it would not drop the news program from its long-held time slot.

Under fire from cable programs, the Internet, video on demand, and scores of new outlets for news and information, the networks found that there was a sizable audience for nonfiction storytelling: people *were* interested in reality, if it were timely, packaged skillfully, and made dramatic. Scandal worked, celebrity news worked, docudrama worked, but, overall, compelling stories always worked.

In the 1990s, with the example of *60 Minutes*, a relatively inexpensive program that yielded a fortune in profits, looming large, the networks acted as though they had an imperative to program other news magazines. Once they hit on the programs that sustained an audience, they appeared to need to keep duplicating the product so that each celebrity journalist could earn his or her keep by fronting a weekly magazine show. By the mid-1990s, television had become an unthinkable oxymoron, a "vast wasteland," not of foolish or escapist entertainment, but of news programs, with prime time filled with hours and hours of personality profiles, sting operations to embarrass petty crooks, scandals of every type, and touching portraits of individuals who were both brave and unfortunate in life.[19]

Conclusion

In the 1970s, the networks learned a set of powerful lessons from local television stations, mainly from WABC and WNBC in New York, but also from WJZ in Baltimore, KYW in Philadelphia, and others too numerous to mention. Unfortunately, the lessons were not good for the overall state of television news. Local taught national that news could draw large audiences and earn substantial profits if the news product were put together using the right mix of ingredients. There had to be likable anchors (and likability would need to be quantified and tested so managers could be certain); the members of a television news "cast"—the players—would have to interact comfortably, as if they liked working together, and might even resemble a family or a group of friends getting together after work. The content itself would need to be "juiced"—on-the-street, in-the-air, in-your-face journalism that came on strong and didn't let go.

Aggressive news coverage certainly is not bad in itself, and the product of this type of thinking was often good, solid reporting. But what the local executives and news consultants were after wasn't mainly the right content. It was instead the right "tone" or "feel" or "texture." In the end, atmospherics mattered more than journalism, although many television news professionals in America will vehemently deny this. In any event, networks learned the bad lessons well, learned storytelling from *60 Minutes*, gritted their teeth and learned tabloid tricks from *A Current Affair*, *Hard Copy*, and *Inside Edition*, learned other lessons from Phil Donahue and Oprah Winfrey, and finally were instructed by their corporate supervisors to learn the lessons that could never be dismissed by a news-for-profit link in a media-conglomerate chain. Earnings per share. The expense of maintaining foreign bureaus. (Foreign bureaus, to be blunt, were an expensive way to get news from other countries. Over the years, a thoroughly global network of suppliers of news video grew up, including Reuters Television, Eurovision, Asiavision, and Associated Press Television [APTV]. Even with the video news services, there remained the problem of having no correspondent in the region to supply an on-the-scene presence as well as historical and political context.)[20] The need to maximize the output of a small number of reporters in Dallas or Omaha or even Washington. "Sexy," ideas for news programs. Over-the-top promotional campaigns waged using local stations' own air time.

By 2002, it also could be said that the networks and the conglomerates chose not to study the lessons of the best cable and local stations, whose work was innovative, community-based, and successful in making complex subjects understandable to the audience. The networks and conglomerates did not learn from C-SPAN that there was an audience made up of every kind of American that was hungry for those dry details of governance that everyone assumed were anathema. They didn't appear to notice that people liked American history and culture. They even liked forty-eight hours of *Book TV*, of all things, on C-SPAN every weekend. The networks and conglomerates did not fully accept the useful lessons of the civic journalism movement, of taking on a mission to find out what really was happening in a community (or a country) and what could be done about it.

Local stations worried too often over whether a particular lead story would lose viewers—not about ways to cover the same story in a more viewer-friendly way. Of course, they had to be concerned about making important issues viewer-friendly. But they acted on those concerns not nearly enough. After at least seventeen failures, NBC did find the right prime-time vehicle for news. But those failed programs that preceded *Dateline* often were given less than a month to find their sea legs and an audience. Is the news no different from the speedily canceled *Bob Patterson*? Are Connie Chung, Jane Pauley, and Lloyd Dobyns no different from *Seinfeld's* George Costanza?

Finally, there are some lessons drawn from the terrorist attack on America that should be remembered long into our electronic future. Americans are a good people, capable of caring for one another and with a serious stake in the continuation of our most treasured social institutions. When it matters most, they can be counted on to act with courage and conviction. For much of the last twenty-five years, however, television news has left that community of millions of viewers less well-served than they deserve to be. The example of September 11, 2001, illustrates that ordinary Americans have a fierce interest in their community, whether it be the financial center of lower Manhattan, a neighborhood in the borough of Queens, or the United States of America. Whatever the countervailing circumstances—the need to make money, the lack of resources, competition for people's time, the tyranny of deadlines, the inherent problems of organizations, the undernourished tradition of public service in the United States—in the end there is no reason why electronic journalism cannot or should not match the genuine public concerns and the demonstrated moral intelligence of its audiences.

Notes

1. Electronic Journalism in a New Era

1. The character Gordon Gekko, played by actor Michael Douglas, made the comment in *Wall Street*, a 1987 film written and directed by Oliver Stone.

2. Michael Eisner, "Letter to Shareholders," Walt Disney Company, Annual Report 2000, p. 6.

3. See Walter Goodman, "What Parson Rather Left Out of His Sermon," *New York Times*, October 17, 1993, p. H33.

4. "Rather Decries 'Hollywoodation' of Journalism," *Columbia University Journalism Alumni Journal*, Winter 1994, p. 1.

5. Angus Finney, "Gutter and Gore," *New Statesman and Society*, September 9, 1988, p. 47.

6. Geraldo Rivera, "TV's Wave of the Future," *New York Times*, December 16, 1988, p. A39.

7. See Albert Scardino, "A Debate Heats Up: Is It News or Entertainment?" *New York Times*, January 15, 1989, p. H29.

8. Axel Madsen, *60 Minutes: The Power and the Politics of America's Most Popular News Show* (New York: Dodd, Mead, 1984), p. 23.

9. See Richard Campbell, *"60 Minutes" and the News* (Urbana: University of Illinois Press, 1991).

10. *Viewpoint*, "The Media and O.J. Simpson," ABC Television, July 22, 1994.

11. Ibid.

12. Interview by author, May 16, 1994.

13. See Ken Auletta, *3 Blind Mice: How the TV Networks Lost Their Way* (New York: Vintage, 1992), pp. 76–77.

14. Dan Rottenberg, "And That's the Way It Is," *American Journalism Review*, May 1994, pp. 34, 36.

15. Interview by author, March 21, 1994.

16. Interview by author, July 26, 1994.

17. Richard Zoglin, "TV News Goes Hollywood," *Time*, October 9, 1989, p. 98.

18. Interview by author, May 19, 1994.

19. Ibid.

20. Ron Powers, *The Newscasters: The News Business as Show Business* (New York: St. Martin's Press, 1977), p. 1.

21. See Marc Gunther, *The House That Roone Built: The Inside Story of ABC News* (Boston: Little, Brown, 1994), p. 17.

2. Beginnings: The Ethic of Commercialism

1. Gleason L. Archer, *History of Radio: To 1926* (New York: American Historical Society, 1938), pp. 112–13.

2. See Eric Barnouw, *A Tower in Babel: A History of Broadcasting in the United States*, vol. 1 (New York: Oxford University Press, 1966), p. 91.

3. Ibid.

4. See Ray Lyman Wilbur and Arthur Mastick Hyde, *The Hoover Policies* (New York: Charles Scribner's Sons, 1937), pp. 207–15.

5. Kendrick A. Clements, *Hoover, Conservation and Consumerism* (Lawrence: University Press of Kansas, 2000), p. 5.

6. Hoover Papers, Commerce—Radio, Box 498, "Radio Is 'Acting Up,' Says Hoover," *Philadelphia Public Ledger*, April 16, 1926.

7. Barnouw, *A Tower in* Babel, p. 209.

8. See Eugene S. Foster, *Understanding Broadcasting* (Reading, MA: Addison-Wesley, 1978), p. 47.

9. Barnouw, *A Tower in Babel*, p. 160.

10. Susan Smulyan, *Selling Radio: The Commercialization of American Broadcasting 1920–1934* (Washington, DC: Smithsonian Institution Press, 1994), p. 165.

11. Ibid.

12. Eric Barnouw, *The Golden Web: A History of Broadcasting in the United States*, vol. 2 (New York: Oxford University Press, 1968), pp. 17–19.

13. Christopher H. Sterling and John M. Kittross, *Stay Tuned: A Concise History of American Broadcasting* (Belmont, CA: Wadsworth, 1978), p. 176.

14. 12. See Edward Bliss Jr., ed., *In Search of Light: The Broadcasts of Edward R. Murrow 1938–1961* (New York: Alfred A. Knopf, 1967), pp. 4–5.

15. Ibid., p. 35.

16. See Harry Reasoner, *Before the Colors Fade* (New York: Alfred A. Knopf, 1981), pp. 82–83, and David Halberstam, *The Powers That Be* (New York: Alfred A. Knopf, 1979), pp. 133–157.

17. Halberstam, *The Powers That Be*, p. 136.

18. Reasoner, *Before the Colors Fade*, p. 81.

19. Ibid., p. 82

20. Ibid.

21. See A. William Bluem, *Documentary in American Television* (New York: Hastings House, 1965), pp. 42–56.

22. Ibid., p. 51.

23. Liz-Ann Bauden, ed., *The Oxford Companion to Film* (New York: Oxford University Press, 1976), pp. 500–02. See also Eric Barnouw, *Documentary: A History of the Non-Fiction Film.* (Oxford: Oxford University Press, 1983); Richard Meran Barsam, *Nonfiction Film: A Critical History* (New York: E.P. Dutton, 1973); and Lewis Jacobs, *The Documentary Tradition*, 2nd ed. (New York: W.W. Norton, 1979).

24. See Bluem, *Documentary in American Television*, p. 34.

25. Ibid., pp. 35–40.

26. *CBS News With Douglas Edwards*, CBS Television, April 7, 1949, collection of the Museum of Television and Radio, New York.

27. *Camel News Caravan*, NBC Television, September 4, 1950, collection of the Museum of Television and Radio, New York.

28. Edward Bliss Jr., *Now the News: The Story of Broadcast Journalism* (New York: Columbia University Press, 1991), p. 235.

29. Ibid., p. 236.

30. See Bluem, *Documentary in American Television*, p. 94.

31. Bliss, *Now the News*, p. 237.

32. See Eric Barnouw, *The Image Empire: A History of Broadcasting in the United States*, vol. 3 (New York: Oxford University Press, 1970), p. 46.

33. Ibid., p. 52.

34. Ibid.

35. See Joseph E. Persico, *Edward R. Murrow: An American Original* (New York: McGraw-Hill, 1988), p. 423. See also Alexander Kendrick, *Prime Time: The Life of Edward R. Murrow* (Boston: Little, Brown, 1969), pp. 335–83; and A.M. Sperber, *Murrow: His Life and Times* (New York: Freundlich Books, 1986), pp. 474–535.

36. See Persico, *Edward R. Murrow*, p. 427, and Sperber, *Murrow*, pp. 532–33.

37. See Bluem, *Documentary in American Television*, p. 100.

38. Bliss, *Now the News*, pp. 359–60.

39. Ibid., p. 364.

40. Persico, *Edward R. Murrow*, p. 468.

3. The Era of Network Dominance

1. See Barnouw, *The Image Empire*, pp. 227–38; Bliss, *Now the News*, pp. 335–39; Robert J. Donovan and Ray Scherer, *Unsilent Revolution: Television News and American Life* (Cambridge: Woodrow Wilson International Center for Scholars and Cambridge University Press, 1992), pp. 58–70.

2. Bliss, *Now the News*, p. 338.

3. Barnouw, *The Image Empire*, pp. 227, 234.

4. William A. Mindak and Gerald D. Hursh, "Television's Function on the Assassination Weekend," in *The Kennedy Assassination and the American Public*, Bradley S. Greenberg and Edwin S. Parker, eds. (Stanford, CA: Stanford University Press, 1965), p. 141.

5. Barnouw, *The Image Empire*, p. 234.

6. Donovan and Scherer, *Unsilent Revolution*, p. 70.

7. Michael J. Arlen, *Living-Room War* (New York: The Viking Press, 1969). See also Arlen, *The Camera Age* (New York: Farrar, Strauss and Giroux, 1981); and Sterling and Kittross, *Stay Tuned*, pp. 412–13.

8. Chris Kaltenbach, "Giant of TV News Dies," *Baltimore Sun*, March 5, 1998, p. E1.

9. Don Hewitt, *Tell Me a Story: Fifty Years and 60 Minutes in Television* (New York: PublicAffairs, 2001), p. 51.

10. Barbara Matusow, *The Evening Stars: The Making of the Network News Anchor* (Boston: Houghton Mifflin, 1983), p. 66.

11. Ibid., p. 75.

12. Quoted in Matusow, *The Evening Stars*, p. 78.

13. See Gary Paul Gates, *Air Time: The Inside Story of CBS News* (New York: Harper and Row, 1978), p. 211. See also Matusow, *The Evening Stars*, p. 129.

14. Gates, *Air Time*, p. 83.

15. Ibid., p. 155.

16. Ibid., p. 156.

17. Quoted in Matusow, *The Evening Stars*, p. 41.

18. Ibid., p. 3.

19. Robert Goldberg and Gerald Jay Goldberg, *Anchors: Brokaw, Jennings, Rather and the Evening News* (New York: Birch Lane Press, 1990), p. 9.

4. *60 Minutes* and the News Magazine

1. For an account of Don Hewitt's career, see Don Hewitt, *Minute by Minute . . .* (New York: Random House, 1985); Madsen, *60 Minutes*; Reasoner, *Before the Colors Fade*; Mike Wallace and Gary Paul Gates, *Close Encounters: Mike Wallace's Own Story* (New York: William Morrow, 1987).

2. Reasoner, *Before the Colors Fade*, p. 161.

3. Ibid., p. 158.

4. Hewitt, *Tell Me a Story*, p. 91.

5. Hewitt, *Minute by Minute . . .* , p. 26.

6. Hewitt, *Tell Me a Story*, p. 93.

7. Hewitt, *Minute by Minute . . .* , p. 27.

8. Hewitt, *Tell Me a Story*, p. 105.

9. Wallace and Gates, *Close Encounters*, p. 123.

10. Dan Rather joined Safer and Wallace on the broadcast in 1976. After a stint with ABC, Harry Reasoner returned as the fourth correspondent in 1979. In 1981, Ed Bradley replaced Rather. In 1984, Diane Sawyer became the fifth correspondent.

11. Wallace and Gates, *Close Encounters*, p. 161.

12. Ibid., p. 353.

13. Reasoner, *Before the Colors Fade*, p. 161.

14. See James W. Carey, "Foreword," in Richard Campbell, p. xii.

15. See Edward Jay Epstein, *News from Nowhere* (New York: Random House, 1973), pp. 4–5.

16. Ibid, p. 152.

17. Ibid., pp. 164–65.

18. Elsa Walsh, *Divided Lives: The Public and Private Struggles of Three Accomplished Women* (New York: Simon and Schuster, 1995), p. 67.

19. Wallace and Gates, *Close Encounters*, pp. 468–69.

20. Ibid., p. 469.

21. Hewitt, *Tell Me a Story*, p. 136.

22. Ibid., p. 137.

23. *PrimeTime Thursday*, ABC Television, June 14, 2001.

24. Quoted in James Fallows, *Breaking the News: How the Media Undermine American Democracy* (New York: Vintage Books, 1997), p. 56.

25. Hewitt, *Tell Me a Story*, p. 194.

5. Tabloid Television and a World of Talk

1. Powers, *The Newscasters*, pp. 29–30.

2. Ibid., p. 33.

3. Ibid., pp. 78–79.

4. Ibid.

5. Ibid., pp. 40–41.

6. See Pauline Kael, *When the Lights Go Down* (New York: Holt, Rinehart and Winston, 1980), pp. 219–24.

7. Pierre de L'Estoile, *L'Information en France Avant le Periodique*, cited in Mitchell Stephens, *A History of News: From the Drum to the Satellite* (New York: Viking Penguin, 1988), p. 8.

8. Maury Povich with Ken Gross, *Current Affairs: A Life on the Edge* (New York: G.P. Putnam's Sons, 1991), pp. 51–52.

9. Ibid., pp. 61–62.

10. Ibid., p. 124.

11. Kevin Glynn, *Tabloid Culture: Trash Taste, Popular Power and the Transformation of American Television* (Durham, NC: Duke University Press, 2000), pp. 22–23.

12. Ibid., p. 118.

13. Ibid., pp. 100–01.

14. See James B. Twitchell, *Carnival Culture: The Trashing of Taste in America* (New York: Columbia University Press, 1992), p. 237.

15. *U.S. News & World Report*, July 25, 1994, pp. 46–54.

16. Ibid., p. 53.

17. Since 1990, I have directed more than 200 graduate and undergraduate students at the University of Maryland in the systematic analysis, both descriptive and quantitative, of programs in various news and information genres. The data reported here are drawn from programs that aired between June 12 and July 31, 1995. The quantitative content analysis was done by Natasha Holmes, with additional work done by Kathy Hettleman.

18. Matthew C. Ehrlich, "The Journalism of Outrageousness: Tabloid Television News vs. Investigative News," *Journalism & Mass Communication Monographs* 155 (February 1996): 7–8.

19. Howard Fast, "The Bobbitt Case Raises THE Important Question," *Greenwich Time*, January 20, 1994, p. 1.

20. Elizabeth Bird, *For Enquiring Minds* (Knoxville: University of Tennessee Press, 1990), p. 92.

21. Ibid., p. 112.

22. See Haynes Johnson, *The Best of Times: America in the Clinton Years* (New York: Harcourt, 2001), pp. 107–41.

23. Ibid.

24. Paul Thaler, *The Spectacle: Media and the Making of the O.J. Simpson Story* (Westport, CT: Praeger, 1997), p. 10.

25. Ibid., p. 133.

26. Ibid., pp. 133–34.

27. Ibid., p. 147.

28. See Janice Schuetz and Lin S. Lilley, eds., *The O.J. Simpson Trials: Rhetoric, Media, and the Law* (Carbondale: Southern Illinois University Press, 1999), pp. 141–43.

29. Virginia Graham's *Girl Talk*, David Suskind's *The David Suskind Show*, and Mike Wallace's *Nightbeat* are among the predecessors of the contemporary talk show. *Girl Talk* was an early 1960s talk show that brought women together to chat informally. The Suskind show, which aired late at night, usually featured either celebrities or guests who had deviant beliefs or practices. Wallace's show was an intense one-on-one encounter with people in the news, often controversial and out of the mainstream.

30. Phil Donahue, *Donahue: My Own Story* (New York: Simon and Schuster, 1979), p. 97.

31. Ibid., p. 99.

32. Joshua Gamson, *Freaks Talk Back: The Tabloid Shows and Sexual Nonconformity* (Chicago: University of Chicago Press, 1998), pp. 25–26.

33. Geraldo Rivera, appearance on *The Charlie Rose Show*, PBS, September 8, 1995.

34. Ibid.

35. Tom Shales, "We're Mad as Hell at Daytime TV, Getting Sleazier by the Minute," *Washington Post*, March 19, 1995, p. G5.

36. Ibid.

37. See Howard Kurtz, *Hot Air: All Talk, All the Time* (New York: Times Books, 1996).
38. Ibid., p. 125.
39. Ibid., p. 120.
40. Alicia C. Shepard, "The Pundit Explosion," *American Journalism Review*, September 1995, p. 25.
41. Ibid.

6. Hard News—Soft News

1. See Peter J. Boyer, *Who Killed CBS? The Undoing of America's Number One News Network* (New York: St. Martin's Press, 1988), p. 17.
2. Matusow, *The Evening Stars*, pp. 5–42.
3. Michael Massing, "CBS: Sauterizing the News," *Columbia Journalism Review*, March/April 1986, p. 28.
4. Interview by author, June 5, 1996.
5. Boyer, *Who Killed CBS?*, p. 133.
6. Ibid., p. 164.
7. Ibid., pp. 164–65.
8. Massing, *CBS*, p. 28.
9. Ibid., p. 30.
10. Ibid., p. 31–32.
11. Boyer, *Who Killed CBS?*, p. 391.
12. Ibid, pp. 392–93.
13. Ibid., p. 403.
14. Interview by author, June 5, 1996.
15. Ibid.

7. Prime-Time News Values

1. Lloyd Grove, "Kiss of the Anchorwoman," *Vanity Fair*, August 1994, p. 92. The author acknowledges the assistance of Kristin Wedemeyer in research for this chapter.
2. Interview by author, March 19, 2002.
3. Interview by author, July 18, 1995.
4. Quoted in David Zurawik and Christina Stoehr, "Eclipsing the Nightly News," *American Journalism Review*, November 1994, p. 34.
5. Ibid., p. 38.
6. Gunther, *The House That Roone Built*, p. 94.
7. Ibid.
8. Interview by author, July 22, 1995.
9. Gunther, *The House That Roone Built*, p. 95.
10. See Linda Ellerbee, *And So It Goes: Adventures in Television* (New York: G.P. Putnam's Sons, 1987).
11. Ibid. See also Kristin Wedemeyer, "'Dateline NBC': Perspectives on a News Magazine's Success" (unpublished manuscript), College of Journalism, University of Maryland.
12. See Wedemeyer.
13. Ibid.
14. Ibid.
15. Ibid.

16. David Zurawik and Christina Stoehr, "Money Changes Everything," *American Journalism Review*, April 1993, p. 27.

17. NBC News Online, "About Us: Dateline NBC," www.msnbc.com/news.

18. Zurawik and Stoehr, "Money Changes Everything," p. 28.

19. Ibid.

20. See Zurawik and Stoehr, "Eclipsing the Nightly News," pp. 32–35.

21. Zoglin, p. 98.

22. Ibid.

23. Ibid.

24. Interview by author.

25. Richard Morin, "Big Breasts and a Bogus Broadcast," *Washington Post*, May 19, 1996, p. C7.

26. Interview by author, May 16, 1994.

27. Interview with Tony Burton, May 18, 2001.

28. Grove, pp. 130–31.

29. Ibid., p. 132.

30. Robert Lissit, "Out of Sight," *American Journalism Review*, December 1994, p. 31.

31. Interview by author, October 4, 1994.

32. Jeff MacGregor, "Diluting the News Into Soft Half-Truths," *New York Times*, June 4, 1995, p. H25.

8. The Impact of CNN

1. Interview by author, July 22, 1995.

2. Interview by author, May 16, 1994.

3. Interview by author, May 19, 1994.

4. Porter Bibb, *It Ain't as Easy as It Looks: Ted Turner's Amazing Story* (New York: Crown, 1993), pp. 32–33.

5. Ibid., p. 43.

6. See Robert Goldberg and Gerald Jay Goldberg, *Citizen Turner: The Wild Rise of an American Tycoon* (New York: Harcourt Brace, 1995), p. 147.

7. Hank Whittemore, *CNN: The Inside Story* (Boston: Little, Brown, 1990), p. 29.

8. Ibid., p. 33.

9. Ibid., p. 105.

10. Ibid., pp. 142–52.

11. Ibid., p. 260.

12. Ibid., pp. 289–98.

13. Ibid.

14. Tom Rosenstiel, "How CNN Wrecked Television News," *New Republic*, August 22–29, 1994, p. 27.

15. Interview by author, July 29, 1994.

16. Rosenstiel, p. 28.

17. Chuck Taylor, "Analysis Is the Buzzword with MSNBC Launch," *Seattle Times*, July 16, 1996, p. E8.

18. Ibid.

19. Kelly Heyboer, "Cable Clash," *American Journalism Review*, June 2000, p. 25.

20. NBC News Online, "Welcome to MSNBC," www. msnbc.com/aboutmsnbc.

21. Marshall Sella, "The Red-State Network," *New York Times Magazine*, June 24, 2001, p. 28.

22. Ibid., p. 30.

23. Ibid., p. 29.

24. Ibid., p. 30.

25. Seth Ackerman, "The Most Biased Name in News," *Extra!*, August 2001, p. 11.

26. Ibid., p. 16.

27. Sella, p. 28.

28. Ibid., p. 28.

29. Ibid., p. 56.

30. Interview by author, September 27, 1994.

31. William Shawcross, *Murdoch: The Making of a Media Empire* (New York: Simon and Schuster, 1992), p. 297.

32. See Ken Auletta, "The Lost Tycoon," *New Yorker*, April 23–30, 2001, pp. 138–53. See also Paul Farhi, "Nothing Left But Billions," *Washington Post*, April 4, 2001, p. C1.

9. Celebrity News

1. Interview by author, January 10, 1995. Van Messel served as executive producer of *Entertainment Tonight* from the beginning of 1987 until July 1995, when he was replaced by Linda Bell, the former executive producer of *Hard Copy*, a Paramount-owned, syndicated tabloid news program. His predecessors included Jim Bellows, Jack Reilly, and David Nuell.

2. Ibid.

3. Ibid.

4. The program was broadcast on January 10, 1995.

5. John Dempsey, "More Mags Will Fly in the Fall: Too Much of a Good Thing?" *Variety*, April 12, 1989, p. 1. See also Richard Zoglin, "That's Entertainment?" *Time*, October 3, 1994, p. 85.

6. Interview by author.

7. Ibid.

8. Ibid.

9. See Curtis Prendergast with Geoffrey Colvin, *The World of Time Inc.: The Intimate History of a Changing Enterprise* (New York: Atheneum, 1986). See also Peter Prichard, *The Making of McPaper: The Inside Story of USA Today* (Kansas City: Andrews, McMeel and Parker, 1987).

10. See Neal Gabler, *Winchell: Gossip, Power and the Culture of Celebrity* (New York: Alfred A. Knopf, 1994). See also Harold Brodkey, "The Last Word on Winchell," *New Yorker*, January 30, 1995, pp. 71–78.

11. Brodkey, p. 78.

12. Prendergast, *The World of Time Inc.*, p. 431.

13. Ibid., p. 433.

14. Ibid., pp. 439–40.

15. Ibid., p. 440.

16. Sperber, *Murrow*, pp. 424–25.

17. Ibid., p. 517

18. See Peter McCabe, *Bad News at Black Rock: The Sell-Out of CBS News* (New York: Arbor House, 1987), pp. 35–36.

19. Interview by author, March 21, 1994.

20. Ibid.

21. Interview by author, March 21, 1994.

22. Ibid.

23. Ibid.

24. See Jean Marbella, "A Pool of Emotions," *Baltimore Sun*, March 11, 1995, pp. 1D-2D.

25. Richard Harrington, "Is He History?" *Washington Post*, June 18, 1995, p. G1.

26. Quoted in Powers, *The Newcasters*, p. 163.

27. Ibid., p. 164.

28. See Powers, *The Newcasters*, p. 163. See also Gwenda Blair, *Almost Golden: Jessica Savitch and the Selling of Television News* (New York: Avon Books, 1988), p. 155.

29. Geraldo Rivera with Daniel Paisner, *Exposing Myself* (New York: Bantam Books, 1991), p. 232.

30. Ibid., p. 236.

31. See Matusow, *The Evening Stars*.

32. Quoted in Matusow, *The Evening Stars*, p. 262.

33. Roger Mudd, address at Washington and Lee University, May 6, 1995.

34. See Campbell. See also Walsh for a discussion of Don Hewitt's approach to crafting *60 Minutes* stories and, especially, to working with correspondent Meredith Vieira.

35. Wallace and Gates, *Close Encounters*, pp. 468–69.

36. Brodkey, p. 78.

37. Neil Postman, *Amusing Ourselves to Death: Public Discourse in the Age of Show Business* (New York: Viking Penguin), 1985, p. 106.

38. Ibid., p. 105.

39. Ibid., p. 101.

40. Twitchell, *Carnival Culture*, p. 9.

41. Ibid.

42. Ibid., p. 117.

43. Gerald Howard, "Mistah Perkins—He Dead," *The American Scholar* 58: 3 (Fall 1989): 355–69.

10. Local News

1. See Howard Rosenberg et al., "Bad News," *American Journalism Review*, September 1993, pp. 18–27.

2. Howard Rosenberg, "The Cult of Personality," *American Journalism Review*, p. 18.

3. Ibid., p. 19.

4. Ishmael Reed, "It's Racist," *American Journalism Review*, p. 22.

5. Max Frankel, "Body Bags at 11," *New York Times Magazine*, April 2, 1995, p. 24. See also Matthew R. Kerbel. *If It Bleeds, It Leads: An Anatomy of Television News* (Boulder, CO: Westview Press, 2000).

6. Ibid., p. 26.

7. Paul Steinle, "Production over Coverage," *American Journalism Review*, September 1993, p. 25.

8. Interview by author, April 30, 2002.

9. Interview by author, June 15, 1996.

10. Jamie Malanowski, "Murder Travels," *American Journalism Review*, September 1993, p. 21.

11. Interview by author, June 15, 1996.

12. Interview by author, March 18, 1996.

13. Interview by author, March 8, 2002.

14. Ibid.

15. Jan Schaffer, "Introduction," *Civic Journalism Is . . .* (San Francisco: Pew Center for Civic Journalism, 2000), p. 1.

16. Gary Walker, "About Reinvigorating Coverage," *American Journalism Review,* September 1993, p. 8.

17. Pat Ford, "Gaming the News: New Entry Points," *Civic Catalyst,* Spring 2002, pp. 1, 14–15.

18. See Steve M. Barkin, "Local Television News," *Critical Studies in Mass Communication* 4:1 (March 1987): 79–82.

19. See Colin Bell and Howard Newby, *Community Studies: An Introduction to the Sociology of the Local Community* (New York: Praeger, 1973).

20. Barkin, p. 79.

21. Ibid., p. 80.

22. Bell and Newby, *Community Studies,* p. 24.

23. Reese Schonfeld, *Me and Ted Against the World: The Unauthorized Story of the Founding of CNN,* (New York: Harper Collins, 2001), pp. 267–68.

24. Interview by author, January 10, 2001.

25. Interview by author, February 3, 2001.

26. Interview by author, January 11, 2001.

27. Ibid.

28. Interview by author, December 10, 2000.

29. Ibid.

30. Ibid.

31. Womack interview.

32. Horner interview.

33. Ibid.

34. Interview by the author, March 17, 2001.

35. Ibid.

36. Interview by the author, March 19, 2002.

37. Ibid.

38. Ibid.

39. Interview by author, January 10, 2001.

40. Houston interview.

41. Interview with the author, January 10, 2002.

42. Schonfeld, 19.

43. *Public Engagement Guide for the PBS Series: Local News* (Waltham, MA: Roundtable, 2000), p. 7.

11. Network News and the New Environment

1. The author heard Lack make the remarks, which were broadcast on closed-circuit television, at the NBC Washington bureau on October 20, 1994.

2. See "Who Owns What" at the *Columbia Journalism Review* Web site, www.cjr.org.

3. Jim Rutenberg and Seth Schiesel, "Doubted as Business, Network News Is Still Hanging On," *New York Times,* March 18, 2001, p. D1.

4. Ibid., p. D4.

5. Ibid.

6. Ibid.

7. Ibid.

8. Ibid.

9. See, for example, Robert W. McChesney, *Corporate Media and the Threat to*

Democracy (New York: Seven Stories Press, 1997), and McChesney, *Rich Media, Poor Democracy: Communication Politics in Dubious Times* (New York: The New Press, 1999).

10. McChesney, *Corporate Media and the Threat to Democracy*, p. 5.

11. Jurgen Habermas, *The Structural Transformation of the Public Sphere*, trans. Thomas Burger with Frederick Lawrence (Cambridge, MA: MIT Press, 1989). Originally published in German in 1962.

12. See Richard Campbell, *Media and Culture: An Introduction to Mass Communication* (Boston: Bedford/St. Martin's, 2002), pp. 536–64.

13. "600 Vermonters Turn Out for Town Meetings to Oppose Corporate Control of the Media," press release, Office of Rep. Bernie Sanders, April 30, 2002, p. 1.

14. Ibid., p. 3.

15. See Ben H. Bagdikian, *The Media Monopoly* (Boston: Beacon Press, 2000).

16. See Mort Rosenblum, *Who Stole the News?* (New York: John Wiley & Sons, 1993); John McManus, *Market-Driven Journalism: Let the Citizen Beware!* (Thousand Oaks, CA: Sage, 1994); Dennis Mazzocco, *Networks of Power: Corporate TV's Threat to Democracy* (Boston: South End Press, 1994).

17. McManus, *Market-Driven Journalism*, p. 12.

18. McChesney, *Corporate Media and the Threat to Democracy*, pp. 9–17.

19. Bagdikian, *The Media Monopoly*, p. vii.

20. See Paul Farhi, "Premature Obit," *American Journalism Review*, May 2002, p. 40.

21. See Gunther, *The House that Roone Built*, pp. 34–35.

22. Interview by author, May 8, 2002.

23. Ibid.

24. See, for example, Marc Fisher, et al., "Covering the Horror," *American Journalism Review*, October 2001, pp. 18–33.

25. "Serious Agenda, Serious Interest," *Baltimore Sun*, December 24, 2001, p. C1.

26. Ibid., p. C3.

27. Howard Kurtz, "ABC Stops Replay of Endless Tragedy," *Washington Post*, September 19, 2001, p. C1.

28. See "For the Record," *Columbia Journalism Review*, March/April 2002, p. 7.

29. See *Crisis Journalism: A Handbook for Media Response* (Reston, VA: American Press Institute, 2001, p. 21.

30. Paul Farhi, "Getting the Story Out," *Washington Post*, October 8, 2001, p. C4.

31. Ibid., p. C1.

32. Leonard Downie Jr., and Robert G. Kaiser, "Does 9/11 Make a Difference?" *Columbia Journalism Review*, March–April 2002, p. 59.

33. Ibid.

12. Electronic Journalism and the Public Interest

1. See Barrie McDonald, *Broadcasting in the United Kingdom* (London: Mansell, 1993), pp. 2–36.

2. Ibid., pp. 76–83.

3. Ibid., pp. 85–99.

4. See John C. Merrill, *Global Journalism: Survey of International Communication* (New York: Longman, 1991), pp. 106–24.

5. See C.L. Heatherly, ed., *Mandate for Leadership* (Washington, DC: Heritage Foundation, 1981).

6. See Patricia Aufderheide, *Communications Policy and the Public Interest: The Telecommunications Act of 1996* (New York: Guilford, 1999), pp. 27–29.

7. Ibid. Also see Mark Fowler and D. Brenner, "A Marketplace Approach to Broadcast Regulation," *Texas Law Review* 60: 207–57.

8. Aufderheide, *Communication Policy*, pp. 61–79.

9. Ibid., p. 67.

10. See McChesney, *Rich Media, Poor Democracy*, p. 120.

11. Ibid.

12. Ellen Ulman, "No One Was Supposed to Own the Net," *The Washington Post*, January 16, 2000, p. B3.

13. Ibid.

14. McChesney, *Rich Media, Poor Democracy*, p. 141.

15. Jay G. Blumler and Michael Gurevitch, "The New Media and Our Political Communication Discontents: Democratising Cyberspace," unpublished paper, 2002, p. 9.

16. See Gaye Tuchman, *Making News: A Study in the Construction of Reality* (New York: Free Press, 1978).

17. Interview by the author, February 26, 2002.

18. Ibid.

19. In an address to the National Association of Broadcasters in 1961, Federal Communications Commission Chairman Newton Minow said that anyone who viewed a full day of television would find a "vast wasteland" of violence, repetitive formulas, irritating commercials, and sheer boredom. See Sydney W. Head et al., *Broadcasting in America: A Survey of Electronic Media* (Boston: Houghton Mifflin, 1998), pp. 272–73.

20. See Christopher Paterson, "Global Television News Services," in Annabelle Sreberny-Mohammadi et al., eds., *Media in Global Context: A Reader* (New York: St. Martin's Press, 1997), pp. 145–60.

Selected Bibliography

Ackerman, Seth. "The Most Biased Name in News." *Extra!*, August 2001, 11.
American Journalism Review. "Bad News." *American Journalism Review*, September 1993: 18–27.
Archer, Gleason L., *History of Radio: to 1926*. New York: American Historical Society, 1938.
Arlen, Michael J. *Living-Room War*. New York: Viking, 1969.
———. *The Camera Age*. New York: Farrar, Strauss and Giroux, 1981.
Aufderheide, Patricia. *Communications Policy and the Public Interest: The Telecommunications Act of 1996*. New York: Guilford, 1999.
Auletta, Ken. *3 Blind Mice: How the TV Networks Lost Their Way*. New York: Vintage, 1992.
———. "The Lost Tycoon." *New Yorker*, April 23–30, 2001, 138–153.
Bagdikian, Ben H. *The Media Monopoly*. Boston: Beacon Press, 2000.
Barkin, Steve M. "Local Television News." *Critical Studies in Mass Communication* 4:1 (March 1987): 79–82.
Barnouw, Eric. *Documentary: A History of the Non-Fiction Film*. Oxford: Oxford University Press, 1983.
———. *A Tower in Babel: A History of Broadcasting in the United States*. Vol. 1. New York: Oxford University Press, 1966.
———.*The Golden Web: A History of Broadcasting in the United States, 1933 to 1953*. Vol. 2. New York: Oxford University Press, 1968.
———. *The Image Empire: A History of Broadcasting in the United States*. Vol. 3. New York: Oxford University Press, 1970.
Barsam, Richard Meran. *Nonfiction Film: A Critical History*. New York: E.P. Dutton, 1973.
Bauden, Liz-Ann, ed. *The Oxford Companion to Film*. New York: Oxford University Press, 1976.
Bell, Colin, and Howard Newby. *Community Studies: An Introduction to the Sociology of the Local Community*. New York: Praeger, 1973.
Bibb, Porter. *It Ain't as Easy as It Looks: Ted Turner's Amazing Story*. New York: Crown, 1993.
Bird, Elizabeth. *For Enquiring Minds*. Knoxville: University of Tennessee Press, 1990.
Blair, Gwenda. *Almost Golden: Jessica Savitch and the Selling of Television News*. New York: Avon Books, 1988.
Bliss, Edward, Jr., ed. *In Search of Light: The Broadcasts of Edward R. Murrow 1938–1961*. New York: Alfred A. Knopf, 1967.

———. *Now the News: The Story of Broadcast Journalism*. New York: Columbia University Press, 1991.

Bluem, A. William. *Documentary in American Television*. New York: Hastings House, 1965.

Blumler, Jay G., and Michael Gurevitch, "The New Media and Our Political Communication Discontents: Democratising Cyberspace." Unpublished paper, 2002.

Boyer, Peter J. *Who Killed CBS? The Undoing of America's Number One News Network*. New York: St. Martin's, 1988.

Brodkey, Harold. "The Last Word on Winchell." *New Yorker*, January 30, 1995, 71–78.

Campbell, Richard. *"60 Minutes" and the News*. Urbana: University of Illinois Press, 1991.

———. *Media & Culture: An Introduction to Mass Communication*. Boston: Bedford/St. Martin's, 2002.

Carey, James W. "Foreword," in Richard Campbell, *"60 Minutes" and the News*. Urbana: University of Illinois Press, 1991, xi–xii.

Clements, Kendrick A. *Hoover, Conservation and Consumerism*. Lawrence: University Press of Kansas, 2000.

Columbia University Graduate School of Journalism. "Rather Decries 'Hollywoodation' of Journalism." *Columbia University Journalism Alumni Journal*, Winter 1994: 1.

Cooper, Gloria. "For the Record." *Columbia Journalism Review*, March/April 2002: 7.

Crisis Journalism: *A Handbook for Media Response*. Reston, VA: American Press Institute, 2001.

Dempsey, John. "More Mags Will Fly in the Fall: Too Much of a Good Thing?" *Variety*, April 12, 1989, 1.

Donahue, Phil. *Donahue: My Own Story*. New York: Simon and Schuster, 1979.

Donovan, Robert J., and Ray Scherer. *Unsilent Revolution: Television News and American Life*. Cambridge: Woodrow Wilson International Center for Scholars and Cambridge University Press, 1992.

Downie, Leonard, Jr., and Robert G. Kaiser. "Does 9/11 Make a Difference?" *Columbia Journalism Review*, March/April 2002: 59.

Ehrlich, Matthew C. "The Journalism of Outrageousness: Tabloid Television News vs. Investigative News." *Journalism & Mass Communication Monographs* 155 (February 1996): 7–8.

Ellerbee, Linda. *And So It Goes: Adventures in Television*. New York: G.P. Putnam's Sons, 1987.

Epstein, Edward Jay. *News from Nowhere*. New York: Random House, 1973.

Fallows, James. *Breaking the News: How the Media Undermine American Democracy*. New York: Vintage Books, 1997.

Farhi, Paul. "Nothing Left But Billions." *Washington Post*, April 4, 2001, C1, C4.

———. "Getting the Story Out." *Washington Post*, October 8, 2001, C4.

———. "Premature Obit." *American Journalism Review*, May 2002: 38–41.

Fast, Howard. "The Bobbitt Case Raises THE Important Question." *Greenwich Time*, January 20, 1994, 1.

Finney, Angus, "Gutter and Gore." *New Statesman and Society*, September 9, 1988, 47.

Fisher, Marc, et al. "Covering the Horror." *American Journalism Review*, October 2001: 18–33.

Ford, Pat. "Gaming the News: New Entry Points." *Civic Catalyst*, Spring 2002, 1, 14–15.

Foster, Eugene S. *Understanding Broadcasting*. Reading, MA: Addison-Wesley, 1978.

Fowler, Mark, and D. Brenner. "A Marketplace Approach to Broadcast Regulation." *Texas Law Review* 60: 207–257.

Frankel, Max. "Body Bags at 11." *New York Times Magazine*, April 2, 1995, 24–26.

Gabler, Neal. *Winchell: Gossip, Power and the Culture of Celebrity.* New York: Alfred A. Knopf, 1994.

Gamson, Joshua. *Freaks Talk Back: The Tabloid Shows and Sexual Nonconformity.* Chicago: University of Chicago Press, 1998.

Gates, Gary Paul. *Air Time: The Inside Story of CBS News.* New York: Harper and Row, 1978.

Glynn, Kevin. *Tabloid Culture: Trash Taste, Popular Power and the Transformation of American Television.* Durham, NC: Duke University Press, 2000.

Goldberg, Robert, and Gerald Jay Goldberg. *Anchors: Brokaw, Jennings, Rather and the Evening News.* New York: Birch Lane Press, 1990.

———. *Citizen Turner: The Wild Rise of an American Tycoon.* New York: Harcourt Brace, 1995.

Goodman, Walter. "What Parson Rather Left Out of His Sermon." *New York Times,* October 17, 1993, H33.

Grove, Lloyd. "Kiss of the Anchorwoman." *Vanity Fair,* August 1994, 88–93, 130–35.

Gunther, Marc. *The House That Roone Built: The Inside Story of ABC News.* Boston: Little, Brown, 1994.

Habermas, Jurgen. *The Structural Transformation of the Public Sphere.* Trans. Thomas Burger with Frederick Lawrence. Cambridge, MA: MIT Press, 1989.

Halberstam, David. *The Powers That Be.* New York: Alfred A. Knopf, 1979.

Harrington, Richard. "Is He History?" *Washington Post,* June 18, 1995, G1.

Head, Sydney W., et al. *Broadcasting in America: A Survey of Electronic Media.* Boston: Houghton Mifflin, 1994.

Heatherly, C.L., ed. *Mandate for Leadership.* Washington, DC: Heritage Foundation, 1981.

Hewitt, Don. *Minute by Minute . . .* New York: Random House, 1985.

———. *Tell Me a Story: Fifty Years and 60 Minutes in Television.* New York: PublicAffairs, 2001.

Heyboer, Kelly. "Cable Clash." *American Journalism Review,* June 2000: 21–27.

Howard, Gerald. "Mistah Perkins—He Dead." *The American Scholar* 58: 3 (Fall 1989): 355–369.

Jacobs, Lewis. *The Documentary Tradition.* 2nd ed. New York: W.W. Norton, 1979.

Johnson, Haynes. *The Best of Times: America in the Clinton Years.* New York: Harcourt, 2001.

Kael, Pauline. *When the Lights Go Down.* New York: Holt, Rinehart and Winston, 1980.

Kaltenbach, Chris. "Giant of TV News Dies." *Baltimore Sun,* March 5, 1998, E1.

Kendrick, Alexander. *Prime Time: The Life of Edward R. Murrow.* Boston: Little, Brown, 1969.

Kerbel, Matthew R. *If It Bleeds, It Leads: An Anatomy of Television News.* Boulder, CO: Westview Press, 2000.

Kurtz, Howard. *Hot Air: All Talk, All the Time.* New York: Times Books, 1996.

———. "ABC Stops Replay of Endless Tragedy." *Washington Post,* September 19, 2001, C1.

Lissit, Robert. "Out of Sight." *American Journalism Review,* December 1994: 31.

MacGregor, Jeff. "Diluting the News Into Soft Half-Truths." *New York Times,* June 4, 1995, H25.

Madsen, Axel. *60 Minutes: The Power and the Politics of America's Most Popular News Show.* New York: Dodd, Mead, 1984.

Malanowski, Jamie. "Urder Travels." *American Journalism Review.* September 1993: 21.

Marbella, Jean. "A Pool of Emotions." *Baltimore Sun,* March 11, 1995, 1D–2D.

Massing, Michael. "CBS: Sauterizing the News." *Columbia Journalism Review,* March/April 1986: 27–37.

199

Matusow, Barbara. *The Evening Stars: The Making of the Network News Anchor*. Boston: Houghton Mifflin, 1983.

Mazzocco, Dennis. *Networks of Power: Corporate TV's Threat to Democracy*. Boston: South End Press, 1994.

McCabe, Peter. *Bad News at Black Rock: The Sell-Out of CBS News*. New York: Arbor House, 1987.

McChesney, Robert W. *Corporate Media and the Threat to Democracy*. New York: Seven Stories Press, 1997.

———. *Rich Media, Poor Democracy: Communication Politics in Dubious Times*. New York: The New Press, 1999.

McDonald, Barrie. *Broadcasting in the United Kingdom*. London: Mansell, 1993.

McManus, John. *Market-Driven Journalism: Let the Citizen Beware!* Thousand Oaks, CA: Sage, 1994.

Merrill, John C. *Global Journalism: Survey of International Communication*. New York: Longman, 1991.

Mindak, William A., and Gerald D. Hursh. "Television's Function on the Assassination Weekend." In *The Kennedy Assassination and the American Public*, Bradley S. Greenberg and Edwin S. Parker, eds. Stanford, CA: Stanford University Press, 1965, 137–149.

Morin, Richard. "Big Breasts and a Bogus Broadcast." *Washington Post*, May 19, 1996, C7.

NBC News Online. "About Us: Dateline NBC." www.msnbc.com/news.

———. "Welcome to MSNBC." www. msnbc.com/aboutmsnbc.

Paterson, Christopher. "Global Television News Services." In Annabelle Sreberny-Mohammadi et al., eds., *Media in Global Context: A Reader*. New York: St. Martin's Press, 1997.

Persico, Joseph E. *Edward R. Murrow: An American Original*. New York: McGraw-Hill, 1988.

Postman, Neil. *Amusing Ourselves to Death: Public Discourse in the Age of Show Business*. New York: Viking Penguin, 1985.

Povich, Maury, with Ken Gross. *Current Affairs: A Life on the Edge*. New York: G.P. Putnam's Sons, 1991.

Powers, Ron. *The Newscasters: The News Business as Show Business*. New York: St. Martin's Press, 1977.

Prendergast, Curtis, with Geoffrey Colvin. *The World of Time Inc.: The Intimate History of a Changing Enterprise*. New York: Atheneum, 1986.

Prichard, Peter. *The Making of McPaper: The Inside Story of USA Today*. Kansas City: Andrews, McMeel and Parker, 1987.

Reasoner, Harry. *Before the Colors Fade*. New York: Alfred A. Knopf, 1981.

Red, Ishmael. "It's Racist." *American Journalism Review*. September 1993: 22.

Rivera, Geraldo. "TV's Wave of the Future." *New York Times*, December 16, 1988, A39.

Rivera, Geraldo, with Daniel Paisner. *Exposing Myself*. New York: Bantam Books, 1991.

Rosenberg, Howard. "The Cult of Personality." *American Journalism Review*. September 1993: 18.

Rosenblum, Mort. *Who Stole the News?* New York: John Wiley & Sons, 1993.

Rosenstiel, Tom. "How CNN Wrecked Television News." *New Republic*, August 22/29, 1994, 27–33.

Rottenberg, Dan. "And That's the Way It Is." *American Journalism Review*, May 1994, 34–36.

Rutenberg, Jim, and Seth Schiesel. "Doubted as Business, Network News Is Still Hanging On." *New York Times*, March 18, 2001, D1.

Sanders, Representative Bernie. "Address on Corporate Control of the Media." Released on April 30, 2002.

Scardino, Albert. "A Debate Heats Up: Is It News or Entertainment?" *New York Times*, January 15, 1989, H29.

Schaffer, Jan. *"Introduction. Civic Journalism Is . . . "* San Francisco: Pew Center for Civic Journalism, 2000.

Schonfeld, Reese. *Me and Ted Against the World: The Unauthorized Story of the Founding of CNN*. New York: Harper Collins, 2001.

Schuetz, Janice, and Lin S. Lilley, eds. *The O.J. Simpson Trials: Rhetoric, Media, and the Law*. Carbondale: Southern Illinois University Press, 1999.

Sella, Marshall. "The Red-State Network." *New York Times Magazine*, June 24, 2001, 26–33, 56–63.

"Serious Agenda, Serious Interest." *Baltimore Sun*, December 24, 2001, C1.

Shales, Tom. "We're Mad as Hell at Daytime TV, Getting Sleazier by the Minute," *Washington Post*, March 19, 1995, G1, G5.

Shawcross, William. *Murdoch: The Making of a Media Empire*. New York: Simon and Schuster, 1992.

Shepard, Alicia C. "The Pundit Explosion," *American Journalism Review*, September 1995, 24–29.

Smulyan, Susan. *Selling Radio: The Commercialization of American Broadcasting 1920–1934*. Washington, DC: Smithsonian Institution Press, 1994.

Sperber, A.M. *Murrow: His Life and Times*. New York: Freundlich Books, 1986.

Steinle, Paul. "Production over Coverage." *American Journalism Review*. September 1993: 25.

Stephens, Mitchell. *A History of News: From the Drum to the Satellite*. New York: Viking Penguin, 1988.

Sterling, Christopher H., and John M. Kittross. *Stay Tuned: A Concise History of American Broadcasting*. Belmont, CA: Wadsworth, 1978.

Taylor, Chuck. "Analysis Is the Buzzword with MSNBC Launch." *Seattle Times*, July 16, 1996, E8.

Thaler, Paul. *The Spectacle: Media and the Making of the O.J. Simpson Story*. Westport, CT: Praeger, 1997.

Tuchman, Gaye. *Making News: A Study in the Construction of Reality*. New York: Free Press, 1978.

Twitchell, James B. *Carnival Culture: The Trashing of Taste in America*. New York: Columbia University Press, 1992.

Ulman, Ellen. "No One Was Supposed to Own the Net." *Washington Post*, January 16, 2000, B3.

Walker, Gary. "About Reinvigorating Coverage." *American Journalism Review*. September 1993: 8.

Wallace, Mike, and Gary Paul Gates. *Close Encounters: Mike Wallace's Own Story*. New York: William Morrow, 1987.

Walsh, Elsa. *Divided Lives: The Public and Private Struggles of Three Accomplished Women*. New York: Simon and Schuster, 1995.

Wedemeyer, Kristin. "'*Dateline NBC*': Perspectives on a News Magazine's Success." Unpublished manuscript, College of Journalism, University of Maryland.

Whittemore, Hank. *CNN: The Inside Story*. Boston: Little, Brown, 1990.

Wilbur, Ray Lyman, and Arthur Mastick Hyde. *The Hoover Policies. New York*: Charles Scribner's Sons, 1937.

Zoglin, Richard. "TV News Goes Hollywood," *Time*, October 9, 1989, 98.

———. "That's Entertainment?" *Time*, October 3, 1994, 85.

Zurawik, David, and Christina Stoehr. "Money Changes Everything." *American Journalism Review*, April 1993: 26–35.

———. "Eclipsing the Nightly News." *American Journalism Review*, November 1994: 32–39.

Index

About the Author

Steve M. Barkin earned a master's degree from the Columbia University Graduate School of Journalism and a Ph.D. in communication from Ohio State University. He teaches at the University of Maryland, where he is the director of the Media, Self and Society honors program. Barkin was coeditor of *Mass Communication Review Yearbook* (Sage, 1985 and 1987) and coauthor of *The Formation of Campaign Agendas* (Earlbaum, 1991), a comparative analysis of U.S. and British party politics and campaign news coverage. His professional experience in journalism includes work at WSB in Atlanta, an ABC affiliate, as a reporter and assignment editor, as a host-producer for National Public Radio in Ohio, and as an editor at the *Washington Star*, the *Baltimore Sun*, and the *Philadelphia Inquirer*. Barkin was the founding editor of *College Park*, the University of Maryland alumni magazine.

He and his wife live in Columbia, Maryland.